House of Cc

Culture, Media and Sport Committee

A LONDON OLYMPIC BID FOR 2012

Third Report of Session 2002–03

*Report, together with
Proceedings of the Committee,
Minutes of Evidence and Appendices*

Ordered by The House of Commons *to be printed 21 January 2003*

HC 268

Published on 23 January 2003 by authority of the House of Commons
London : The Stationery Office Limited
£16.50

CULTURE, MEDIA AND SPORT COMMITTEE

Remit

The Culture, Media and Sport Committee is appointed by the House of Commons to examine the expenditure, administration and policy of the Department for Culture, Media and Sport and its associated public bodies.

Membership

Mr Gerald Kaufman MP	(*Labour, Manchester Gorton*) (Chairman)
Mr Chris Bryant MP	(*Labour, Rhondda*)
Mr Frank Doran MP	(*Labour, Aberdeen Central*)
Michael Fabricant MP	(*Conservative, Lichfield*)
Mr Adrian Flook MP	(*Conservative, Taunton*)
Alan Keen MP	(*Labour, Feltham and Heston*)
Miss Julie Kirkbride MP	(*Conservative, Bromsgrove*)
Rosemary McKenna MP	(*Labour, Cumbernauld and Kilsyth*)
Ms Debra Shipley MP	(*Labour, Stourbridge*)
John Thurso MP	(*Liberal Democrat, Caithness, Sutherland and Easter Ross*)
Derek Wyatt MP	(*Labour, Sittingbourne and Sheppey*)

Powers

The Committee is one of the departmental select committees, the powers of which are set out in House of Commons Standing Orders, principally in Standing Order No.152. These are available on the Internet via www.parliament.uk.

Publications

The Reports and evidence of the Committee are printed by The Stationery Office by Order of the House. All publications of the Committee (including press notices) are on the Internet at

http://www.parliament.uk/parliamentary_committees/culture__media_and_sport.cfm.

A list of Reports from the Committee since 1997 is set out inside the front cover.

Footnotes

In the footnotes of this Report, references to oral evidence are indicated by 'Q' followed by the question number. References to written evidence are indicated by the page number, for example, 'Ev 10'.

Contact

All correspondence should be addressed to the Clerk of the Culture, Media and Sport Committee, Committee Office, House of Commons, 7 Millbank, London SW1P 3JA. The telephone number for general inquiries is: 020 7219 6188; fax: 020 7219 2130; the Committee's e-mail address is cmscom@parliament.uk.

TABLE OF CONTENTS

THIRD REPORT

The Culture, Media and Sport Committee has agreed to the following Report:

A LONDON OLYMPIC BID FOR 2012

I SUMMARY

Conclusions and recommendations

1. Our conclusions and recommendations are summarised below.

Transparency

(i) The process followed by Government has produced in public no more than an anaemic 12 page summary of a 250 page document containing only impenetrable, estimated, aggregate costs. We were grateful to receive confidential copies of the full report containing financial estimates for a "specimen" Games. However, this was of limited use for the purposes of accountability and none whatsoever with regard to public debate. (Paragraph 9)

Costs

(ii) There are three key questions that the Government needs to answer before being able to commit itself to a bid (and any such commitment will be all the better, easier and the more convincing to the IOC for this work having been done):

— that the costs and risks are understood as far as is possible at this distance from the event, can be afforded, and are justified in comparison with other sporting and wider spending demands on Government;

— that the challenges and implications of delivering the necessary facilities and infrastructure developments on time are understood and catered for; and

— that any infrastructure legacies created will be free from on-going, possibly open-ended, subsidy necessary from the public sector. (Paragraph 17)

(iii) We are confident that the Government has undertaken more and better appraisal than previous bidders in order to tackle the vagaries of estimating the costs for a huge and complicated project nine and a half years away from the final delivery date. We trust that the IOC will take note of the implications of all this effort in any future judgements it may make on a London bid. Crucially, we expect the Government to finalise, and reconcile, the various strands of its appraisal work and to be able to set out clearly and in detail what its conclusions are, their bases, and how they influenced its decision on whether to bid or not. (Paragraph 25)

Legacy

(iv) London might well end up with a stadium at Wembley, specifically built with the capability to host the Olympics without legacy issues, and another in East London, actually built to host the Games, with an uncertain future. If this duplication were in fact to occur much of the responsibility would lie with the sporting bodies and agencies whose discussions with each other, and with Government, have led to this confusion. (Paragraph 28)

(v) The most serious and creative thought needs to be given to the long-term future of an East London stadium before a single word of the design brief is written. All options should be considered from temporary construction and subsequent demolition, to a full range of alternative uses after the Games. Such uses could include sporting, retail, leisure or residential adaptation (or any combination thereof). We recognise, therefore, that there could be a creative legacy option developed in due course. However, we recommend that, for the purposes of the bottom line of the bid, the Olympic stadium be costed on the basis of construction and demolition. (Paragraph 30)

6

(vi) First, however, the Government must satisfy itself that the fundamental proposals for a privately developed village and construction of any kind of stadium are in principle realisable and deliverable between 2005 and 2012. (Paragraph 31)

Delivery

(vii) We cannot insist strongly enough that, whatever new agencies are established, leading unequivocally from the centre should be a Minister, located in the Cabinet Office or even No. 10, and with an explicit cross-governmental remit and the power and personality to make things happen. This should be established from day one, 31 January 2003, and should include arrangements for liaison between that Minister and the Prime Minister as a matter of course. The leadership issue cannot be allowed to languish for one minute if a positive decision has been taken. (Paragraph 35)

Transport

(viii) The Government must provide clarity on transport issues if announcing a decision to go forward with a bid:

— what capital projects are required for, or before, 2012;
— what investment will be required in measures to improve levels of service;
— the costs involved and the risks of their escalation (always greater when the pace of construction is being dictated by an external deadline);
— the risks of non-delivery and related contingency plans and/or resources;
— a strategy, in outline at least, for the "unprecedented" management of the London transport network (including demand management) recommended to cope with Olympic transport needs; and
— any apportionment of these costs, or elements of them, to the Olympic balance sheet. (Paragraph 38)

Conclusions

(ix) It is clearly desirable in principle that London should host an Olympic and Paralympic Games. But it should not do so at any price. (Paragraph 39)

(x) The Government must assure itself, before deciding to support a bid, that it understands what it is committing itself, London and the country as a whole, to spend and to deliver. (Paragraph 40)

(xi) The Government could have been much more transparent in this process; reflecting the recommendations of our predecessor Committee. The Arup summary published, for what it was worth, was an abridgement too far. The Government should publish Arup's work in full, as well as its own subsequent calculations on costs and delivery of facilities and infrastructure, before a decision is taken. If release is not possible in the time available then the Government must publish a full account of the facts and figures on which it has based its decision, to allow the proper degree of scrutiny and accountability to take place. (Paragraph 42)

(xii) In answer to the question as to whether 2012 was London's only chance to host the Olympics for the foreseeable future, possibly ever, the Secretary of State said "... you are not categorically right in what you say, but there are certainly judgments that would support your view." We took this as a "yes". (Paragraph 43)

(xiii) If we are right in interpreting the evidence of the Secretary of State to mean that 2012 is indeed the last chance to host the Olympic Games in this country, the decision to be made by the Cabinet next week is of fundamental importance. We therefore urge the Government to take full and careful account of the issues set out in this Report. (Paragraph 44)

II INTRODUCTION

The inquiry

2. We decided on 17 December 2002 to hold a short inquiry into the Government's decision-making process on whether to support a London bid for the 2012 Olympic Games. Over 14 and 15 January we took oral evidence from: Mr Mark Bostock, Project Director, Mr Sam Higginson, Project Manager, and Mr Nick Banks, Senior Consultant, *Arup*; four London boroughs, Mr Max Caller, Chief Executive of *Hackney*, Mr Simon White, Chief Executive of *Waltham Forest*, Mr Norman Turner, Director of Culture and Leisure, *Newham* and Mr Ray Gerlach, Corporate Director of Customer Services, *Tower Hamlets*; Mr Craig Reedie, member of the *International Olympic Committee* (IOC); Mr Reedie also appeared subsequently in his separate role as Chairman of the *British Olympic Association (BOA)*, accompanied by Mr Simon Clegg, Chief Executive, Sir Steven Redgrave, Vice-President, and Mr David Luckes, London Olympic Bid Co-ordinator; Rt Hon Tessa Jowell MP, Secretary of State for Culture, Media and Sport, Rt Hon Richard Caborn MP, Minister for Sport and Mr Robert Raine, Head of Commonwealth Games Division, *Department for Culture, Media and Sport*; Mr Richard Sumray, the Mayor's representative on the 2012 Olympic Bid Stakeholders Group, *Greater London Authority* (GLA), Mr Tony Winterbottom, Director of Strategy Implementation and Project Development and Mr Michael Ward, Chief Executive, *London Development Agency (LDA)*, Mr Jay Walder, Managing Director, Finance and Planning and Mr Barry Broe, Director of Strategic Planning, *Transport for London*; Sir Rodney Walker, Chairman, and Mr John Scott, Director of International Relations and Major Events, *UK Sport* and Mr Roger Draper, Acting Chief Executive, and Mr Ian Fytche, Director of Strategy, *Sport England*.[1]

3. We were grateful to our witnesses, and those who submitted written memoranda, for their efforts at relatively short notice.[2] We sought evidence from the Organising Committee of the Athens 2004 Games but unfortunately this could not be arranged within the time available.

4. To achieve expeditious publication of our conclusions, all the written evidence we received—apart from that submitted in confidence—is published together at the back of this volume after the oral evidence. The transcripts of the oral evidence have been available on the Parliamentary website since 16 January.[3]

The Olympic Movement and the Olympic and Paralympic Games

5. The Olympic Movement brings together all those who agree to be guided by the Olympic Charter and who recognise the authority of the International Olympic Committee (IOC): the international federations of Olympic sports; the national Olympic committees and associations; ad hoc organising committees (such as Athens 2004); athletes and other sports men and women; judges, umpires and referees; associations and clubs; as well as other partner organisations and institutions recognised by the IOC. The IOC itself, established in 1894, is an international, independent, non-governmental, non-profit making organisation owning all rights to the Olympic symbols, flag, motto, anthem and Olympic Games. Its main responsibility is oversight of the organisation of summer and winter Games, a process which includes selection of the host city. By agreement between the IOC and the International Paralympic Committee (IPC), the Olympic and Paralympic competitions are hosted each Olympiad by the same city.

[1] See Ev 1-50
[2] See Ev 51ff
[3] http://www.publications.parliament.uk/pa/cm/cmcumeds.htm

6. The modern Olympic and Paralympic Games are one of the largest regular international gatherings of any kind in the world, let alone the sporting world. For athletes, and for host cities, it is sport's richest prize. It is also the most expensive.

Host city, date and cost — £m 2002 prices[4]					
Munich	1972	1,430	Atlanta	1996	1,481
Montreal	1976	2,436	Sydney	2000	2,534
Moscow	1980	2,622	*Athens*	*2004*	*3,937*
LA	1984	567	*Beijing*	*2008*	*9,775*
Seoul	1988	3,746			
Barcelona	1992	8,057	*London*	*2012*	*2,614[5]*

The Games together involve about 15,000 athletes and an almost equal number of coaches, officials and members of the 'Olympic family'. Twenty thousand media representatives, 7,000 thousand sponsors and, of course, the equivalent of nearly 500,000 spectators a day are also likely to attend.[6] In the background about 60,000 operational personnel will be working to keep everything running smoothly. This event is awarded, seven years in advance, by the IOC to the Candidate City which puts forward what the 126 active IOC members vote to be the best bid against a range of criteria.

---

[4] The comparisons are approximate. Some cities have incorporated infrastructure costs in their Olympic expenditure and others have not. For Barcelona and Beijing (planned) the figures include substantial associated development and redevelopment across the cities concerned. Exchange rates and purchasing price parity issues also apply—at London prices the Sydney Games would have cost about £3,248 million. See Ev 53.
[5] This is the Arup baseline forecast (using Mills Mead village and athletics stadium legacy options and without discounting). The latest DCMS estimate for total cost, at 2002 prices, is £3,822 million.
[6] From London Olympics 2012, Costs and Benefits, Arup, 21 May 2002, published summary, November 2002, p2 - hereafter "The Arup summary".

III BACKGROUND

Development of a London bid for the Olympics

7. The timetable of key events and decisions relating to bidding for the 2012 Olympics is summarised in the table set out below.

Date	Event/action	Comment
Sept 1993	Sydney awarded the 2000 Olympic and Paralympic Games. Manchester fails for a second time, having bid also for the 1996 Games. Third loss for a British bid (Birmingham beaten by Barcelona for 1992).	The Olympics have been held in the UK in London in 1908 and 1948 (when the Stoke Mandeville Games began which grew into the Paralympics).
1995	National Olympic Committee of the BOA (representing 35 sports governing bodies) decided that the next bid would be from London.	A review of IOC members in 1994 indicated London as the only British city able to attract enough votes to win a bid.
1997	Manifesto commitment by the Labour Party to bring the Olympics to the UK. The BOA decided to focus on 2012 as the next possible date for a bid.	BOA felt that a European host for 2004 and a strong Beijing candidacy did not augur well for the UK in 2008.
1997 – 2000	Feasibility study of a London Olympic bid conducted by the BOA and London International Sport: village, transport, facilities and sustainability examined. Largely in parallel, proposals for a new national stadium at Wembley emerge and develop. Progress of the design and financial arrangements, including a £120 million Lottery grant, was and remains the subject of controversy.	Report delayed by withdrawal of athletics in 1999 from proposals for a new Wembley national stadium. Originally designed for dual use (field sports and athletics). The Funding Agreement includes obligations for the stadium to be available for major athletics events including the Olympics.
1999	The IOC responded to allegations of corruption with an inquiry by a special IOC Commission. The Commission recommended reform and punishment of offenders: there were four resignations, six expulsions and ten official warnings. Reform centred on the bid process, transparency of financial matters and changes to the constitution of the IOC: 115 members (under the age of 70)—15 active Olympic athletes elected by their peers, 15 from the national Olympic committees, 15 from international sports federations and 70 individual members.	Other particular measures included: – abolition of visits by IOC members to Candidate Cities; – a reduced term of office for IOC president; – establishment of an IOC Ethics Commission; – publication of reports on sources and use of the Olympic Movement's income; – IOC Session opened to the media for the first time.
15 Dec 2000	Confidential report submitted to the Government by the BOA on options for a London Olympics.	East and West London options were assessed (but not an East/West village/stadium mix).
Feb – May 2001	Presentations of the BOA report to a range of stakeholders and other parties.	These include, in March, one to the new Mayor of London.
Nov 2001	Confidential report by surveyors Insignia Richard Ellis to a "Stakeholders Group" (Government, GLA/LDA and BOA) on land availability for a London Olympics.	The report identified 4 main sites all in East London (on the basis of IOC criteria and study of previous Olympic bids).

Date	Event/action	Comment
Jan 2002	Arup commissioned by the Stakeholders Group to estimate the costs and benefits of a London Olympic and Paralympic Games in 2012. The Government began its analysis.	Arup was asked to assess the implications of a Games staged in the Lower Lee Valley, East London.
May 2002	Submission of Arup's conclusions to the Stakeholders Group	—
May 2002 – Jan 2003	Government seeks to clarify its position, assessing: – the costs and revenues identified by Arup as a basis for long-term public expenditure planning (involving a critical appraisal of risks and contingencies, a probability analysis, and benchmarking against the Sydney 2000 Games); – the possible diversion of funds from other schemes and projects; – the most effective delivery vehicle for the Games (including the role for Government); – transport arrangements based on existing infrastructure and traffic management (and costings where possible); – the potential for a football club to take on the new main stadium; – legacies in former Olympic host cities; – potential legacies in the UK for élite and grassroots sport; – the impact of the Games on the current Thames Gateway Regeneration plan for the Stratford area; – the economic impact for the UK of staging the Games; – the likelihood of London winning the bid; and – public opinion	
Sept 2002	Submission of "winnability" study by UK Sport to Government.	Government's other key tests are: cost, delivery and legacy.
26 Sept 2002	Wembley National Stadium project achieved financial close and work commenced to clear the site for construction.	Original multi-sport design, and contractual obligations regarding athletics, remain in place.
1 Nov 2002	Publication of Arup study summary	Limited detailed information.
28 Nov 2002	Interim report to IOC Session from its Olympic Games Study Commission (remit: the means by which the costs, complexity and size of the Games can be controlled).	The report recommended amending the Olympic Charter to emphasise the importance of the Games legacy in host cities.

Transparency

8. Both the Secretary of State and the Minister for Sport suggested that the Government had followed the Committee's process as recommended in previous Reports.[7] We do not altogether agree. A key factor in the recommendations of the previous Committee was the timely publication of the relevant material for the purposes of clarity in public debate. The previous Committee recommended that, in advance of any decision to bid for a London Olympic Games, the Government should:

- seek and publish the views of Sport England and UK Sport on the BOA's Olympic Games feasibility study of December 2000;

- set out its overall rationale, the objectives of staging the Games and the strategy to ensure enduring economic, social and regenerative benefits;

---

[7] QQ 162 and 152

- publicise its views on where in London an Olympic bid should be concentrated and be explicit about how to preserve the opportunity to use the identified sites, while not jeopardising regenerative development there;

- publish an assessment of the facilities for a London Olympics, specifying for each facility the likely sources of funding;

- set out its proposals for a main stadium including specifics about the site, funding arrangements for both stadium and surrounding infrastructure, proposed design concept and long-term use and viability;

- publish an assessment of the transport and wider infrastructure changes required, clearly distinguishing between investment that would be justified on other grounds and costs specific to the Games; and

- commission and publish independent analysis of the likely total cost of a London Olympic Games, accompanied by a statement from the Government about the extent of the Exchequer commitment both to meet these costs and to underwrite the Games.[8]

9. At the time the Government welcomed the Committee's views on what should inform the decision on whether to bid for the Olympics as helpful and timely. It noted the Committee's decision not to make definitive recommendations at that stage and appreciated the range of relevant issues identified. The Government stated that it would "assess the viability of any BOA bid before giving support and ... work closely with the Government Office for London, the Mayor of London, the GLA, and the BOA" in doing so.[9] **So far the process followed by Government has produced in public no more than an anaemic 12 page summary of a 250 page document containing only impenetrable, estimated, aggregate costs. We were grateful to receive confidential copies of the full report containing financial estimates for a "specimen" Games. However, this was of limited use for the purposes of accountability and none whatsoever with regard to public debate.** At our request the Department submitted, for publication, a supplementary memorandum on its own further analysis of Arup's high level cost estimates (and this material is discussed below).[10]

---

[8] Third Report, 2000-01, *Staging International Sporting Events*, HC 286, see pages xlixff
[9] Government Response to the Third Report from the Committee, Session 2000-2001, Cm 5288
[10] See Ev 60ff and, below, paragraph 20

The timetable to 2012

10. The timetable of IOC deadlines, planned developments in London and other relevant events from now, in 2003, until 2012 is set out below (entries relating to the IOC schedulc for the 2012 bidding process are in *italics*).

Date	Action/event
30 January 2003	Cabinet deadline for a Government decision on whether to support a bid. If Government decides to back a bid, work will need to start immediately to meet the November 2004 deadline for submission of the required file.
May 2003	*Invitation to National Olympic Committees to nominate Applicant Cities.*
15 July 2003	*Deadline for nomination of Applicant Cities.*
15 January 2004	*Deadline for submission of response to Applicant Questionnaire (end of phase one process).*
May/June 2004	*Selection of Candidate Cities by the IOC Executive Board (start of phase two process).*
13-29 August 2004	Athens Olympic & Paralympic Games.
15 November 2004	*Deadline for submission of full bid (Candidate File).*
February-March 2005	*IOC Evaluation Commission visits Candidate Cities.*
May 2005	*Evaluation Commission report to IOC.*
July 2005	*Election of Host City for 2012 by IOC.*
5-14 August 2005	World Athletics Championships, Paris.
2006	(i) Planned opening of Wembley National Stadium. (ii) Central Line upgrade to deliver increased peak services. (iii) Possible date for completion of upgrade to Stratford regional station (subject to availability of funds).
11 June 2006	Last possible sitting day, under statute, of the 2001 Parliament.
2007	Planned date completion of the Channel Tunnel Rail Link, St Pancras to Stratford International.
25 July -10 August 2008	Beijing Olympic & Paralympic Games.
2008	Planned date for completion of the extension of the DLR to Stratford (subject to availability of funds).
2009	Planned date for completion of the Jubilee Line upgrade (including replacement of the signalling system) leading to 45 per cent increase in capacity.
May 2012	Planned date for commencement of Crossrail Line 1 train service assuming a November 2003 start to the programme (Line 2 planned to be operational in 2014).
August 2012	Summer Olympic & Paralympic Games of the XXX Olympiad.

IV BIDDING FOR THE OLYMPICS

‫ the Games

11. The potential for significant benefits to flow from hosting the Olympic and Paralympic Games was the subject of much of our evidence. Sir Steven Redgrave, Vice-President of the BOA, and Olympic gold medallist said "it is not just the legacy that is left from the material things that the Games will deliver ... If we deliver a successful Games then people will be interested in being involved in those sports."[11] The British Paralympic Association wrote that "a London bid will enhance the growing reputation of Great Britain's élite disabled athletes and firmly demonstrate HM Government's commitment to their sporting success. The present administration's current commitment to sport and the legacy it leaves through social inclusion, health, education and facilities can have few clearer illustrations than in supporting a Paralympic Games in London. The benefits that would accrue to Great Britain's disabled people through the demonstration of national commitment to their sports would be immense and tangible."[12]

12. The BOA's evidence sets out a great number of areas that would benefit from staging an Olympic Games: a feel good factor across the nation as a whole; increased élite sporting performance, grassroots participation and facilities; the reduction of youth crime; the promotion of education[13]; a new culture of volunteerism; social inclusion; regeneration in the form of new housing and better transport infrastructure; employment (with about 9,000 new jobs, of which 3,000 would be in the local economy); tourism and the convention industry; UK investment and exports; and all British cities through the preparation and training camps for overseas teams as well as the football and sailing competitions.[14]

13. Representatives from the London boroughs of Hackney, Newham, Tower Hamlets and Waltham Forest made a variety of points on the impact of the Games. Mr Max Caller, Chief Executive of Hackney, and Mr Simon White, Chief Executive of Waltham Forest, argued that the pressure and profile of the Olympic Games could act as a catalyst for action on moribund regeneration plans, especially transport infrastructure, where issues "keep turning up and they keep on never getting a decision."[15] Mr Norman Turner, Director of Culture and Community at Newham, pointed to an array of positive social and health gains that might be extracted and sustained from the culture clash between 11,000 of the world's best athletes performing in areas with some of the country's worst rates of mortality and coronary heart disease.[16] Mr Ray Gerlach, Corporate Director of Customer Services at Tower Hamlets, also referred to the opportunity to celebrate the cultural diversity of the borough as well as to shift the centre of gravity in London a little "so that the East End did not just see this as a one-off ... and then disappear; we are looking beyond the Games".[17]

---

[11] Q 92
[12] Ev 74
[13] See also Mr Duncan Goodhew's evidence on the positive impact of exercise on children's cognitive performance, Q 80, HC 418, 2001-02.
[14] Ev 67-68, paragraphs 24ff
[15] Q 37
[16] Q 35
[17] QQ 35, 40 and 41

14

14. We received three memoranda from local community groups which disagreed with the concerted local authority stance. The Southern Lea Valley Federation and the Hackney Environment Forum and the New Lammas Lands Defence Committee argued vigorously against siting the Olympics in the Lee Valley as they regarded the area, not just as 'derelict land needing restoration', but rather a 'tranquil and precious green lung' close to central London.[18] The importance of consultation with, and involvement of, the local community in a project of this nature should not be under-estimated no matter how enthusiastic are the relevant local authorities. Experience in Manchester with regard to the Commonwealth Games bears this out.

15. We would disagree with very little that we heard or read in regard to the potential for benefits from hosting the Olympic and Paralympic Games. Indeed our predecessor Committee concluded in 1998 that "International sporting events can bring considerable gains to a nation. They can promote economic and social development and bring a 'feel good factor' to the host country. There is no doubt that seeking to stage events is worthwhile. Indeed, this country cannot afford not to attract and stage international sporting events."[19] The fact remains that a substantial amount of these benefits will rest on public expenditure on an extremely large scale.

Preparing to bid

The Government's approach to costs

16. The Government's approach appears to be twofold: seeking to pin down costs and reduce the range of uncertainty on estimates to a minimum; and making a judgement about the affordability of the identified spend, and the implications of its under-writing of the project risks in relation to its other priorities for sport and other policy areas. This attitude seems entirely appropriate for this stage of the project. So long as Ministers can manage a racing gear-change to full-on enthusiasm and commitment in the event of support for a bid being agreed in Cabinet, the Government can—and indeed must—be as hard-nosed and sharp-eyed in crawling over the estimated figures as it likes. However, we can say little about the Government's actual performance and implementation of this approach at this stage because of the lack of transparency over the detail, as we have discussed above.

17. **We believe there to be three key questions that the Government needs to answer before being able to commit itself to a bid (and any such commitment will be all the better, easier and the more convincing to the IOC for this work having been done), namely:**

- **that the costs and risks are understood as far as is possible at this distance from the event, can be afforded, and are justified in comparison with other sporting and wider spending demands on Government;**

- **that the challenges and implications of delivering the necessary facilities and infrastructure developments on time are understood and catered for; and**

- **that any infrastructure legacies created will be free from on-going, possibly open-ended, subsidy necessary from the public sector.**

---

[18] See Ev 105, 106 and 107
[19] Fourth Report, 1998-99, *Staging International Sporting Events*, HC 124, paragraph 47

18. The bedrock for the Government's analysis is the assessment of the costs and benefits of a London Olympics in East London undertaken by Arup between January and May 2002. Arup developed a "specimen" Games and undertook an estimate of the costs and revenues based on the information available. We were concerned by the term "specimen" with its hypothetical overtones. In fact the "specimen" identified by Arup is the culmination of all the relevant feasibility work going back to 1997; a "prototype" London Games might capture the meaning better. Mr Richard Sumray, representing the GLA, told us "the specimen proposal is not going to be exactly what the end result is, and, in fact, if you look at the history of bids, the end result is never quite what is even bid for. It is pretty well there or thereabouts and we believe that what Arup has come up with is actually sustainable and robust."[20] Of course the Mayor of London's department is so far committed to providing, at most, a tiny fraction of projected expenditure. Arup themselves were confident that the financial profile of the Games presented in their report could be improved upon in development[21]; but how late in the process that might be is not clear.

19. Arup describes its appraisal as a hybrid between a cash flow business plan and a conventional cost benefit analysis. Arup calculated "attributable costs and incomes for bidding, preparing and staging the Games, made provision for risk, and estimated the residual value of assets created", generating a total direct cash flow for a prospective organising committee and the public sector agencies involved.[22] Arup said that the resulting deficit must then be justified by additional benefits, both quantified and unquantified.[23] The Arup figures, including some quantifiable additional benefits are set out below.[24]

Bidding and staging	Expenditure	Income	Balance
Bid	13	7	− 6
Staging	779	864	85
Elite sport development programme	167	0	− 167
Capital investment in facilities	403	0	− 403
Land purchase (residual value)	325	431	106
Sub-total	1,687	1,302	− 385
Risk	109	0	− 109
Total	1,796	1,302	− 494
Wider benefits	Expenditure	Income	Balance
Additional tourism	103	280 to 610	+280 to +507
Other benefits	0	69	69
Grand total	1,899	1,651 to 1,981	− 145 to +82

---

[20] Q 166
[21] Q 9
[22] The Arup summary, p4
[23] The Arup summary, pp4 and 11
[24] Drawn from the Arup summary, pp5 and 6

20. The Government described the Arup conclusions as "a good baseline" and said that it had re-examined them as a basis for long-term public expenditure planning using three techniques: critical appraisal of risk and contingency; probability analysis; and benchmarking.[25] Adding the effect of inflation to produce outturn figures increased the figure for the cost of the Games by £1,762 million from Arup's total of £1,796 million to £3,558 million (and of course did the same for revenues: from Arup's £1,302 million to £2,450 million). Critical appraisal by the Department turned up a number of additional items and risks, adding a further £1,116 million to estimated costs and reducing estimated revenues by £400 million. The resulting total outturn cost was £4,674 million[26] with public subsidy set at £2,624 million by the DCMS. The table below sets out the changes in more detail.

DCMS's revised costs and revenues (outturn prices)	£m[27]
Arup cost baseline	*3,558*
Increased allowance for *construction contingency*.	26
An extra 10 per cent on Arup's *staging contingences* reflecting a "general concern" about uncertainties in a complex 10 year project—in line with New York's 2012 bid assumptions)	225
The uprating of Arup's Sydney-based costs to reflect *price parity* between London and Sydney	70
An allowance for street dressing and cleaning to improve the *Look of London* based on spending in Manchester on the Commonwealth Games	40
The high-end estimate for additional investment in station capacity and service enhancement to enable *transport* requirements to be met	500
Allowance reflecting updated estimates for *land* acquisition from the London Development Agency	55
Allowance for a risk that suitable indoor competition *venues* and training centres in East London will not be available without further investment	50
Allowance for higher than estimated *administration costs* to attract the right number and quality of Games administrators	150
DCMS revised total costs	4,674
Arup revenue baseline	*2,450*
Allowance for a 16 per cent shortfall in revenue against estimates on the basis that Arup's assumptions about ticket prices and sales were relatively high.	400
DCMS revised total revenues	2,050
Arup public subsidy estimate	*1,108*
DCMS revised total public subsidy	2,624

---

[25] Ev 51 and Ev 60
[26] This estimate would be £3,822 million if turned back into 2002 prices
[27] Ev 60-1

21. Arup disagreed with some of the Department's further work[28] but overall Arup emphasises that a full appraisal of the project must include an assessment of wider benefits as these will always be the deciding factor given the inevitability of a significant funding deficit.[29] Arup said that the potential public subsidy must be considered in the context of quantifiable benefits but also the range of non-quantifiable benefits which were identified in its report but not incorporated into its figures. Of course, "quantifiable" expenditure will turn out to be a precise sum. Wider benefits, even those described as quantifiable, are far less precise and much more subjective.

22. Despite this work on critical appraisal and the resulting estimate for total public subsidy of £2,264 million, the probability analysis undertaken led the Department to indicate, later in the same memorandum, that "the key figure is the assessment of a 90 per cent probability that the public subsidy would be no more than £2.1 billion".[30] We realise that very different appraisal techniques are being used to assess the project but we find the Department's apparent inconsistency peculiar.

23. The Secretary of State emphasised in oral evidence the risks involved in budgeting for the Games with reference to the experience of Sydney and Athens. She said that both had found their outturn to be about double their estimated costs.[31] We asked the DCMS what work had been undertaken to assess and avoid the failures of Sydney and Athens in predicting costs. The DCMS reported the New South Wales Auditor General's opinion that the assumptions within the Sydney bid were "superficial", with the work undertaken being primarily aimed at winning the competition to host the Games. We were amazed to see that Sydney's budget had excluded capital costs for facilities, infrastructure and security as well as post-Games costs such as redundancy payments and indirect costs. The estimated public sector contribution to the Sydney Games turned out to be about six times greater than the figure in its original bid. Similarly, Athens undertook no detailed cost benefit analysis for the 2004 bid but worked off the baseline provided by the figures for its unsuccessful 1996 bid.[32]

24. The Commonwealth Games in Kuala Lumpur, and the Sydney Olympic and Paralympic Games were said to have "raised the bar" for Manchester in 2002, which contributed to its budgeting difficulties. We were concerned lest there were any potential for a similar effect before 2012. The DCMS told us that the technical specifications for the Olympics were far more tightly defined than was the case for the Commonwealth Games and that a Beijing Olympics was likely to be very different in style to any London Games and thus unlikely to bear direct comparison.[33]

25. We hope to have explained the apparently ludicrous range for the estimated total costs of the Games, often quoted erroneously in the media, as anywhere between £1.8 billion (2002 net present values) up to £5 billion (2012 outturn costs plus the maximum risk provision). We do not criticise the Government for taking a cautious attitude to risk. The perceptions of the project in the media will be critical to its progress (despite vigorous campaigns to secure a positive outcome to this first stage in some quarters). An estimate, for example, of £2 billion where outturn soon looks like £3 billion, has the potential to inhibit progress, winnability and success in a way that an estimate of £5 billion, and a likely outcome of £4 billion, would not—despite the balance of absolute expenditure. **We are confident that the Government has undertaken more and better appraisal than previous bidders in order to tackle the vagaries of estimating the costs for a huge and**

[28] Memorandum submitted by Arup, Ev 64
[29] The Arup summary, pp4 and 11
[30] Ev 61, table 1, and Ev 62
[31] Q 128
[32] Ev 62-3
[33] Ev 63

18

complicated project nine and a half years away from the final delivery date. We trust that the IOC will take note of the implications of all this effort in any future judgements it may make on a London bid. Crucially, we expect the Government to finalise, and reconcile, the various strands of its appraisal work and to be able to set out clearly and in detail what its conclusions are, their bases, and how they influenced its decision on whether to bid or not.

Legacy

26. The heart of a modern Olympic bid appears to be the binary development of the main stadium and Olympic Village and their inter-relationship. UK Sport was adamant that a bid that did not contain a compact stadium and single village concept was doomed to fail, as it did not reflect the Olympic ideal of 'bringing the world together'.[34] Sir Steven Redgrave told us that coming together to live and compete in, more or less, a single location was what distinguished, for athletes, the Olympics from a series of world championships held in rough proximity.[35] Both John Scott from UK Sport and Sir Steven also referred to the practical, and ever more important, issue of maintaining a high level of security; something that is obviously easier with fewer perimeters.[36]

27. The Arup report contains no provision for village development as it is assumed that the construction would be undertaken by others for the legacy on a commercial basis and that therefore only the land cost/value is attributable to the Olympic budget.[37] We have no evidence that this proposal has been researched or market-tested beyond looking at what other Olympic hosts have done. Confidence over delivery of the village development in this form cannot therefore be assumed.

28. An East London Olympic bid needs an 80,000 seat athletics stadium but East London itself does not. The Government gave us evidence of the difficulties faced by a number of former hosts of the Games in relation to their legacy stadia.[38] We were concerned about the role of a new Wembley national stadium whose capability of hosting athletics, including the Olympics, was one very controversial strand in a web of dispute and contention during that project's development. The evolution of both projects, Wembley and an Olympic bid, is set out in supplementary memoranda from Sport England and from the BOA, reflecting their respective interests and priorities.[39] From these it is clear that there was, to say the least of it, some shortfall in strategic thinking across the two projects. **London might well end up with a stadium at Wembley, specifically built with the capability to host the Olympics without legacy issues, and another in East London, actually built to host the Games, with an uncertain future. If this duplication were in fact to occur much of the responsibility would lie with the sporting bodies and agencies whose discussions with each other, and with Government, have led to this confusion.**

29. It was unclear from the evidence we received whether the timetable for design and construction of an Olympic stadium in East London would fit with the timetable for decision on the bid set by the IOC. It is essential that the Government assure itself as to these schedules in order to avoid being left with significant work done in relation to a stadium for which it has no use.

---

34 QQ 203 and 205
[35] Q 103
[36] QQ 103, 203 and 205
[37] The Arup summary, p5
[38] Q 147
[39] Ev 69ff (BOA) and Ev 88-9 (Sport England)

30. **The most serious and creative thought needs to be given to the long-term future of an East London stadium before a single word of the design brief is written. All options should be considered, from temporary construction and subsequent demolition, to a full range of alternative uses after the Games. Such uses could include sporting, retail, leisure or residential adaptation (and any combination thereof). We recognise, therefore, that there could be a creative legacy option developed in due course. However, we recommend that, for the purposes of the bottom line of the bid, the Olympic stadium be costed on the basis of construction and demolition.**

31. **First, however, the Government must satisfy itself that the fundamental proposals for a privately developed village and construction of any kind of stadium are in principle realisable and deliverable between 2005 and 2012.**

Choices and opportunity costs

32. Clearly, the point of the financial and economic scrutiny was to assess the scope of the guarantee that the Government would have to give and the risks that all or some of this guarantee would be called upon. The Secretary of State told us that "we have to accept that at the end of the day the provider of last resort is the taxpayer and that is why we are looking at this...as being potentially a major public expenditure commitment that would have to be set alongside the commitment to building new hospitals, new schools and so forth, all the priorities that our Government was elected to deliver."[40] Tessa Jowell pointed to the opinion polling which showed the Olympics to have a higher priority amongst the general public than reducing taxes but came below schools, hospitals and pensions.[41] She said "if we decide to bid...we have decided because, in full understanding of the consequences, this is such a great thing for Britain; and if we do not bid it will be because we have decided after rigorous examination that the costs are just too great and other very precious priorities, not just of the Government but of people up and down the country, would have to suffer if we were to do this."[42]

33. Another choice was whether to pursue regeneration in East London, in part at least, by way of an Olympic Games. Tessa Jowell told us that the cost of directly delivering the estimated regenerative benefits of a Lee Valley Olympics, without actually bidding for and staging the Games, was estimated at £300 million.[43] The Secretary of State made the point that Barcelona and Beijing had been clear that they were going to use the Olympics to drive the regeneration (with commensurately higher 'Games' costs). She contrasted this with the position of East London where there was a plan and regeneration was going to take place "anyway".[44] As we have set out above, this is not the perception of the borough officers, who told us that a catalyst or accelerator was necessary: "for this bid to succeed, the day Government says, 'yes, we want to do it', is the day they have got to go forward on the transport infrastructure, or it will not be built."[45]

Organisation and the role of Government

34. For the effective delivery of a bid for, and the staging of, the Olympic Games, the management, decision-making and administrative mechanisms have to be absolutely right. The strategy and objectives have to be clear, as does the allocation of responsibilities. We do not believe that the Government can adopt a hands-off or arms-length approach. We were encouraged to hear from the Secretary of State that "If we decide we are going to go for it we will go hell-for-leather to win and all the commitment of Government will be

[40] Q 142
[41] Q 148
[42] QQ 142, 148
[43] Q 127, but see Q 185
[44] Q 131
[45] Q 37

deployed".[46] The DCMS submission said: "Work on the structure of the organisation required for both the bid and staging is being undertaken. This will examine, amongst other things, whether the organisation should be run centrally by the Government, should be at arm's length from Government or should be set up according to another model".[47]

35. **We cannot insist strongly enough that, whatever new agencies are established, leading unequivocally from the centre should be a Minister, located in the Cabinet Office or even No. 10, and with an explicit cross-governmental remit and the power and personality to make things happen. This should be established from day one, 31 January 2003, and should include arrangements for liaison between that Minister and the Prime Minister as a matter of course. The leadership issue cannot be allowed to languish for one minute if a positive decision has been taken.**

Transport

36. A key challenge of the Games is transport: within the Olympic zone; throughout the city; and the links with terminals for inbound overseas visitors. Getting everyone to the venues, between venues and away again in the context of a congested and busy city like London should not be under-estimated. The East London site was selected because of the conjunction of empty land and existing and planned transport infrastructure. Mr Jay Walder, of Transport for London, told us that the "site that has been selected benefits from four tube lines, two national rail lines and the Docklands Light Railway. That is a very, very significant transport capacity."[48] On transport, Arup said that London could cope with the 125,000 extra 'Games' commuters, even without Crossrail, if the network was managed to "an unprecedented degree".[49] Mr Walder said "the Olympic Games would add about one per cent to the daily transport flows that we deal with in London, a range that the system has to accommodate on a fairly regular basis. The real issue in terms of transport is...the concentration of activity in a very small area. That will likely necessitate some improvements...nowhere near the complexity of the other items that you have mentioned."[50]

37. We were concerned with conflicting views of the timescale for progress with Crossrail and its inter-relationship with staging the Olympics. There were so many versions of the place of Crossrail in providing communication to an East London Olympic venue that it is impossible to know which to believe. The Arup study looked at the Games both with and without Crossrail concluding that the link could not be relied upon.[51] In November 2002 the Mayor of London stated that "without Crossrail you would [not] want to run the risk of trying to move everybody around the city [for the Olympics]".[52] On 14 January he was quoted in the press as stating: "I am more confident than I have ever been that within a few months we will have the go-ahead for the development of Crossrail".[53] However, Crossrail itself does not expect to have prepared the *application* for statutory consent for Crossrail line 1 before November 2003; although it hopes that this is the start of a programme and timetable that will lead to completion of construction in 2011 (subject to obtaining powers, finance and procurement). On this schedule the Line 1 train service itself would be in place by May 2012, *i.e.* in time for the Games.[54] On the other hand Transport for London have ruled Crossrail out from their assessment of available transit

[46] Q 139
[47] Ev 52, paragraph 15
[48] Q 170
[49] The Arup summary, p5
[50] Q 169
[51] The Arup summary and Q 3
[52] London's Bid for the 2012 Olympic Games, London Assembly's Culture, Sport and Tourism Committee, January 2003, paragraph 4.4, quoting the Mayor's Advisory Cabinet, 12 November 2002.
[53] The Evening Standard, 14 January 2003
[54] Ev 80

links for a Games in 2012 and this view was endorsed by the Secretary of State.[55] We wonder which, if any, of these views is accurate?

38. With regard to the overall transport situation, the Secretary of State agreed with the thrust of both the Arup report and of Transport for London's evidence. She stated that the Government's position was that "transport is not an obstacle to a bid, and I think it is very important to be clear about that."[56] We are not convinced that this would be the view of many regular users of London's public transport networks or congested roads. It does not seem to have been the view, two days earlier, of the Minister for Sport, Rt Hon Richard Caborn MP, who was reported by UK Sport to have said "on the transportation, it's a major factor moving people around. We've been looking at a number of cities that have hosted the Olympics and that's the one thing they say to us 'get the transport right'. Everyone knows that there are major problems with moving people around in London, therefore that's got to be a serious consideration."[57] **The Government must provide clarity on transport issues if announcing a decision to go forward with a bid, namely:**

- **what capital projects are required for, or before, 2012;**

- **what investment will be required in measures to improve levels of service;**

- **the costs involved and the risks of their escalation (always greater when the pace of construction is being dictated by an external deadline);**

- **the risks of non-delivery and related contingency plans and/or resources;**

- **a strategy, in outline at least, for the "unprecedented" management of the London transport network (including demand management) recommended to cope with Olympic transport needs; and**

- **any apportionment of these costs, or elements of them, to the Olympic balance sheet.**

---

[55] See Q 169
[56] Q 133
[57] UK Sport Newsletter, 14 January 2003

V CONCLUSION

39. Great Britain is a fully signed up member of the Olympic movement and London has hosted the Games on two previous occasions in 1908 and 1948. London is a "world" city in every sense.[58] It is the wealthiest city in Europe, the most culturally diverse in the world, as well as the most popular destination in terms of inbound visitors.[59] We are a sporting nation and both our athletes and armchair enthusiasts deserve the practical advantage and sheer euphoria that an Olympics on home soil would entail. The potential boost from a successful Games—well-hosted and with a goodly haul of medals—to civic and national pride, prestige and well-being, to a more active lifestyle throughout the nation and, arguably, to the wider economy was the subject of much of the evidence submitted to us. Partly in recognition of these factors, and partly to demonstrate them, **it is clearly desirable in principle that London should host an Olympic and Paralympic Games. But it should not do so at any price**.

40. The question is whether a bid for the Games in 2012 can go ahead on 30 January 2003. Those submitting evidence to us were almost unanimous that it should; a recent report from the London Assembly's Culture, Sport and Tourism Committee also gave it the thumbs up;[60] and public support for the proposal, according to DCMS research, is extremely strong, at between 73 and 81 per cent across the UK.[61] However, hosting the Olympics, the most 'mega' of mega-events, is a challenge and involves a substantial commitment of funding, attention and energy over an extended period and, crucially, the whole-hearted backing and financial under-writing of it all by the Government.[62] The bulk of these resources, and of course the overall guarantee, will be from taxpayers' money for which the Government is accountable to Parliament and this Committee. Nine and a half years out we could not, and do not, expect the bill to be calculable down to the last penny with delivery of each facility signed off, but **the Government must assure itself, before deciding to support a bid, that it understands what it is committing itself, London and the country as whole, to spend and to deliver.**

41. It is our role to scrutinize the uses to which public money has been, and will be, put and to examine closely the basis on which decisions are to be made. As we have discussed above, it has been a peculiar feature of this inquiry that almost all the significant information is under wraps—contrary to the firm recommendations of our predecessor Committee. This seems to have been because of a perceived need to protect normal market conditions over prospective sites, the integrity of any eventual tender processes and, uniquely, details that may be useful to competing cities in rubbishing a London bid. We have acquiesced to the confidentiality of a number of relevant documents provided to us. As often is the case, public discussion has been clouded, rather than informed, by partial disclosure of some details and figures in the media (with consequent partial rebuttals from stakeholders). We do not blame the press for this but rather the absence of authoritative documentation on which to base open debate.

42. This Report therefore identifies the questions that we believe must be asked and answered by the Government before it can decide that the country and its taxpayers will seek to put on the greatest sporting show on earth—writing effectively a blank cheque. **The Government could have been much more transparent in this process, reflecting the recommendations of our predecessor Committee. The Arup summary published, for what it was worth, was an abridgement too far. The Government should publish**

---

[58] Ranked, with New York, Tokyo and Paris, as an "Alpha" world city by Loughborough University's *Globalisation and World Cities Study Group and Network.*

[59] Barclays Private Clients, 16 May 2002. London First, 9 December 1999. Travel Business Partnership, City Profiles, No. 6, November 2002.

[60] London's Bid for the 2012 Olympic Games, London Assembly's Culture, Sport and Tourism Committee, January 2003

[61] See annex to this report and http://www.icmresearch.co.uk/reviews/2003/dcms-olympic-bid-dec-02.htm

[62] See, for example, Q 139

Arup's work in full, as well as its own subsequent calculations on costs and delivery of facilities and infrastructure, before a decision is taken. If release is not possible in the time available then the Government must publish a full account of the facts and figures on which it has based its decision, to allow the proper degree of scrutiny and accountability to take place.

43. We raised with Ministers the option of deferring a bid to a time later than 2012. Given that London was the only British city likely to be considered seriously by IOC members, and given the limited availability of suitable sites within the M25 and other plans for their use, the question arose as to whether 2012 was London's, and therefore the UK's, only chance to host a Games for the foreseeable future, possibly ever. The Secretary of State said that: "In looking at the balance sheet for and against...the aspirational balance sheet, the actual costs in the balance sheet, the opportunity costs in the balance sheet, the legacy benefits in the balance sheet, that is obviously a factor."[63] When asked the question again, Tessa Jowell replied "It is a judgment rather than a fact. The judgment is that it is in East London that you get the synergy between the space required for Olympic development and the planned regeneration, so that is correct, yes. It is also likely that after 2012 if those sites are not used for Olympic facilities they will be developed for other purposes. There is a third element, which again is more art than science, there is a feeling, a belief dependent on decisions like where the 2010 Winter Olympics will be held, that 2012 will be a European Games and after that the IOC will move to another continent. So you are not categorically right in what you say, but there are certainly judgments that would support your view."[64] **We took this as a "yes".**

44. **If we are right in interpreting the evidence of the Secretary of State to mean that 2012 is indeed the last chance to host the Olympic Games in this country, the decision to be made by the Cabinet next week is of fundamental importance. We therefore urge the Government to take full and careful account of the issues set out in this Report.**

---

[63] Q 155
[64] Q 156

ANNEX: THE PRESENTATION OF RESEARCH
INTO PUBLIC OPINION BY THE DCMS

The Department's summary of the ICM opinion poll on the merits of the 2012 bid, which appears on the ICM website and which was submitted to this Committee, is inconsistent to say the least. In the summary there were ten findings identified. In eight out of these ten, different strengths of response applied (*i.e.* statements were offered and respondents were invited to agree or disagree, strongly or slightly). Two of these eight findings can be characterised as negative towards a bid for the 2012 Olympics and six as positive. For the two negative findings, the 'strongly' and 'slightly' categories were added up together to give the figure for the summary. In relation to five of the six positive findings, only the figure for 'strong' agreement was given in the summary. In one case, legacy in East London, the figure suggested was just plain wrong. The detail is set out below. We do not believe there to have been any malign intent in these infelicities; especially in view of the free availability of the full survey data on the ICM website and reference to that fact within our memorandum. However, the Department needs to take more care with such matters to avoid the appearance of incompetence or worse. We trust that the Government's conclusions on the other matters on its long list of analyses will be much more carefully and accurately presented and explained.

Figures in **bold** were given in the DCMS summary of the survey	Agree strongly	Agree strongly & agree slightly
Negative		
Money better spent on grassroots/school sport in communities	30%	**56%**
Majority of the investment, for example in sporting facilities, will be in London therefore no gain for the rest of the UK	27%	**51%**
Positive		
Hosting Olympics will bring UK prestige and 'feel good' factor	**70%**	94%
Commonwealth Games in Manchester proved UK to have the experience and track record to run a successful Games	**71%**	92%
The hosting of the Olympic Games will bring economic benefits such as more employment and more investment	**60%**	90%
A London Olympic bid will leave a legacy of a redeveloped East London with excellent sporting facilities - **figure given: 60%**	45%	81%
The hosting of the Olympics will create more sporting opportunities for young people	**65%**	88

PROCEEDINGS OF THE COMMITTEE RELATING TO THE REPORT

TUESDAY 21 JANUARY 2003

Mr Gerald Kaufman, in the Chair

Mr Chris Bryant	Ms Debra Shipley
Alan Keen	John Thurso
Miss Julie Kirkbride	Derek Wyatt
Rosemary McKenna	

The Committee deliberated.

Draft Report (A London Olympic Bid for 2012), proposed by the Chairman, brought up and read.

Ordered, That the draft Report be read a second time, paragraph by paragraph.

Paragraph 1 postponed.

Paragraphs 2 to 8 read and agreed to.

Paragraph 9 read, amended and agreed to.

Paragraphs 10 to 13 read and agreed to.

A new paragraph (now paragraph 14) brought up, read, amended and inserted. —(*The Chairman.*)

Paragraphs 14 and 15 (now paragraphs 15 and 16) read and agreed to.

Paragraph 16 (now paragraph 17) read, amended and agreed to.

Paragraphs 17 to 23 (now paragraphs 18 to 24) read and agreed to.

Paragraph 24 (now paragraph 25) read, amended and agreed to.

Paragraphs 25 and 26 (now paragraphs 26 and 27) read and agreed to.

Paragraphs 27 to 29 (now paragraphs 28 to 30) read, amended and agreed to.

Paragraph 30 to 38 (now paragraphs 31 to 39) read and agreed to.

Paragraphs 39 and 40 (now paragraphs 40 and 41) read, amended and agreed to.

Paragraph 41 (now paragraph 42) read and agreed to.

Paragraph 42 (now paragraph 43) read, amended, and agreed to.

A new paragraph (now paragraph 44) brought up, read and inserted. —(*The Chairman.*)

Postponed paragraph 1 again read, amended and agreed to.

An annex (The presentation of research into public opinion) brought up, read and inserted.—(*The Chairman.*)

Resolved, That the Report, as amended, be the Third Report of the Committee to the House.—(*The Chairman.*)

Ordered, That the Chairman do make the Report to the House.

Ordered, That the provisions of Standing Order No. 134 (Select committees (reports)) be applied to the Report.

Several Papers were ordered to be appended to the Minutes of Evidence taken before the Committee.

Several Papers were ordered to be reported to the House.

The Committee deliberated.

[Adjourned till Tuesday 28 January at Three o'clock.

LIST OF WITNESSES WHO GAVE ORAL EVIDENCE

LIST OF APPENDICES TO THE MINUTES OF EVIDENCE

MINUTES OF EVIDENCE

TAKEN BEFORE THE CULTURE, MEDIA AND SPORT COMMITTEE

TUESDAY 14 JANUARY 2003

Members present:

Mr Gerald Kaufman, in the Chair

Mr Chris Bryant	Miss Julie Kirkbride
Mr Frank Doran	John Thurso
Alan Keen	Derek Wyatt

Examination of Witnesses

MR MARK BOSTOCK, Project Director, MR SAM HIGGINSON, Project Manager, and MR NICK BANKS, Senior Consultant, Arup, examined.

Chairman

1. Gentlemen, I would like to thank you very much indeed for making yourselves available for this inquiry. As you will know better than most, this is a week of concentrated consideration and three sittings of this Committee, plus the debate in the House of Commons this afternoon. The British Olympic Committee have very kindly provided us in confidence with a copy of your report, and we understand and accept entirely the commercial confidentiality of your report and we will therefore not be referring to its contents, though there is a published executive summary of which we can take advantage. Could I just make one point before we begin which is that the acoustics in this room are pretty terrible and in the past people in the public area, particularly at the back, have been unable to hear very well so I would be most grateful if you could speak more loudly than normal, and I say that to my colleagues on the Committee as well. Gentlemen, could you please, first of all, clarify to me a couple of aspects relating to costing infrastructure? The understanding is that if we were to obtain the Olympics for 2012 there would have to be a new stadium in East London together with additional swimming pools and the construction of a village. Could you please, therefore, clarify, first of all, what the role of Wembley Stadium in your view would be, taking into account that the stipulation of Sport England was that Wembley Stadium should be of dual use for football and athletics, and could you tell us how precise any calculations you have that you can make public are with regard to (a) the cost of the building of the new stadium and the village and (b) completion dates? How confident are you that they could be completed in time? I have one other question while we are at it: if there were to be a new stadium in East London then access to it by Crossrail is regarded as very important. Crossrail on the present timetable, as I understand it, is due for completion by 2016 and the Games would be held, if the bid were to go ahead and be successful, in 2012, therefore could you relate the completion time for Crossrail with the communications situation to the new stadium, if it were built in East London?

(Mr Bostock) Thank you, Mr Chairman. There are three very specific points there. Could you just give me a few minutes to give you the context of the work

we did, and then I would like to answer those three specific points very clearly? I have a very short introduction to start with because I think it is very important for you to understand the context in which the work was done. My name is Mark Bostock; I am a director of Arup and was project director for the particular study which is the subject of the discussion today. First of all, very quickly, Arup is a very large, global multi disciplinary, planning, project management and engineering practice with a very large resource base here in London. We were commissioned, appointed, to undertake this work in association with Insignia Richard Ellis following a competitive tender, and during the 16-week elapsed time for this work we met with our steering committee approximately every two weeks and a pretty rigorous programme was set out, and that steering committee comprised representatives from the Greater London Authority, the British Olympic Association, the London Development Agency, UK Sport, Sport England, Her Majesty's Treasury and the Department of Culture, Media and Sport, and we had the Cabinet Office's Performance and Innovation Unit with observer status. We reported on 21 May last year, 2002. After approximately five months Government put into the public domain the 12-page summary report which you made reference to, and I need to emphasise again that the main report is not in the public domain and I am very pleased you have made reference to that in your introduction. I would like to make a comment on the scope of work. What we were commissioned to do was to establish the outline construction costs for all the permanent and temporary sport facilities and all the sporting infrastructure; we were asked to look at the costs for bidding for and staging the Games; we were asked to establish the benefits of bidding for and staging the Games and establishing the residual legacy costs and benefits. What we were not asked to do was examine winnability, nor were we asked to examine the opportunity costs of Government spending, and I must make that very clear. Coming closer to the points in the context of the answers that I will give you in a second, we developed our own specimen Games—and I must emphasise specimen Games—and these were centred on an Olympic zone in the Lower Lee Valley in East London, so that provided the basis of our appraisal. During our work

[**Chairman** *Cont*]

and in our report we have been totally transparent in terms of all the various assumptions that we have made in our evaluation and I need to say, with great emphasis, that the financial appraisal methodology was accepted by the Treasury. We always anticipated, as we did this work and completed it, that each of the key stakeholders—the Government, the London Government and the Britain Olympic Association—would evaluate the project from their own point of view, including risks, risk assessment and mitigation of that risk in order to examine the impact of a possible Olympic Games on their respective organisations, and I need to make this very specific point, because risk assessment from the point of view of each of the key stakeholders was not part of our commission. What I want to make absolutely clear, therefore, is that in providing an independent assessment of whether London should or should not bid or stage for the London Olympic Games we concluded very strongly that the key stakeholders needed to enter into a concordat, and I would be very happy to indicate what that meant, because this is planning for a major event in 12 years plus a legacy thereafter, and we have concluded that in the event that an appropriate concordat cannot be entered into between the three stakeholders there is absolutely no point in proceeding with these propositions. Also, we have indicated in the summary report five areas where we felt more work needed to be done from the time we completed our work in May and June and a decision which we thought would have been made in November—it is January now—and that additional work is very clearly set out in section S16 of the summary report. Finally, we also included in our work a decision matrix tree, with important decision milestones that needed to be achieved before making that decision. Mr Chairman, thank you for allowing me to make that statement and can I now answer the three questions you asked. First of all, Wembley. Wembley participates in our specimen proposal as being the place for the final of the football. We are envisaging in the specimen Games that there will be a new stadium within the Olympic zone meeting, as I am sure you know, the aspirations of the IOC charter and their requirements, and if London is to put in a bid that has any credibility there needs to be a degree of compactness and wholeness about that proposition so that the relationship between the village and the stadium and other facilities is a vital part. In answer to the specific issue of Wembley, therefore, Wembley in our specimen proposal is where the finals of the football will be played.

2. Could I interrupt, and it may well be that it is not a fair question to put to you in which case please be very frank about that: if you are stipulating, and obviously understandably you do not have any specific responsibility, that Wembley should be the location for the finals of the football, is it not rather puzzling that the whole condition which Sport England laid down for providing £120 million for Wembley Stadium was that it should be convertible for athletics?

(*Mr Bostock*) I cannot possibly comment on that: I am afraid it is well beyond the scope of our work. Can I just make an observation? The British Olympic Association, and I am sure you will want to ask them, have done a huge amount of work on the Olympics:

they started this work several years ago. Secondly, the London Development Agency retained Insignia Richard Ellis to look at suitability of sites. Thirdly, there has been a lot of work done on which part of London the Games should be. All I can say to you is that, from the point of view of our brief, we were asked to look at the sites that we have indicated and I have to say to you that the Stratford area is very important because it is a very significant transport hub. I am sure you will know about the issue of access and egress which is a key issue, so that the transport infrastructure around Stratford and the commissioning of the Channel Tunnel Rail Link is a very important asset. You ask about the costs of building the stadium and the village: I am afraid that is in our main report and it is not something that we can comment on at the moment. I would like to say that Arup knows about engineering, building and designs, and I am sure you are aware that Arup had a very heavy involvement in the design of the Manchester stadium and we are very comfortable with our estimates for both those two elements. On the issue of the location of the stadium and Crossrail I am going to ask my colleague Nick Banks to make an observation.

(*Mr Banks*) May I add one point to what Mark said about the infrastructure for the stadium and the Olympic village, because I think you asked whether it can be completed on time. It is easy enough to build the facilities on time but it is important to make sure that we are not on a construction programme which leaves the building incomplete very shortly before the Games because then costs can rack up very terrifically and there is an enormous amount of stress. The critical path issue is the acquisition of the land and it will be necessary to start serving compulsory purchase orders very shortly in order to make sure that the timetable is not boxed in at the end of the process and the costs go up, but that is something that probably you would be better pursuing with the LDA.

3. You were not precise, and maybe you were unable to be, on the previous question I put about the completion of Crossrail, whose completion date is 2016 for a Games which is due to take place if the bid is successful by 2012.

(*Mr Banks*) My understanding is that the current programme for Crossrail is for completion in 2012 but it is a very tight timetable and leaves no slack for delays of any sort. It would in our view be very foolish to go ahead with an Olympic proposal that relied on Crossrail. We therefore evaluated the proposal on a worse case basis and on what we described as a reference case basis from the demand point of view, and we did it with and without Crossrail to show the differences.

4. Finally, you have talked repeatedly about a concordat. Is your assumption that the preparations for the Games and the running of the Games would be joint by the different organisations which were part of such a concordat, taking into account that we had a rough equivalent prior to the Commonwealth Games and if that had continued and the Prime Minister had not appointed the minister in charge, it is very difficult to anticipate the Commonwealth Games could have been the success they were?

[Chairman *Cont*]

(*Mr Bostock*) I think that is absolutely correct and the way that we have looked at this and our basic assumption in coming to the conclusions that we have is that the driving and the delivery of this whole major event plus its legacy will be driven in partnership between the public and the private sector, and we have assumed that the private sector efficiency drivers are implicit in that. The complexities of the IOC contract, and you and your members will know about this, require joint and several responsibility. The application is taken from the BOA from the specific city, but there is a huge amount of underwriting that the Government needs to enter into, and in the body of our report we have discussed that. It is our strong argument that if that is not all in place right at the beginning of what is a major event, and there is not clear identification at the outset on the output specification of what is going to be delivered after 15 years which includes all the legacy, and if there is not agreement between the three main stakeholders—the BOA, the London Government and the UK Government—covering all eventualities, then there is not a proposition to go forward.

Derek Wyatt

5. You say you are a worldwide company and you have won many projects all over the world. Your budget seems to be £2 billion out from the Government's and you seem to have a huge difference. Can you explain it to us so we can understand it?

(*Mr Bostock*) I am going to ask my colleague, Sam Higginson, just to comment but I would like to say this: we are not going to be commenting on anything that is not in the media and in the press. The methodology that we have used to do this high level cost benefit is very strong and I would like to ask Sam to tell you exactly what we have found.

(*Mr Higginson*) I think the starting point for this is that there are two issues: (1) about the individual cost items which we do not feel able to talk about in any detail today but perhaps the most important issue and the reason for the big difference in the figures is there is a difference in methodology. Our first step was to identify all the cost and revenue items and put them into 2002 prices in the particular year where they would fall. For example, you would have the stadium costs in 2002 prices in the years running up to the Games. What we then did was we discounted all of those numbers using the accepted Treasury approach and a discount rate of 6%, so that you get back to what it costs today to run the Games and what revenues you would get today for the Games. The advantage of using that approach is that basically what you are doing is you are valuing a pound in your pocket today more than a pound in your pocket tomorrow. What Government has done with a lot of the numbers you have seen floating around is taken a different approach. They have started from exactly the same base position where they have all their numbers in 2002 prices in different years but inflated all those numbers to get, if you like, to money of the day. The disadvantage we would contend with that approach is that it values the pound tomorrow more than a pound today, so that

is why you get a big discrepancy in the two sets of numbers although they are basically both starting off from the same position.

(*Mr Bostock*) Additionally, first of all, our costing is based on a functional Games, and I am happy to try and define this, if you would like me to. Secondly, the costs, revenues and benefits are based on our skill, knowledge, and experience. We have already reported in our summary report that we have underestimated the benefits and one has to be looking at that in the round, and again I think we would be very happy to give you some indication of the extent to which those have been underestimated. Whilst we did this work during our 16-week study we might have missed one or two costs, and if we have we will put up our hands and say we have missed some. It is very difficult to make sure that one has the totality of these costs but the only costs that we would be interested to put into this are those which are directly attributable. The principle of what we put in is very clear and we are going to stick to this: first of all, there must be excess revenue over costs of staging the events; secondly, we anticipate that the net costs of infrastructure is going to be negative and, thirdly, there are benefits to off-set that financial balance. These are the important issues that one has to be looking at and concentrating on. In our report, which you say you have seen, we have done some sensitivity tests which are the what-if scenarios in terms of if there are changes in those assumptions both on costs and revenues on the base case, and the results are sensitive to some of those changes.

6. Thank you for that long answer but given that you also said in your preamble that you were meeting with PIU, Treasury and CMS, what we cannot understand is why disagreements come after all that, but let me leave that aside. What were the lessons of the Commonwealth Games for your particular report?

(*Mr Bostock*) The Manchester Games? There are at least four points that I think are very interesting. The management of the Games and the total commitment of the city council in terms of its promotional aspect were very significant; the value that is created from volunteers and the whole impact of volunteers and the economic argument to support the benefit of that has been particularly good; and the fact that the scale of the venues are affordable for Manchester and the impact that the development of some of those venues will have on the regeneration of east Manchester are all very important lessons. The other point I feel very strongly about is that I do not think Manchester, when it set out to get the Commonwealth Games, sat down and did what we have done which is look at the cost and benefits of hosting and try to get the budgets and the costs and the revenue flows right, and I think in a sense, taking on from Manchester, what we are trying to do is get that upfront analysis so a proper decision can be taken.

7. Can I put to you that the reason why the Athletics was such a jumble is that nobody owned it in the UK? It was not owned by a single organisation, including the GLA, and the reason the Commonwealth Games worked was because

[Derck Wyatt *Cont]*
Manchester City Council owned it. If there is to be a British bid and it has to be London, it seems to me it has to be absolutely totally owned by the GLA.

(*Mr Bostock*) I would agree.

8. We have London Heathrow just inside the M25, London Gatwick outside, London Stansted way outside and London Luton economical with the truth. What other sites have you looked at that are not in East London for a bid and what discussions have you had, bearing in mind that Queen Mary College and University College were thinking of combining to be a university, with university colleges inside London University to create a brand new campus site to be the focus of an Olympic bid?

(*Mr Bostock*) Firstly, it was not within our brief to identify sites. We were given that as part of our commission and we have executed that. Secondly, on the issue of the universities and hospitals and the village, I will ask Mr Banks to answer.

(*Mr Banks*) Can I have one crack at the first question as well? When you are looking for a site for an Olympic Games there are three important criteria. The first is that you need a large area of land to build the Olympic zone; secondly, you need good access to central London and, thirdly, you need accessibility to the zone itself. Knowing London, looking around London, there is nothing like Stratford, and in our view it is not likely there will be anything like Stratford. In answer to your second question, no, we did not talk to universities about the idea of building a new university campus and having these facilities about it. However, we did discuss the question of having a substantial amount of student accommodation in the overall Olympic village dwelling mix, and that is something that can be taken forward and developed in the next stage if it is decided to go and bid. So I think it was not part of our specimen Olympic Games proposal to be costed.

Mr Bryant

9. I should confess from the outset that I personally believe that a London Olympic bid, whilst it might seem superficially attractive, would be a foolhardy mistake because I think the money could be spent better elsewhere. I think a bid based on the East End of London simply is not going to deliver anything for the rest of the United Kingdom, and I think there are major transport problems which you touch on in your report. Having read the whole of your report, I must confess that my predilections and concerns are compounded because I look at the figures and they seem remarkably "fag packety", if you do not mind my saying so, to invent a word, and one of the reasons I would suggest there is a major difference between what Government is saying about the figures and what you are saying on the likely £2 billion or £5 billion or £6 billion cost is there are a series of imponderables which are not really tied down in your report. For instance, you refer to the legacy issues and clearly there will be a very significant difference in the amount of money that would be attributable to the cost of the Games and therefore to the Exchequer if any of the different options for the stadium itself and for the village come to pass. Now, those are not really outlined in your public report. Would you like to comment on them?

(*Mr Bostock*) Let me come back to legacy in a moment. Can I just remind you, Mr Bryant, that what we are looking at here is a specimen Games. We had to have something on which we were going to look at the costs and the benefits and it is very clearly stated in our summary report that we believe that that specimen Games can be improved in terms of its financial performance and its regenerative effects, so there is a lot of work that has to be done before that bid is won.

10. So your £1.2 billion is based on a best case scenario in terms of legacy, a worse case, or somewhere in between?

(*Mr Bostock*) In our report we had to have several alternatives, as you well know. We looked at two alternative locations for the village and two alternative legacy uses for the stadium. The stadium costings included the conversion costs to whichever appropriate use is finally decided on. On the specific legacy costs I will ask Mr Higginson to answer.

(*Mr Higginson*) We have not included, for example, any on-going legacy costs for the running of the facilities after the Games because we would argue to a certain extent (a) it may not be attributable and (b) you need to think about what revenue benefits you would get from that as well. Our costing brief was for the relevant period of the Games.

11. But this is a major issue for Government then, the legacy, because it is one of the four criteria that the Government has set, and it seems from what you are saying that this is still pretty imponderable?

(*Mr Bostock*) More work has to be done on the issue of legacy, and we said that right up front. We were very transparent on that specific issue.

12. Can I ask about what I would think is an imponderable but you seem to think is a tidied up ponderable—media income for the Olympics? You say, "We have not included a provision for reduced media income because it is just as likely to be higher than estimated as lower". I would suggest to you that is an over optimistic view of the media market and for Olympic bidding rounds next time round.

(*Mr Higginson*) I would disagree with you on that point. You have to understand that when the media contract comes up for renewal it will be in several years' time; it will not be in today's economic climate.

13. In 2008 it comes up.

(*Mr Higginson*) Yes, so not in today's economic climate—

14. The major bidders are the public service broadcasters and the public service broadcasters around the world for the most part are not going to be seeing massive changes in their media market over the next five years, I would suggest, and certainly the EBU, the European Broadcasting Union, which is the major bidder which has all the rights in Europe and the European Union and is one of the biggest players in this, is not going to be significantly increasing and may well be decreasing its bid.

(*Mr Bostock*) Well, we are going to stick to our proposition at the moment, and do remember the figures that we have taken are net figures as the payment comes into the committee and the IOC make their retention. We have done a lot of analysis on that and that is the position we have taken.

[Mr Bryant Cont]

15. On a different issue, one of the points you make—and I do not think this is a commercially sensitive bit of the main document so I do not think I am breaking any confidences—is about levering investment, and how important this is in terms of an Olympic bid and you cite, "Both Atlanta and Sydney claims that the global marketing options created by the Olympics was instrumental in attracting inward investment"—and you add rather tellingly—"but neither final report is explicit as to the extent of this effect", so you seem to be making a quasi political point which is that London would be able to attract greater investment into the UK by virtue of an Olympic bid but then withdrawing it by saying there is no clear indication whether this has been the case for Sydney or Atlanta at all?

(Mr Higginson) I think the point is that within our report itself we were being particularly conservative with the wider benefits, and we divided those up into those you could quantify and those you could not—ie, they did not become parts of the analysis—and inward investment in this particular case fell into the category of those you could not quantify because we did not feel it was possible to put a specific number on it.

16. One of the things that perplexes me about the whole idea of the bid and one of the elements that seems to be being put across is that this would be an opportunity to launch London as a worldwide capital city. It may be that Atlanta and Sydney needed that but London is already, if not the greatest, then one of the three/four greatest cities in the world and hardly needs relaunching.

(Mr Bostock) There is no question about that but it requires refreshing, we would argue, so there are a whole lot of non quantifiable benefits. We have not put a value on this, which we believe needs to be identified as part of the non quantifiable benefit which is all part of this equation. As you have heard we have not put a value on inward investment but, as a clear demonstration that London remains and is one of the world's leading cities, it works and it can deliver, so the Games give a good feel factor, a celebratory factor, all of which is very difficult to quantify in monetary terms.

Alan Keen

17. I am a sports enthusiast and I want to convince the sceptics that we should go ahead with it. We all want the east side of London to be regenerated and, although this report is confidential, can you tell us in broad terms a bit more about the regeneration?

(Mr Bostock) Can I quickly respond? We provided an independent assessment. We looked at the costs and the benefits and the circumstances where the benefits would exceed the costs. I need to say that we have an impartiality on this, and I make that very clear.

(Mr Banks) On regeneration, the first thing to bear in mind is that we did not go into detail on how you dovetailed the Olympics and the regeneration proposals for East London in order to take greatest advantage of each. That was, in our view, a task that was far too complex for our study. You can argue, I think, that Stratford City and the development to the north of the station on the railway lines is already

planned and will go ahead with or without the Olympics. It is a lot less certain what the situation is for the rest of the Lower Lea area, and there is about 5 kms between Hackney Wick and the river so it is a big area. It is a high priority for the London Development Agency and there is an awful lot to do, as anybody who goes to visit can see. The problems are, amongst other things, a lack of infrastructure, a run down environment and a poor image. The Olympics can offer lots—flagship facilities, land assembly on a large scale, infrastructure with an obvious legacy, physical connections through the area and a wholesale environmental improvement which would have a long term benefit, and probably as much as anything it can have the advantage in raising the profile of the whole area so that it becomes a location which for all time would have an Olympic caché attached to it. Profile is important in East London, so the extent to which it is possible to capture this is a difficult question because there will be things needed for the Olympics that are not so attractive for the legacy but it is how to fit the two together on a common regeneration programme which is the complex and tricky task that would need to be addressed.

(Mr Bostock) Can I just add—and you will get bored with this word and I do apologise—that we have done a specimen Olympics. We have had no discussion with any of the local authorities as we concluded the work, so that is one of the reasons why one cannot be more specific on the regeneration, but we know that area very well and one has a good feel in terms of what those opportunities might be. My previous experience on putting Olympic Games together, and when I have looked at the issue of Manchester I agree, it is the championing of the city there and using the Commonwealth Games; all part and parcel of their regeneration strategy. That is a very important statement and for London I would argue, very similarly, that there has to be a purpose in doing this, and we are arguing that there is a catalytic impact from a major event like the Olympic Games coming in to help in the regeneration of part of London which so desperately needs it and is part and parcel of the London plan. I put that as a very strong point.

18. If we decide to bid and the bid is successful, it is essential that the media is behind the UK on this because it is a national bid and we have to remove any of the issues that can cause controversy. The new stadium has already been mentioned, and we spent so much time on the Wembley issue that we are a little bit sensitive about it I think, and there has already been mention in the press about the legacy of the main stadium. It is hard to see what that is going to be used for in the future and there is no way anybody can tell us whether either Spurs or West Ham, for instance, would want that stadium afterwards. What are your comments on that—and I do not want to make it a major issue because it is something that will be solved in the years in between.

(Mr Bostock) There are two questions there, and if I can take your first question and give you an answer, I think you were talking about what are the benefits to the United Kingdom, and I think that is very important because one has to see this basic proposition in that context. I think there are three or

[**Alan Keen** *Cont*]
four major arguments that we have put forward that there are some non London venues—Bisley, Weymouth, the equestrian, and the finals of Wembley Stadium in north London. Secondly, there is the whole impetus that this can give to tourism, and to get the whole of the tourism industry going. People are going to visit London and go on to the rest of the country so you will get very much a holistic offering, and, thirdly, there is our training facilities for Olympic teams coming over. So the whole of the United Kingdom should be behind London in terms of the benefits and advantages. On the specific issues of venue, I have to tell you upfront that an 80,000 seater is a very complex issue. On the one hand, the new President of the IOC is wanting to descale these and to reduce the scale of some of these facilities. If it is going to be a stadium for football and long term use, then the stadium in our proposal will be designed for a 50,000 seater and there will be temporary seating to take it up to 80,000, and that cost will be part of the legacy cost. If it is going to be used for athletics, it will be designed for a smaller number of a capacity which is appropriate for an athletics stadium. That is all I can say, but a lot more work needs to be done on getting clarity as to what the legacy is going to be, and we have said that the work needs to be done on that.

Alan Keen: That is very helpful

Miss Kirkbride

19. Could you take us through a little bit on what the upfront costs to the taxpayer might be and the risks? What is the chronology, if we were to go ahead with the bid, of how we go about pursuing it? Who pays the compulsory purchase? Who puts up the money for the stadium? Who looks at the village? Where is the money going to come from and in what order, and who is going to be paying it?

(*Mr Bostock*) Can I just deal with the bidding costs? The figure we have in the summary report is that the present value of the bid costs is £13 million and in 2002 prices that is £15 million, of which we are assuming approximately 50% will be raised in the private sector. It depends on how the bidding committee is established, but half that amount has to come from the private sector in some form or other. If we are then looking at the infrastructure costs, we are assuming that one of the pre-conditions of going forward is a very effective development agency with suitable powers to acquire and secure the rights for development.

20. And that would be public sector backing it?
(*Mr Bostock*) Yes.

21. The taxpayer backs that bit?
(*Mr Higginson*) Yes. I am sure you are aware that the LDA is currently very active in that area of London and what we were assuming is that they take on that role, so the other costs that would come in would be land acquisition costs.

22. Paid for by whom?
(*Mr Higginson*) By Government but they would be off-set by land disposal revenues, so when you move forward you move forward with a development agency that has a plan A and a plan B. Plan A is you win the Games in 2005 and then you go on and develop the Olympic facilities and deliver the Games, and plan B is you do not win the Games in 2005 but you go on and deliver a significant amount of development in the area anyway.

(*Mr Bostock*) The issue of risk was not part of our commission and it seems to me—and it is for you to ask the Secretary of State when she gives evidence—that Government has been going through its own risk evaluation to look at the bottom and upper limits of the contingency positions that they need to make from the public sector, but that is not for us to make any comment on but for Government and each of the stakeholders.

23. In terms of your professional competence, if they are bought on compulsory purchase does that make a difference to the price as opposed to the open market, because clearly if the Olympic bid is successful then it is more valuable, and it is the taxpayer picking up the bill?

(*Mr Banks*) I think you should probably ask the LDA that when you speak to them because they are responsible for that but compulsory purchase buys at current value, broadly speaking.

24. Current value, not expected?
(*Mr Banks*) Yes.

25. In terms of how this would work if we were to go forward, you say in the report that there are enough hotel spaces; we have touched on but not really clarified the issue of Crossrail and the transport infrastructure; but can you go into a bit more detail and elucidation as to how people would get there, where they would stay, what transport they would use in the absence of Crossrail, and how much disruption the rest of us who live in London would have to cope with if this went ahead?

(*Mr Bostock*) That is a good question and we will try and answer it, but one of the great attractions of London, of course, is the very high quality of existing hotel stock and that is particularly appealing to the members of the IOC, so we have assumed that all those are going to be in the West End and West End hotels—

26. What about the rest of us? Where are we going to put the competitors and the spectators? How will they get there? What transport infrastructure will they be using in the absence of Crossrail, and in summary how much disruption to the rest of our lives is there going to be for the glory of having the Olympics?

(*Mr Banks*) I will just briefly take you through the methodology. Our first step was to try and work out what the demand would be and how many people would come to the Olympics, and some of them are fairly straightforward because they are the Olympic family and the athletes and the media and those people. The spectators were more difficult and we had to make an estimate which we based, broadly speaking, on the number of tickets and assumed that all the tickets would be sold. We then added on the people who accompany people going to the Olympics but who are not actually attending it, and we apportioned those people between those who will stay with friends and relatives, those in hotels and hostels, those who are day visitors and those who are international and those who are British. That gave us our demand scenario and we worked out where the

[Miss Kirkbride *Cont*]
accommodation was, and for those in hotels and hostels we apportioned them according to where they are located. As far as the friends and relatives are concerned, we assumed those international visitors would have the same behaviour as domestic visitors to the Games. So that gave us our pattern of origins for the journeys, and it also gave us the scale of the demand needed to be catered for on the network. Here I think it is very important to describe our approach to transport because it is absolutely essential to our thinking about it. Essentially, you can either adopt an infrastructure-led approach to Olympic transport or a management-led approach or something in between. We went for the management-led approach because the infrastructure-led approach has a long history of problems because it is very expensive and there is risk of being late and all these difficulties, and very often it does not make a lot of sense to build a whole new bridge or whatever for the sake of a six-week Games. The infrastructure has to be needed in the long term if it is worth investing in. It is difficult to believe sometimes but London has a very large and very flexible set of transport networks, albeit very congested, but it is also in many ways very inefficiently used. Our argument is that if the traffic flows are heavily managed during the period of the Games and it is planned for seven or eight years before the start of the Games, the capacity can be allocated efficiently and you have a long time for the existing people in London to decide how they are going to react towards that during the Games. A big part of the Sydney experience was that everybody pitched in during the Games and there was a big celebration, and that is something that probably the BOA can probably tell you about more than I can. Now, with all those things in place our approach was to allocate as much as possible on to the rail networks and then to provide for the rest with dedicated routes and shuttle coach services, but there would also be facilities park and ride and all the rest so that was the essential pattern. What we would aim to do was minimise the infrastructure investment and, in fact, infrastructure investment only ever provides for a small part of the overall travel demand because it comes from many directions.

John Thurso

27. I want to ask you about risk and risk assessment but before I do can I follow on from the question you have just answered and perhaps ask you to give a definition of what "heavily managed" means? Are you expecting the congestion charging to clear the roads for you, or are you asking people not to get on the tube and go to work?
(*Mr Banks*) I think the first thing is that for those attending the Olympic Games there would be mechanisms to ensure that when you bought your ticket you were also buying a particular route to travel to the event wherever possible, so you can use that mechanism to allocate people to different bits of the transport network, but it also means that you need a transport agency with proper powers as they had in Sydney, and it means you have to have thought about all the individual aspects of what could go wrong and have contingency plans for it. It also means you have street management during the

duration of the Games which keeps the key routes clear, and in terms of the totality of London there are not so many key routes that you need to be clear. Then you ensure you have all those pieces in place and that the agency has the powers to direct people who are not very keen on this, so that you deliver a result.

28. It sounds very easy!
(*Mr Banks*) It is not easy. I certainly do not want to give you that impression.

29. Can I come to the question of risk. Here I do not want to ask you about financial sensitivity. In other words, this is not a question of how much you have built into your various scenarios—but actually the risks to the project going through. What assessment have you made of those events or actions that may or may not take place on the critical path which are likely to or could have the effect of derailing the project? What are the things that put most at risk the viability of the project?
(*Mr Bostock*) I will repeat what I have said already—we are assuming that the delivery of the Games and its legacy will engage the expertise of the private sector. I assume right upfront, and I am going to come back to this concordat, that the budgets are agreed and there are funds available for what needs to be done in that highly project-managed approach for the delivery of that project. Right upfront there is no argument as to where the funds are going to be delivered. Our assumption is that there is a very strong transport authority put in place, and that there is a development authority also in place. I have to make those assumptions; and we have to make those assumptions. Because if you haven't got those, then you haven't got a concordat and there is not a basic proposition. For the delivery of the infrastructure under those assumptions we are fairly confident; but there is a whole range of things outside those that we have been discussing, such as revenue; interestingly enough, security has not come up, and there are three or four main areas which are totally outside the control of the delivery mechanism provision, which are very difficult to put probabilities to, but which are high risk. We did an evaluation of a 'what if' situation if there was a terrorist attack three years before, and the impact that would have, and that is a disaster scenario in terms of the consequences, in terms of reduced revenues, attendance all the rest of it. I assume that the Government, in terms of their risk evaluation from the point of view of public sector risk, will be looking at all those, and coming up with an overall provision. I would expect that to be the case.

30. You mentioned that one of the risks you saw was the private sector not engaging in the process. Perhaps this is what you have just said, but would it not be fair to say that the biggest risk is, surely, Government not engaging in the process?
(*Mr Bostock*) Yes.

31. The lesson of Manchester must surely be that, unless there is ministerial involvement from the outset and leadership from Government, that it is doomed to failure?
(*Mr Bostock*) The answer to that is: absolutely correct. Implicitly I was trying to say that.

[**John Thurso** *Cont*]

32. Now you have said it explicitly.

(*Mr Bostock*) It has been quite interesting—as we have been going round (and I am giving you a personal view and not a view of Arup) there is a lot of consultation with all the relevant ministries we have dealt with—that Government is a portfolio of silos, and it is the delivery of the totality of Government which is absolutely critical for this. The Manchester experience is directly relevant. I am going to go stronger to say, if there is not a political will to do this which is cross-Party (and I am expressing a personal view) forget it.

33. You would also say that in order to get that responsibility it really is one minister who is responsible for this and takes the lead role in Government?

(*Mr Bostock*) Correct.

Chairman

34. Thank you gentlemen. We are very grateful to you indeed, first of all, for coming and, secondly, for providing us with this very illuminating insight into the way you have conducted your work. Thank you.

(*Mr Bostock*) Thank you, Chairman. You have asked us some quite difficult questions. If you want any further views from us we would be very happy to respond.

Chairman: Much obliged.

Examination of Witnesses

MR MAX CALLER, Chief Executive (Hackney), MR NORMAN TURNER, Director of Culture & Community (Newham), MR RAY GERLACH, Acting Corporate Director of Customer Services (Tower Hamlets), and MR SIMON WHITE, Chief Executive (Waltham Forest), examined.

Chairman

35. Gentlemen, thank you very much for coming before us this morning. We are much obliged to you, particularly with the short notice we have had to give you. Could I start by asking you what I suppose is the key question for you as boroughs, namely, could you describe to us briefly, taking into account the time constraints, how you see the regenerative possibilities for your boroughs of an Olympic Games located in East London? Each of you, all of you, any permutation of you, is welcome to respond.

(*Mr Turner*) It will be a little informal, Chairman. We are not well rehearsed, but we will do our best. Could I just say that the four boroughs support in principle the Olympic Games bid based in the Lower Lea Valley. We want to work together closely to try and influence matters as they might evolve. As you suggested, Chairman, we believe that hosting the Games would bring significant benefits to the people who live in the four boroughs. We would be keen to ensure that any potential benefits are maximised, which include acting as a stimulus to regeneration, and creating or renewing the infrastructure of the area. I guess a caveat from the boroughs would be that the end result must be a sustainable and real benefit to local people. The legacy tends to be regarded in terms of actual physical infrastructure and economic development. We are strongly of the belief that the social infrastructure, the social development of East London, and our four boroughs in particular, can be greatly enhanced by the Olympic Games. The four boroughs do share a number of quite startling characteristics in terms of demography, economic and social characteristics: it will be around age, ethnicity, poverty, health etc. If I may just give three specific figures to put that into context. We are the youngest community in the UK. Looking at the percentage of population under 30, for example: there is a UK figure of 37%; a London figure of 41%; and the four boroughs in aggregate

have 48%. In terms of ethnicity: UK 7%; London 31%; the projection to 2011 for the four boroughs together is 50%—a quite startling contrast. The mortality rate per hundred thousand of population from coronary heart disease in the under 65s is: for England and Wales 37%; London 39%; and the four boroughs in aggregate 55%. We could replicate that scale of difference in terms of the characteristics that the four boroughs share. Taking those points, with the young population for example, having 11,000 athletes coming to the Olympic Games would give role models; it would give us a whole programme of development around personal achievement, aspiration and a focus for endeavour for our young people. We could use the Games to promote a healthy lifestyle in a constructive way, in partnership with other partners such as the health trusts. A central issue for us in our earlier discussions was the concept that the Games would be based around the theme of cultural diversity; and that there would be a four-year festival and celebration as part of the preamble into the Games. We would see that as a major vehicle for the promotion of social cohesion. I would not want to go through the other elements in light of the time, but there are a whole range of key social impacts. We are working together but the scale of the problem, of multiple deprived, is such that it needs something of a world significance to really shift matters in the timescale required, so that is a particular attraction of the Olympic Games.

(*Mr Caller*) Hackney needs jobs; and Hackney needs access to jobs. The statistics are quite clear, and I have put those round in a note which I have given to the Committee. We think that this is the best opportunity to get the investment in the infrastructure, to ensure that people in Hackney can access jobs wherever they might be in London, and they do not have that opportunity at the moment.

(*Mr Gerlach*) We would echo those things in Tower Hamlets as one of the poorer boroughs in the country. All of these issues are of tremendous

[Chairman *Cont]*

importance for us. The opportunities to accelerate the enhancement of regeneration and employment are key features for us. Also the celebration of diversity is a key theme for us. Our recently launched cultural strategy is on this. We do look to celebrate our differences and to actually build on those through our community cohesion programme. We see this as playing a role within the overall infrastructure for us within Tower Hamlets.

(*Mr White*) The issues in Waltham Forest are similar to Hackney. Most of our economically active workforce work outside the borough, so we are very keen that this bid should accelerate the developments that are going on in East London, and should not get in the way of it. Perhaps just to add a gloss to what was said about the regenerative possibilities that a bid would offer—we have all got experience of working together on regeneration issues, particularly in fact around sports and health. In Waltham Forest, for example, we are using the regeneration of Whipps Cross Hospital as a way of trying to engage with the Health Service and with local populations to get real long-term benefits for local people above and beyond the simple investment in that hospital. As the bid becomes more concrete we would hope to be fully engaged to make sure that any developments which are in our borough or about our borough we are able to shape, so that we can apply the lessons we have learnt in other regeneration initiatives to this.

Mr Bryant

36. As a former Hackney councillor, I have a lot of sympathy with the Chief Executive of Hackney—just to be Chief Executive of Hackney Council! Sorry, a cheap jibe!

(*Mr Caller*) It is getting better!

37. I have a great deal of sympathy with the regeneration argument, but I could make exactly the same case for the Rhondda, which has probably worse, if not similar, figures on mortality rates on coronary heart disease, on diabetes and blindness, all these different issues; but nobody is going to be putting in a bid for the Rhondda to be hosting the next Olympics. You are making this argument for regeneration, but would there not be better ways of achieving the same regeneration in the East End of London—which nobody would deny is a vital part of regenerating the whole of the capital city—and it would actually be cheaper to the Exchequer and more effective for local people?

(*Mr Caller*) That is an interesting argument, but the proposals to promote regeneration through transport infrastructure, through a range of activities, have been around for a very long time. They keep turning up and they keep on never getting a decision. So in one sense forcing a decision, because for this bid to succeed, the day Government says, "Yes, we want to do it", is the day they have got to go forward on the transport infrastructure or it will not be built. It is a catalyst, but it also brings a large number of things together. There is an issue about piecemeal development and the time it takes to make things happen. I do not want to trade statistics between Hackney and Rhondda; and I am not going to do this on the basis of graveyard-type activity; but it is a great opportunity and we need to seize it.

38. As I understand it, what you are saying is, part of the reason you are backing the bid is because you think this will force the Government to finally make up its mind on a whole series of transport and regeneration issues in the East End, whether or not the Olympics ends up coming to London?

(*Mr Caller*) They are a crucial precursor to a successful bid.

39. One of the other dangers presumably is that through this process one might be forcing decisions to be made which would not be made in the long-term interests of London without the Olympic bid happening? For instance, you might be rejigging the whole of the transport system in London towards delivering for the Olympics rather than towards delivering the long-term economic benefits that London needs?

(*Mr Caller*) Our analysis of the transport proposals show that they are necessary whatever. This just provides the catalyst.

40. We heard earlier it seems likely that the IOC might be attracted by coming to stay in some of the best hotels in the world, because they will be in the West End of London. As far as I can see, they are going to be staying in the Ritz and the Savoy, the IOC themselves, and then travelling out to the Olympics. How exactly would they do that, do you think? What would be the route from the West End, where most of the hotels are, to the Olympic site?

(*Mr Gerlach*) Maybe we do not see it quite as black and white as you have outlined there; insomuch that as part of an infrastructure that we would be looking for as a benefit would be to have hotel accommodation within the east part of London, not necessarily the west part of London. I think there are two issues there. One is that as part of an infrastructural sustainability we would be looking for the longer term, so that the East End did not just become a one-off drop-off point and then disappear; we are looking beyond the Games, and about what that infrastructure would bring in legacy terms, in real terms, for a solid accommodation base so that the East End will not be in the same position as it is now.

41. That is interesting. You are suggesting that there would be more hotels based in the East End of London?

(*Mr Gerlach*) Absolutely.

42. Because historically it has been very difficult to get tourists to stay in the East End of London. I remember when the Holiday Inn Express was built at Old Street, the Holiday Inn was saying, "That's as far east as we're going".

(*Mr Turner*) Having worked for many years in the west of Scotland, I appreciate your comment on the Rhondda and the demographics and social characteristics but there is an issue of scale in East London. There are a million people in a very small area. In terms of the regeneration which is taking place anyway, there was an issue discussed between the four boroughs and others about the potential problem of blight in relation to the CTRL and Stratford City development. That was the subject of a meeting at the end of last year with the developers. As a result of discussions there, there was a unanimous view that the Olympic Games would give

[Mr Bryant *Cont]*

a further acceleration to the existing process, and would not divert or take it off a strategic direction but would speed up the rate of improvement. One of the features so far of regeneration in East London has been the growth of the hospitality industry, and the fact there are four hotels together as far east as the A13 just on the Barking border. In the two years finishing the end of 2003, there will be over 2,000 bedroom spaces that will have been created in the Lower Lee Valley alone. We only go up as far as three star at the present time, I must say, so perhaps there will not be a great attraction to the IOC, but for many others the budget range which is also developing would be attractive. There is strategy of developing visitor support and increasing the hospitality sector. One thing which perhaps would have been unthinkable even five years ago is that a Holiday Inn Express has opened in the heart of Canning Town, which is surprising enough; but the good news on that is that 80% of employees are from the Canning Town area. It is a micro detail but gives the flavour of the broader picture.

(*Mr White*) I think the Holiday Inn have calmed their fear of East London. They even opened a hotel at the Villa Road Roundabout, which I think would trump yours! The point is that East London is changing rapidly anyway. The centre of London is changing. The Olympic bid could be a way of accelerating developments which we believe are going to happen in any case.

Derek Wyatt

43. One of the principle debates missing in the GLA first elections is, what is the definition of a global city? It seems to me that Paris is a global city. It has over 50 Olympic swimming pools and London has—seven, five, two or one?

(*Mr White*) One.

44. When we compare and contrast and go into this bid for 2005 we have three years basically for the GLA to make up its mind about what an international city should be, and we will not resolve it by 2005. Paris is resolved. New York is not. How do you feel about that aspect? The bid is going to be weaker because actually London has not taken on board what a global city should be.

(*Mr Turner*) The element in terms of swimming is accepted. Wearing my sporting hat, that is absolutely incredible.

45. Crystal Palace, we do not know whether that is going to come or go. Wembley, which we thought was going to be the centre of an Olympic bid, and it was in 1999, has now been written off.

(*Mr Turner*) There is an infrastructure either in place or planned that could accommodate the various sports involved in the Olympic Games—a whole bunch of them within the Lower Lee Valley area. I know later you will be speaking to the British Olympic Association and UK Sport who can give you some more specific evidence. Part of the legacy that has been discussed with the four boroughs, to take an example, is to get a 50 metre pool for East London. Various options, Walthamstow and Newham, have been looked at for that.

46. We got the legacy wrong, in a sense, in the Festival of Britain in 1951; and we got the legacy wrong with the Dome. We did not get the legacy wrong with the Games in Manchester. The legacy is a pretty critical part. Are you saying that if persuaded, say, the Imperial or Queen Mary College to physically move and become a new university, the catalytic impact of a university with 15,000 students, would have a much greater impact quicker than bidding for a major Olympic Games which we may not get?

(*Mr Turner*) I think, from a personal view, that the Olympic Games is on such a scale it is unique, and would be the largest single gathering in the history of mankind, and it could provide an impetus that nothing else may do. Even at this stage, with the Olympics, we have been discussing with the various organisations, including the University of East London, how they might develop in terms of the legacy arrangements, and work with the boroughs and other partners to look at a sustainable use of a whole range of potential physical facilities that would be located. Obviously that is a point of detail that will be further down the road. The scale of land available within our four boroughs would be a configuration which would supply all the Olympic needs and provide a whole range of legacy issues which would involve, by definition, the community.

47. It is on an opportunity cost basis model that the costs of moving a new university out of a London university is, say, £700 million and it produces exactly what you want, your legacy, but should the Government go for that or should it go for the Olympic Games?

(*Mr White*) It is very difficult to speculate about the potential opportunity costs. One of the issues for us is that there is the prospect of an Olympic bid right now, and we are being asked if we support it in principle, subject to a great many caveats, many of which the Committee has raised. You would need a different meeting and a different proposition to get our views on some of the possible alternatives.

48. The previous speaker said that he thought the GLA should own the Games. Do you have the confidence that the GLA has the capacity to actually organise and run those Games?

(*Mr Gerlach*) As a single entity, I think anything of the magnitude of the Olympic Games is mind-blowingly enormous. What we are talking about here is the biggest sporting event in the world. I think that in itself takes some getting round in terms of trying to imagine what that is, and the impact of that, and the organisation of that. If one looks at the organisation of the last two major events in this country, Euro '96, the football event, and the Commonwealth Games, I think that our track record of organising and being able to deliver these sorts of top range games is very good. I think it is a logical step to take a look at hosting the two biggest, the World Cup and the Olympic Games. I would say our track record in organisation ability is very good. There are a lot of lessons we have learnt from those two experiences that would stand us in good stead on how to go about that, and the best way of putting an infrastructure together which could deliver it. I agree, to think through the detail that it would take is an enormous piece of work that needs to be done.

[Derek Wyatt *Cont*]

49. Do you think we have enough time if the Cabinet says, "Yes", on 30 January, with all the things that are now coming out about costing etc, to actually get a bid ready for June?

(*Mr Caller*) I think there is enough time, provided that the Government is prepared to make the commitments, rather than a wait and see—we put the bid in and then we put the investment in. I said at the outset that when we decide to go for the bid there are a number of requirements, and those have got to be committed to at the same time. I endorse the point made by Arup, about having a minister that is going to sponsor the event and carry it through. You can have an organisation umbrella, but actually many of the decisions that need to be taken are going to be taken by central Government; and central Government have got to be part of it, and they have got to carry it through, because these things will not come to pass if they are left uncoordinated without the commitment. There is enough time if we do it.

(*Mr Turner*) That certainly is a general view: it is not an issue of time; it is an issue of will.

Alan Keen

50. Simon White said the centre of London moved—for me it was when Ray Gerlach went from Hounslow to Tower Hamlets. It is nice to see you! How much involvement have you had so far in this process and the stage that is reached now?

(*Mr Turner*) The four boroughs and other colleague boroughs have been meeting together for three and a half years. We have been meeting regularly. We have been fed into, been advised and kept up-to-date with the Arup process, for example, through that mechanism.

51. You have met with Arup on a number of occasions?

(*Mr Turner*) Through London International Sport we have been involved in the process as it has evolved.

52. If the bid goes ahead what involvement are you hoping to have in the planning?

(*Mr Turner*) We would like to have the maximum position of influence in terms of the regeneration programme, both in physical and regeneration areas. The delivery vehicles still need to be confirmed to see precisely what our level of involvement is.

53. Do you think you will be given an involvement to the extent to which you would like it? Or are you frightened of being over-run by the LDA and the GLA?

(*Mr White*) There is a tension between the need to have a delivery mechanism which has a single intelligence at its heart, and which can drive the change that is necessary to make it successful, with the need to make sure local communities are engaged with the process. We want to have influence in the way that was devised. I think it is probably possible to have the best of both worlds. From our point of view, the way we would be looking at it is, for those aspects of the bid which most closely touched on real geographic communities, we would want to make sure there was a real engagement with them; and that we were at the centre of that, without trying to create a very ornate consultative structure which would

mean nothing could ever be achieved. Big projects like this need compromise, and a willingness for the whole purpose to be achieved at the expense of some of the more parochial issues, which no doubt would come up in the process.

54. Local government finance is pretty tight, is it not? Have you thought about grouping together as four bodies to have a representative to try and give you a bit more leverage than you will get if you operate independently?

(*Mr Caller*) I do not think we are operating independently. I think we are working as a partnership—that is why we are here today. I do not see any difficulty in us continuing to work as four boroughs together, and with our GLA members, to actually get the influence. I just want to add a small point to what Simon was saying. We do not expect to be at the top table deciding all the big things. What is crucial for us in our involvement is making sure that whatever happens takes account of the cultural diversity of our boroughs; and that the legacy reflects something which all our populations can use. Together I think we are probably the most diverse part of the United Kingdom, in terms of the range of ethnicities that we cover, and that is quite an important thing for us.

55. Are you confident you will be listened to sufficiently?

(*Mr Gerlach*) Certainly we have been involved up to date. The Arup report in section 16 does say that the next stage has to be real negotiations with the local authorities, and we need that to happen. The principle of us supporting this is on the basis that we will have that ability to be heard, to shape and to influence what we need to deliver for local people.

Alan Keen: I have been making the point all the time, as you must guess, because you will have no spare money to contribute in any way. You desperately need to be listened to. I wish you luck with that.

Miss Kirkbride

56. We are very minded of the fact that Wembley has been somewhat stymied by the activities of Brent Council. In my part of the world Solihull did not even get a look in when it came to the siting of the football stadium because Solihull council was not given planning permission. So what about planning permission? Who decides what we are going to have?

(*Mr Turner*) The allocation of planning permission in general is part of the delivery mechanism for the Games: where will there be an Olympic stadium established?

57. Will you reserve the right to decide planning issues; or will it be diversity with another body? Given that an area of land is identified, will it go through your members, or will it have to wait six months whilst they do this and do that? What are you prepared to hand over in terms of powers in planning to make this work?

(*Mr Turner*) That has been our assumption in our earlier discussions, that planning would not be retained by the individual boroughs, because of the need for speedy decisions.

58. What mechanism would that be?

[Miss Kirkbride *Cont*]

(*Mr Turner*) The LDA or the GLA is a more likely vehicle for that. There are proposals and possibilities in the Arup report. There have been discussions within the boroughs at the moment. With the stadium, for example, a stadium could be reduced to football size and there have been discussions between the planning authority in Newham and West Ham Football Club (and it might not be a positive time to discuss West Ham's future at the present time); but the Club has expressed its interest in a location around Hackney/Stratford to become its future home. Discussions are in place and responses have, in general, been positive. I think everybody within the borough would want this to work.

(*Mr Caller*) We certainly see the way it would work is that the boroughs would be consulted, but it is such a strategic decision it would be for the Mayor of London to decide. Like all these big developments, it would fit into that context.

59. If the land was to be compulsorily purchased, at that point you would lose your planning powers. You would obviously expect to be consulted but it would then not have to go through your borough to proceed in any way?

(*Mr Caller*) The boroughs would be consulted. The boroughs would express their views. Like any other strategic planning application, the boroughs would be able to express their views and put proposals forward. I would have thought we would meet together to try and work out a common planning approach; but there is no point in four boroughs considering the detail of these sorts of applications—we need to work together; and we are able to work together to handle these sorts of things.

60. That is very encouraging. It has been a problem in other areas that there has not been that kind of agreement. I would have thought, from the Government's point of view, because they very much support the idea that Ministers have to be actively involved, they are going to want the surety to proceed on the basis that if they are going to take a decision they can pursue that decision without other people having the ability to countermand it. I think that is a very encouraging move. What, in the end, will consultation mean? What will that mean to your residents?

(*Mr White*) The first thing is that the context of any arrangement will be a whole package, so we would be looking for some of the things that Max started off the session with: commitments about investment in infrastructure, proper arrangements about legacy and an absolute guarantee that we were not going to be blighting developments which are dear to us and which are going to happen in any case. So assuming all of those three things happen, the context for the kind of arrangements which colleagues have been talking about, I think, is one that is politically deliverable. Our expertise will be in helping the Mayor, the LDA, or whoever is taking the lead, to engage with the communities, which we already have very rich communication with, and be in a position to lead those communities. So we would see ourselves as midwives in that rather happy way. So you cannot isolate that from an overall package, which we would expect to have bought into very, very shortly.

(*Mr Turner*) There has been work in some authorities already involving the Local Strategic Partnership to make sure the consultation and the engagement is across sector and across parties. The Local Strategic Partnership in Newham, for example, in its cultural strategy, which was adopted in 2000, at that time, had included in its work plan a commitment to work with partners, neighbours, the GLA and others to try and attract major events such as the Olympic Games to the Lower Lea Valley in general. So there has been a level of engagement— 6,000 community consultations—in that particular exercise, but that would be something, obviously, in the next stage that we would all need to notch up a gear.

Chairman

61. Gentlemen, thank you very much indeed. Regardless of whether there is a bid, regardless of whether the bid is successful, regardless of whether the Games are held, as a Member for a deprived area I wish your boroughs every success in regeneration.

(*Mr Turner*) Thank you very much.

Examination of Witness

MR CRAIG REEDIE, CBE, British Member of International Olympic Committee, examined.

Chairman

62. Mr Reedie, we would very much like to welcome you here today. We recognise that you are here wearing two hats and you are, at this moment, under the first hat. If you have anything to say by way of introductory remarks, then it would be very welcome. Otherwise I will call Mr Keen right away.

(*Mr Reedie*) Very briefly, Chairman, I only got back from holiday early on Saturday morning and I told your Secretary that I had not submitted any written evidence. I have no specific opening statement to make. I am one of the two IOC Members in Great Britain, and Matthew Pinsent is the elected athlete Member of the International Olympic Committee. I will be happy to try to answer any of your questions.

Chairman: Thank you very much, Mr Reedie.

Alan Keen

63. Welcome. The bidding process is very expensive, is it not? I have raised this with you before, I think. What changes have been made in the bidding process over the last eight years of the Olympics? It is still very expensive now, is it not?

[Alan Keen *Cont]*

(*Mr Reedie*) The estimates taken, I think, by Arup in the report is their best estimate of the middle market cost of the bidding process for the 2008 Games, which was won by the City of Beijing. There has been a very significant change to the bidding process for Olympic Games. This Committee will know that in 1999 the IOC received much criticism over the bidding process for the Winter Olympic Games in Salt Lake City and they put in place a series of reforms. The major reform was designed to prevent or avoid visits by members to cities paid for by cities and to avoid visits by cities to members. The cost of the exercise has been reduced. At that time the Government, I think (and Tony Banks was the Minister for Sport), made it quite clear that no future bid from Great Britain would go forward until the IOC had changed its rules. The IOC then changed its rules in 2000 at an extraordinary session in Lausanne, and those rules came up for re-examination only as recently as November last year in Mexico City, and the rules were reinforced by a very substantial majority. So the system is much better, in my view, than it was all those years ago. The cost factor is very much what the bidding committee would wish to do, and some of them may be based on geography.

64. I have read in the press in the last few days that the Government does not want to go ahead with the bid unless they feel it has a pretty good chance of being successful—and that is not just because of the estimated £60 million, or whatever it is. There is rotation, as you have just hinted at now, of continents. It is said that if we did not bid this time for the 2012 then it would not be until 2024 that we would have another opportunity. Has the International Olympic Committee thought about, rather than asking for bids, choosing cities to save a lot of money going down the drain and, also, harming the confidence of governments as well. It is not a happy process, is it? Also, downsizing the Games slightly, rather than increasing them. What has actually happened?

(*Mr Reedie*) Can I answer those in reverse order? There is currently a new Commission, the Olympic Games Study Commission, which has produced an interim report. While an attempt will be made to downsize the Games, the IOC have recognised they are now at their optimum size and it is their long-term wish that in the future the Games could be hosted by smaller cities in different parts of the world, although I think the IOC and, in particular, its new President, understand that that may take some time to bring about. As far as the IOC turning round and saying to cities "We would like you to organise the Games", the selection process is a matter of never-ending debate. One of the thoughts given to the IOC some years ago was to create a permanent site in one particular country. This suggestion was in Greece. While that has some historical advantages it may have other practical disadvantages. I think, on balance, the IOC sees a properly organised bidding process as being good for the Olympic movement all round the world; it generates great interest in sport, in generates investment in facilities and, at the end of the day, I would like to think that over the last few years in the main the IOC has got its decision right, no matter the process that it used.

65. I know these questions are not directly involved with the decision that is going to be made by the end of this month, of course, but it is important because I think these things need airing. We are desperate to have regeneration in East London but it is much more desperate in Africa, for instance. Would it not be better to spend the money to regenerate some of the African cities by targeting the Games there—not just in Africa, obviously, but in other undeveloped nations? I know that sponsorship plays a massive part in this, and who is going to go to Harare to pay for hospitality boxes? This is something for which I think the International Olympic Committee has some responsibility.

(*Mr Reedie*) We choose to develop sports on a worldwide basis in a different way rather than saying "We wish specifically to take one event which lasts for 16 days to a particular city". We have, as part of the share of the revenues, a fund called Olympic Solidarity which, in the current Olympiad, will distribute around $450 million to countries all round the world, particularly those national olympic committees who do not have the marketing strength and the commercial advantages that larger NOCs would have. That is the way the IOC tries to spread its funds and make its sporting investment. It does not see that it has a responsibility "to promote a city in Africa". There has been one bid from an African city in recent years and that was a very attractive bid from Cape Town, and Cape Town lost in the process to Athens.

Chairman

66. Could I just follow up Mr Keen's question? When the Olympic Games came to London in 1948 we are told that London agreed to have them to help out the IOC. Los Angeles, as I understand it, got the Games almost *volte demur*. What has happened since Los Angeles that has led to a situation where, in the case of Manchester when it was making its bids, Sir Robert Scott felt obliged to learn the names of the dogs of members of IOC in order to try to establish some personal relationship with them?

(*Mr Reedie*) 1940 was marginally before my time. I suspect that I will have to look through the minutes of the IOC. My guess is that at that time the British Olympic Association might have volunteered to do it, and if they did then they did much good for the Olympic movement at a difficult time just after World War Two. Los Angeles found themselves as the only bidder for the 1984 Games and it is part of Olympic history that when the IOC went to renegotiate the contract they found out that the negotiations were rather different with one single bidder than they might have been with several. What then happened in Los Angeles was that a very entrepreneurial head of the organising committee, Peter Uberoff, made, in Olympic terms, a huge profit out of the exercise. It rather coincided with the development of international television and the whole commercial interest grew hugely in the Games, and from that bid on cities have been very interested in bidding. Thereafter, the intensity of the bidding process developed, there is no doubt. If Bob thought it was better to know the members' names, then that was his call. The IOC clearly were aware that that

[Chairman *Cont*]

intensity got out of hand in 1999 when it then had, for the first time, clear evidence of wrong-doing, and I think it can rightly claim that it puts its house in order.

Miss Kirkbride

67. Obviously, being a member of the IOC, you are at slight difficulty in answering some questions, but can you help to guide us as to what issues and political (with a small "p") considerations (maybe, even with a big "P" considerations) the IOC take into account when they come to choosing cities? You have half mentioned continents and the "It's our turn", sort of thing—Europe's turn. Can you help us as to what they are looking for at the next bid, in terms of what has gone before?

(*Mr Reedie*) The IOC have been blessed by a fairly large number of applications from good cities over the last eight to 10 years, and it has moved more and more to looking at the bids on a technical basis. So its principal concern is to look and see how a Games would be run in the bidding city: how close are the major facilities to the village, for example; how complex is the transport structure; how easily can it be made to work; how much accommodation is there? There is a huge accommodation problem in Athens. That would not be an issue in London. So that technical aspect is what the IOC concentrates on. However, with a diverse group of 125 people, all with different (small "p") political views it does become very much a geo-political decision. Part of that is geography, part of that is favouritism, part of that is sympathy. An example I can give you is that the Athens bid in 1990 in Tokyo for the Centenary Games of 1996 was, in my view, a very poor bid, and Athens lost to Atlanta. When they came back eight years later they had gone to very, very considerable effort to improve the technical presentation of their bid, and in addition there was much sympathy for their loss of the Centenary Games since they hosted the first one. Does that help?

68. Does London fit quite well into what you have just said? Bearing in mind that there is sympathy because the UK has tried three times and has not succeeded, that the Stade de France is quite old and that we have potentially got a purpose-built site that we have been hearing about earlier (with maybe a few transport issues) how would you see the London bid fitting into those criteria that you have just been talking about?

(*Mr Reedie*) If I looked at the likely list of candidates, there has been a huge list of quotations in newspapers of cities who say they might bid but saying that "we might bid" is very different to actually coming to the table and mounting a bid. The declared cities at the moment are New York, which has been selected by the United States Olympic Committee, and Russia declared a bid during the IOC session in 2001. They actually have not said very much about it since then, but on the assumption that they adhere to what their premier said at that meeting, then they are declared. We know there is a contest in Germany; they are looking at five cities and having a domestic contest. We know there is a contest in Spain, probably between Seville and Madrid, and after that there is conjecture that Paris

may bid again—Paris bid last time and lost rather heavily—and there is conjecture that Rio de Janeiro may. Rio de Janeiro have won the contest to run the South American Games in 2007 and I think they see that as, perhaps, a stepping stone towards the greatest prize, which is 2012. If I look at all of that and if I then take into account a decision to be taken in Prague next year, where the 2010 Winter Olympic Games will be held, where there are three candidates, Pyeongchang in Korea, Salzburg in Austria and (I think very significantly) Vancouver and Whistler in Canada, if neither America or Vancouver and Whistler are successful, conventional wisdom is that that is more likely to place the summer games in 2012 in Europe. Therefore, a London bid would be competing with a Spanish city, a German city, with Moscow, with New York and, perhaps, with Paris. The prospect does not over-frighten me. That is a BOA comment, Chairman. I should not have said that, I am sorry.

Derek Wyatt

69. Good morning. I gather the Princess Royal has said that she will come in front of the Committee at the next appropriate occasion, but she is sorry she cannot be here today. We are sorry she cannot be here today. Could I just ask: the Australian bid was fronted initially by Gough Whitlam, a previous Prime Minister, and George Papandreas did huge amounts of work for the Athens bid. In terms of a British bid, is it John Major? Who is it? Is it the Princess Royal? Is she going to give up two years and be pounding on doors for votes? Who is going to do this hard work on behalf of Britain?

(*Mr Reedie*) The process is controlled very strictly under a set of bidding rules introduced and controlled by the IOC Ethics Commission. It is a two-stage process that if we decide to bid we are an applicant city and there is no bidding as such; you may not promote your case until the first cut-off point, which would be in June 2004. On the assumption that—and it is an assumption that I know the British Olympic Association have made consistently—London would pass that first test and move from being an applicant city to a candidate city, it is only then, at that time, that you would have, under the rules, the limited opportunities to promote and sell your case. In my view we will need to have at that stage clear support from Government. I would like to see a clear and charismatic leader of the bid committee and I would like to see a small, able, knowledgeable and dedicated sales team. That would be my package. Mr Wyatt, this is a joint venture, this is a three-stakeholder venture: it is the Olympic Association, it is London and it is the Government, and it would be wrong for any one of these stakeholders to make decisions on that particular issue until a bid has been decided upon.

Chairman

70. Can I just ask a clarificatory question? Derek Wyatt has referred to the role of Gough Whitlam in the Sydney bid in which Gough Whitlam visited—anyway, an Australian bid (you are looking sceptically at me)—most of the countries of Southern

[Chairman *Cont]*

and Central Africa including countries which did not even have a member of the IOC. Does one take it that that kind of procedure would no longer be relevant or available if Britain were to make a bid?

(*Mr Reedie*) It is absolutely and totally forbidden and it got the Australians into one hell of a problem after the decision in Sidney was announced and all of the Salt Lake City issues came into the public domain. That would not be permitted under the new bidding rules.

Derek Wyatt

71. In 2004 you are getting pretty near to a General Election in 2005. If you cannot tell me which politicians should be in charge of it now, by 2004 those politicians will not be available. It seems to me it is incredibly important that there is one political person, possibly a past politician in a sense or it might be someone in the House of Lords. It does not seem to me that anyone has given this any thought.

(*Mr Reedie*) We have brainstormed it ourselves and we have begun those discussions with the Department of Culture, Media and Sport, but, as I said, we think it is a little bit premature to take that decision now when we are told another decision will be taken on 30 January. It would be nice to know a name on the thirty-first.

72. Can I bring you to the opening and closing ceremonies. Many of us on 31 December 1999 had the most wonderful party here in London, especially in the Moor where there were 300,000 of us having a drink or two, not all of us were at the Dome. In fact, in London three million partied and around the world probably 100 million partied. Why do we have to have a boring opening ceremony in a stadium? Why can we not put it to the IOC that we would like to have a different celebration so that we would not need an 80,000-seater stadium?

(*Mr Reedie*) There is absolutely no reason why there should not be a little bit of off-the-wall thinking and then decide if whatever notion you come up with would actually fit into the sales process to attract the event. The name of the game here is winning the Olympic Games and if by winning those Olympic Games you could come up with some form of celebration that was different then that might be appropriate. However, it is part of the Charter that there is an element of Olympic ceremonial, there is the element of the flame, there is the element of the flag, there is the element of the teams. It is a great moment in an Olympic athlete's history to come in and represent his country to the stadium and as yet nobody has been quite brave enough to do what you are suggesting.

73. Take the London Marathon, if you had someone coming down the Mall with a torch in front of 300,000 people it would be sensational. Let us not go there. I am looking at the bid: Bisley does the shooting, Wimbledon does the tennis, sailing is in the Solent or somewhere else, Sheerness might do the windsurfing and the rowing will be in Nottingham. This is not actually a London bid, this is a London bid on behalf of Britain. Why can we not persuade the IOC that it would be much better for the country if the country celebrated the Olympics with London perhaps with a third or a half of the Games?

(*Mr Reedie*) Again, that is a discussion that has been debated in IOC sessions and modern technology would have you believe that you could take it all round the country and drive it by digital television. However, one of the principal aspects of a Games and what makes an Olympic Games unique is the opportunity to put 10,500 of the best athletes of the world in one village for 16 or 17 days and that simply would not be possible if you spread the events all round the country. It is a very important part of the Olympic philosophy that everybody comes together. If you separate the events all round the country then what you have is a series of individual world championships and the international sports federations do not want to go down that route either. So at the moment the IOC Charter says the Games are awarded to a city and that decision has been reinforced by the Games Study Commission which has produced an interim report that it will be a city. The IOC are well enough aware that on occasions that is impossible. For example, Beijing is a landlocked city so sailing will be in Qingdao. It would be difficult to have competitive dinghy sailing in London so it goes down to Weymouth. Substantial investment has been made in Bisley. Bisley is one of the best shooting ranges in the world. It was used by the Commonwealth Games in Manchester. It would be entirely wrong to develop another shooting range in the Lee Valley for the Olympic Games, so we could use Bisley. Wimbledon is the world's greatest tennis venue and it is in London. The rest of the events would be in London other than the football events where FIFA, with IOC encouragement, take it round the country.

74. That is my point exactly. One more question just on corruption. Are you confident that no-one in the IOC has received any money in the bidding process for Greece? Are you aware of anyone receiving £500,000 for that bidding process?

(*Mr Reedie*) No, I am not. The rules which I have in front of me are absolutely clear that the Ethics Commission will investigate any breach. There is now a formal requirement to bring constant and independent audit into the bidding process. Any breach will be made public and that should happen immediately and it certainly would not happen under any substantive inner London bid.

Mr Bryant

75. Obviously one of the key issues that the Government has put on the agenda and everybody else would agree with is the winability of the Games. As far as I can see from what you are saying, one possible outcome is that Vancouver wins the Winter Olympics for 2010 and that would then put Britain in a good position for winning in 2012, but we might be in competition with Paris, somewhere in Spain, somewhere in Germany. Paris did worse than Istanbul last time round, did it not?

(*Mr Reedie*) It did.

76. So how would you estimate the likelihood of Paris doing well?

[Mr Bryant *Cont]*

(*Mr Reedie*) The Paris bid last time—and I served on the IOC's Evaluation Commission looking at the five bids for 2008—was an attractive bid and it brought all of Paris's style and charm to the table, in particular it bought a piece of ground at Stade de Nice, close to the Stade de France, on which they could develop a very complex city centre village. It is my understanding that that ground is no longer available to them. So if Paris come back into this race they will have to re-think their village concept and it is hugely beneficial to any bid to have your village close to the venue for the two major sports in population terms and that is athletics and swimming. If you can build a village close to the main stadium with a swimming pool that is an advantage. I have seen press reports of Paris's favouritism. The first report seemed to me to be entirely wrong because it did not quote accurately what the author of the report said and recently there was a second report indicating that Paris might get somewhere over 40 votes in the first round. That seems to me to be highly unlikely. I would have thought at the moment, just looking down the list of members, and I insist this is only a personal view, I could make a case for London and Paris being pretty equal in terms of attractions to the existing IOC members.

77. Stade de Nice does seem to be out of the equation now so that makes it less attractive. If you were saying it was so attractive last time, why did it do so badly in terms of votes?

(*Mr Reedie*) Perhaps they did not lobby as effectively as they might. Perhaps they did not present as well as they might. You would have to ask individual members for their impression of what Paris did. Personally, I did not think their final presentation to the IOC actually fitted what the IOC wanted, but that is a personal point of view. I also think that they were against the one city in the world which had a very major claim to host the Games and that was Beijing with roughly 22% of the world's population.

78. It seems to be a fairly murky world how the IOC ends up making a decision, how the votes are arrived at and I accept that you have tried to amend your ways of working and tried to make it more transparent and so on, but clearly emotional and geographical issues must play a part in people's eventual decisions and other political issues. Do you think that September 11 will play any role in people's affections for New York?

(*Mr Reedie*) Clearly it will in some ways. I think by the time July 2005 comes that will weigh much less importantly than now. The best example I could give you is that Berlin bid some years ago and had the decision been taken after the fall of the Berlin Wall then I think the Games would have been in Berlin. The decision was taken 18 months later and I think Berlin went out in the first round. So I think the influence of September 11 will be less important by July 2005. I have to say, however, that New York will mount a vigorous and lively campaign. I suspect New York is good at that.

79. There seems to be mixed evidence as to whether having made a previous bid or a recent previous bid makes any difference in terms of feeling, "Oh well, they got close last time, let us give it to them this time." If you look through, Moscow made a bid for St Petersburg for 2004. Is that going to put them in good stead for a further bid even though they only had the Olympics in 1980 and so on? I guess what I am asking is whether London making a bid for 2012 might help us get it in 2016?

(*Mr Reedie*) You can argue the case for consistent bidding and winning eventually. Barcelona comes into that category. I think it started in 1938 and eventually ran the Games in 1992. You can also make a case for cities coming in and winning it the first time. The London situation in my view is quite clear and all the advice we have is that the opportunity exists now because the development possibilities in East London are there now. We will find ourselves in 2016 in perhaps the same situation as Paris finds itself now and that is that the ground is not available. So on that basis, since it is a bid that I think we can win but nobody is guaranteeing that we will win, if the facilities and the will is there now then clearly we should go for it now.

John Thurso

80. You mentioned earlier that the process of evaluation by the IOC has become much more technical and indeed you have also referred to the processes having been cleaned up somewhat compared to what it used to be. Can you describe to us what the IOC will be looking for in a London bid that would make London attractive?

(*Mr Reedie*) I suspect that the best way to do that is to give you some idea of the weightings placed on various areas for the initial applicant city process because on these weightings you move from applicant city to candidate city. There are 11 of them in total: Government support and public opinion is the first one and the weighting is three; general infrastructure, the weighting is five; sports venues, the weighting is four; the Olympic village, the weighting is four; environmental conditions and impact, the weighting is three; accommodation, the weighting is five; transport, the weighting is three; security, the weighting is three; experience from past sports event, the weighting is two; finance, the weighting is two, and the general concept, the weighting is three. I hope that gives you a clearer picture. As a member of the Evaluation Commission process the sports experts, who in the main came from the international sports federations, visited all of the proposed venues or were given discussions on them. The rest of the Evaluation Commission dealt with finance, marketing, security, particularly the village accommodation and all the other aspects. So it is a highly technical process and a very detailed report is produced on the basis of even more detailed bid books from each bidding city. One element is the financial element which is Government guaranteed, but all of that information has been available to the process and all of that information is held in the offices.

81. I do not know if we have already a copy of that, but would it be possible to have a copy?

(*Mr Reedie*) I am sure it would, yes.

[**John Thurso** *Cont*]

82. I am interested in the very first thing on the list, Government support and it has got a weighting of three, which probably represents something like 10 per cent of the total in terms of earning or value. As an IOC member yourself looking at other governments coming in, how typically would you expect an applicant government to demonstrate their support?

(*Mr Reedie*) They should engage clearly in the evaluation process when the commission is here, they should make clear and unequivocal commitments in the bid books which go to all of the IOC members and they should be prepared to undertake the signing of the guarantees that are necessary. If all of that information is made available beforehand then from a financial and a guarantee point of view as a member I would be quite happy for it. I have to say that those guarantees coming from the British Government I think would be cast iron.

John Thurso: Thank you.

Mr Doran

83. Let us go back to the deliverability issue. There is a huge prize in winning the Games but obviously huge risks in the process. I listened carefully when you talked about the new procedures which have been introduced to the Government bidding process. The first thought that occurred to me was that they seem a little bit bureaucratic and I am unsure whether they comply with the spirit of the Olympics, but they suggest quite serious difficulties in the past. Is it fair to say that? Can you say how secure you feel the process now is?

(*Mr Reedie*) Having operated under both regimes, I think it was inevitable that under the huge criticism faced by the IOC they would have to react very firmly and they did. It is interesting that at our session recently in November, particularly on the issue of visits, there was a long and very high quality debate from members who found themselves personally insulted by not being trusted to visit a bidding city and at the end of the day, out of 120 people in the room, 114 people voted in favour of no visit and six voted for change. So while it might be bureaucratic, I think it represents the IOC's wish never again to be faced with the problems that it had.

84. We are still involved in a situation where there will be huge competition. You have mentioned a number of cities and it will obviously be very, very intense, and you have now put in place the rules which may deal with the problem of whether corruption is involved or undue influence. One of the biggest criticisms that has been made in the past about the way the British deal with this situation is that we play by the book and we are not very good at building up the blocks and influencing other voting members. I speak as somebody who has just watched the fishing industry, for example, being signed away in Europe by just that sort of operation, where there was no corruption but lots of little nudges here and support there. How are we going to deal with that problem?

(*Mr Reedie*) That is why I would like to have, first of all, clear and total Government support and in this I agree entirely with Mark Bostock that if the concordat that he talks about cannot be put in place

then we will not bid. Secondly, it would be good to have a charismatic leader of the bid committee. Thirdly, it would be good to have a small and effective sales team and they will be briefed as well as I can possibly brief them on all of the many different alliances that there are within the IOC and even within the IOC within Europe because you made reference to the fishing industry in Scotland and you are well aware that one part of Europe seems to be of one mind and another part is not, it is equally true in the International Olympic Committee.

85. That deals with one aspect of it. You have put together a fairly highly qualified and focused team, but what are their chances compared to their competitors?

(*Mr Reedie*) Everybody will be operating under the same set of rules. There are only so many events which bidding cities can attend. There are a very clear set of rules on what you may or may not do and it is monitored by the IOC and ultimately by its independent Ethics Commission. You have to believe that the rules will work. If you believed that people would simply get round the IOC's rules it would be a very unsatisfactory state of affairs.

86. We want to know in advance that we have a fair chance before we suggest that the Government should put on the line the money and its own credibility. From the outside it does seem to be a very ruthless, bloody process. Sometimes I feel that politicians sitting round this table are pussycats compared to some of your fellow members on the IOC. Is that a fair comment?

(*Mr Reedie*) It is a comment that I have seen in the press. I do not think I would agree with it in quite the sense that you presented it. There are certainly some individuals who would like at least to have others believe that they had influence on the voting blocks or whatever. I think the evidence for all of it is relatively sketchy and I think the IOC is a much more open and a much more democratic place now than it was and that encourages me to think that a well organised and well supported London bid has a more than reasonable chance of success.

Chairman: Mr Bryant, as we have time left you may put your other question.

Mr Bryant

87. It was about broadcasting. Obviously broadcasting is absolutely essential to any Olympic financing and also most ordinary citizens see the Olympics through watching it on TV. As I understand it, in the past the International Olympic Committee has been quite keen to make sure that they take into hefty consideration the public service broadcasters when granting the rights. Is that still going to be true in the future?

(*Mr Reedie*) Can I correct you? The IOC has a policy that the Games will be shown on free-to-air television, they may not necessarily be public service broadcasters. I listened to your earlier question to Mark Bostock of Arup. The principal television deal is done in the American market which is free-to-air, but it is commercial and the IOC have appointed consultants and will be going back into that market on very, very good professional advice at the best

[Mr Bryant *Cont*]

time so to do. Thereafter, the European rights are currently held by the European Broadcasting Union, which in the main is public sector in Germany and France and in Britain. The last time the rights came up for negotiation the IOC turned down a very, very high offer from News Corporation because it was not free-to-air and it stayed with the European Broadcasting Union, a decision for which it was given much credit. The third major area is what is known as the Japan pool, meaning the Japanese companies pooled their efforts. The IOC are very well aware of the difficulties in the television marketplace, but they will simply not be going to negotiate when they think the market is bad, they will be going to negotiate when the market has recovered. They have good advice in that and I am reasonably confident that they will succeed in at least maintaining, if not increasing, the overall television rights fees because the product that they have is hugely attractive.

Derek Wyatt

88. Could you just confirm that there is no relationship between the ISL and the IOC in regard to the sponsorship for television?

(*Mr Reedie*) I do not believe that the IOC have any relationships with ISL. The IOC had left ISL as an agency arrangement many years ago and has been doing all its commercial negotiations in-house by setting up its own marketing department.

89. You do not think there is anyone left in the IOC who has a legacy with ISL?

(*Mr Reedie*) No, that cannot can be the case because there are members of the IOC who have been involved with FIFA for many years and who must have had some relationship through FIFA with ISL, but the fact is that that happened years ago, wearing their IOC hats and there is no relationship with ISL to the best of my knowledge.

Chairman

90. We have been talking about the New York application. If New York were to get it then the United States would have staged the Olympic Games three times in less than 30 years. By 2012 it will be 64 years since Britain has had the Olympic Games. Is that kind of factor taken into account?

(*Mr Reedie*) Yes, it is and it is certainly taken into account as far as the United States is concerned, because you must remember that not only do they have the Olympic Games, they have regularly hosted the Olympic Winter Games, the most recent in Salt Lake City. It is my understanding that the domestic process undertaken by the United States Olympic Committee was to find a city with which USOC would stick in the long term. I think the United States would like to have the Games back at some future date. I do not believe that they are passionate about having them in 2012, although they certainly would not say that.

Chairman: Thank you very much, Mr Reedie. I think we are about to see you again immediately.

Examination of Witnesses

Mr Craig Reedie, CBE, Chairman, Mr Simon Clegg, OBE, Chief Executive, Sir Steven Redgrave, CBE, and Mr David Luckes, London Olympic Bid Co-ordinator, British Olympic Association, examined.

Chairman

91. Mr Reedie, welcome back. Mr Clegg and Mr Luckes, we have had the opportunity of seeing you here before and we welcome you again. Sir Steven, this is the first time you have appeared before this Committee and I would like to say what a privilege it is for the Committee to have you present here today. We much appreciate you appearing.

(*Sir Steven Redgrave*) Thank you very much.

Mr Bryant: It is indeed a privilege to have you, Sir Steven, not least as I tried canvassing you during the 1997 General Election but you were out.

Chairman: We will not proceed along that line of questioning.

Mr Bryant: As you know, I am something of a sceptic about whether this bid is the right thing to go ahead with and part of my reasoning is to do with what it will deliver for UK sport. In your submission to us you said that one of the likely outcomes is that we will win more gold medals and you point to Korea gaining more when they held the Olympics, Spain holding more and Australia holding more. I wonder whether that is a correct correlation. I have worked out that we win far more Olympic gold medals when there is a Labour Government, but I do not think it is a direct correlation—

Chairman: Order. Any more interventions of this kind and I shall move on to the next questioner.

Mr Bryant

92. Could you just clarify a bit more what you think the direct benefits would be for elite sport and grass-roots sports across the whole of the UK?

(*Mr Reedie*) I will ask Simon to start with that and then ask Steve to come in behind him.

(*Mr Clegg*) One of the things that is absolutely critical to how the Games are perceived from a success perspective within the host nation is how the host nation performs on the athletic field and therefore it is absolutely critical that one delivers sporting success when the Games are on your shores. That is why that has been factored specifically in to the cost-benefit analysis and the calculation that has been undertaken is that it would require an additional £167 million-worth of funding to increase our levels of performance to put us in about the top five of the Olympic table. That would be sustained over the whole period of the campaign, kicking off from immediately when the decision is made in 2005 because you need to be investing in people who are going to be reaching the optimum age point in 2012.

[Mr Bryant Cont]

There are many other legacies that are associated with the sporting benefits of floating the Olympics Games, but you specifically asked about sporting performance. In terms of grass-roots, I do not think this is a question of either grass-roots or elite sport. We need to be investing in grass-roots sports and we need to be investing in elite sport as well. Certainly the 35 Olympic governing bodies that form the National Olympic Committee are very excited about the opportunity of running development programmes on the back of the Olympic Games in order to capitalise upon the exposure that we will have and to drive more young children into sport today.

(Sir Steven Redgrave) It is a proven thing that if one has more coverage given to something then young people like getting involved in those things. One of the successes that rowing has had through the 1980s and 1990s and into the 2000s is that the number of people who have become interested in rowing has grown immensely because of the success that we have had, and having the Olympic Games in this country will create so much more attention on young people wanting to get into sport. So it is not just the legacy that is left from the material things that the Games will deliver, it is the enthusiasm and the desire that these people will have at seeing the Games. We have seen what football does for young people and if we have a successful campaign for the championships then everyone wants to go and play football. If we deliver a successful Games then people will be interested in being involved in those sports.

93. But I remember a speech by Matthew Pinsett last year in which he was saying that one of the great successes of the last Olympics for Britain where we did significantly better than we had done for some time in terms of medals was the Lottery. We had invested a lot of money in elite sport and across the board and that was good news. My worry is where is this £167 million that we are talking about across the next 11 years coming from? Will we be hindering our long-term success? Spain has not done very well following the Barcelona Olympics in terms of medals.

(Mr Clegg) I do not agree with that, I think that success can be sustained. It may not be sustained at the same level, but it is certainly sustained at a much greater level of improvement than occurred before the Games. If you look at the number of medals and David will tell you, since 1896 Spain won four gold medals in total up until 1992. In 1992 Spain won—

(Mr Luckes)—13.

94. And in 1996 and 2000?

(Mr Luckes) But Korea won 33 medals in Seoul and maintained that level of medals consistently through subsequent Games. So it all depends on the programme that you put in place. You made the point about Spain and Spain did not win things by coincidence, they won it because they put the programme in place, but what they did not do was continue that programme beyond the hosting of the Games. That is the critical bit that we are looking at. If you look at the Arup Report, that talks about the three years following the 2012 Games for elite sport development.

95. So where is the £167 million coming from?

(Mr Reedie) It will have to come from direct Exchequer funding and I assume it will be directed through the excellent distribution arrangements which are currently run by UK Sport.

(Mr Clegg) But it is in the business plan. So this is not money over and above what has been identified in the business plan?

96. But it is over and above the money that sport would otherwise be receiving, is it not?

(Mr Clegg) Yes.

97. So you could argue that it is a net benefit to sport which would not happen if the bid were not going ahead at all?

(Mr Reedie) Absolutely.

98. One of the other issues is about how you bring the benefits to the whole of the UK rather than just to London because London already receives a vast amount of UK tourism and we find it very difficult to move it out beyond London and similarly, it looks as if we will be putting more elite sporting resources into London but not elsewhere in the UK. I have two questions associated with that. Wales is about to have a 50-metre pool for the first time and London has a 50-metre pool minus six centimetres, as I was told last night. How are we going to improve those national resources on the back of this? How are we going to get them out across the whole of the UK? Would you suspect that the Millennium Stadium in Cardiff might be one of the football stadia?

(Mr Clegg) I think in the last session you addressed how some of the events might be spread all over the country. As I am sure you are aware, we have approached all Premier League clubs as well as suitable facilities in Scotland and Wales and we have had a 100% positive response rate in terms of wishing to be involved in staging the football competition. There is a minimum requirement of 20,000 seats. Currently Northern Ireland has no such facility. If it does by 2012 then we will extend the commitment that we have already made to take football competition into Wales and Scotland to include Northern Ireland as well.

(Sir Steven Redgrave) One of the wider issues is that something that the British Olympic Association have done in previous Games is link with a town or city the build up to that Games and the legacy that is left there is immense. We had a training facility in Tallahassee in the build up to Atlanta and we trained there for four years on a regular basis and teams within the British Olympic Team went there and trained. The same with the Gold Coast just outside Brisbane, the legacy it has left there for those areas is immense. In some ways that is better than the legacy that is left because they do not have to supply an 80,000-seater stadium, so they are more at grass-roots level and for rowing we trained at a place called Hinze Dam. It used to be used for rowing back in the 1930s and 1940s and then it was not used and they used it as an excuse for us coming back in to be able to have that facility revamped and re-done and that legacy now is being used long term. That is the same with all the different activities within Olympic sports. I have spoken to a number of MPs and they are extremely keen to be considered as host venues for countries coming in and that is an immense legacy that a country will get the benefit from sporting wise.

[**Mr Bryant** *Cont*]

(*Mr Clegg*) I think your own Committee visited the Gold Coast and you saw the arrangements that we put in place. We invested over £1 million sterling in the Gold Coast in 1999 and 2000 and we are only one of a 199 national Olympic committees. So there really is a huge opportunity for every large town and city across the country to be able to engage in this type of business. It is a highly lucrative level of business.

99. How significant is the Paralympics as part of the London bid? In Wales we have had a few significant winners so we take a particular interest in it.

(*Mr Reedie*) From the IOC point of view, it is part of an overall agreement with the International Paralympics Committee that any city that bids for the Games will also bid for the Paralympic Games. Greece and Beijing are both incorporating the Paralympics organising section in the main organising committee and they are now beginning to move towards joint marketing arrangements. It is built in entirely. It will not be the same as Manchester where the Games were equally open for athletes with disabilities, but that is possible within the programme for the Commonwealth Games based on the size of the event, the Paralympic Games were held separately, but it would be a major part of the promotion of the bid from a British point of view because we are currently the second and have aspirations to be the leading Paralympics nation in the world.

Alan Keen: Chris Bryant has asked you the advantages of hosting the Games. As I tend to be on your side of the argument, can I give you the opportunity to tell us all the other opportunities?

Chairman

100. But briefly.
(*Mr Clegg*) The sporting benefits?
Alan Keen: All of the benefits.

Chairman

101. That is why I say briefly.
(*Mr Reedie*) In our submission you will notice, pages 4 and 5, (*see Ev 67–8*) one and a half pages are on key benefits because for the last six months we have been involved in a debate which seems to concentrate entirely on costs and nobody talks about benefits and we run through sport, we run through health, primary education. I was rather impressed by the statements made earlier this morning about how the Boroughs saw a major sports event being a catalyst for good there. The volunteer programme developed very successfully in Manchester, hugely successfully in Sydney and at the moment unusually successfully in Greece where there is no history of volunteerism at all is now up to about 50,000 volunteers. We talk about improved social inclusion, we talk about the obvious ones of regeneration and new housing. I personally am not an expert in East London but I would have thought the prize of having 4,000 new housing units where they are needed for the people who need them is a prize that is worth considering. There is the employment costs which have been dealt with in the Arup Report. There is the legacy element not just for sport, all of the practise

arrangements that we would have to put in place will be there. There is clearly a tourism advantage and there is an investment advantage. There is the feel good factor and we take advantage currently of that and it is all there. We think it is a very attractive package and it goes way beyond the benefits of sport. Certainly and personally, where I do have more experience is that I first looked at the Eastland site in Manchester some 18 years ago as part of the Manchester bids and when you look at what was done there and how all of that came together for a Commonwealth Games and there has not been enough said about—maybe I should have concentrated on this a little more in my evidence to you—the dramatic effect on the world's view of this country on the success of Manchester. Every magazine that comes in from a Commonwealth country at the moment talks very highly of what happened in Manchester. International sports officials who came spoke highly and speak highly of what happened in Manchester and every Commonwealth member of the IOC who was there was very impressed by what happened in Manchester.

102. If you are mentioning Manchester, Mr Reedie, and obviously I am extremely proud of the achievement of the Commonwealth Games in Manchester, but if one is looking at what happened in Manchester, the Government did not spend a penny, the taxpayer did not spend a penny on the bid, the taxpayer did not spend a penny on the stadium, the taxpayer did not spend a penny on the village, the taxpayer did not spend a penny on regeneration. I am not saying that public money was not involved, of course it was involved, but what we had were financial guarantees from the Treasury for the Commonwealth Games. What we have here, even for the bid let alone for what would be necessary if the bid were to succeed, is a substantial requirement for taxpayers' investment. I do not expect you to set aside any other view but your commitment to the Olympic Games being held in this country, but would there not be an argument for saying that rather than spending a very substantial amount of money on the bid that money could equally well, if not better, be spent on sporting facilities for young people in this country?

(*Mr Reedie*) Let me deal with that by saying that Manchester found themselves in the same fortunate position as Los Angeles did, there was only one bidder for the Commonwealth Games so there were no bidding costs. I think we should also draw it to everybody's clear attention that the original budget for Manchester was based on the Victoria Games in Canada which bore no relation at all to the scale of the event that was eventually held in Manchester and that was why Government had to come in, as they did substantially and in large degree, to support the organisation of the Games. I think it is entirely possible, but you would have to speak to our experts in that a number of the stadia may attract individual private investment as far as the Olympic Games is concerned, but for the Olympics, Chairman, it is a hugely greater challenge and in my view the benefits are much greater as well. I use Manchester as an example of what can be done. I think the results are

[Chairman *Cont]*

multiplied by whatever factor you care to think of in terms of regeneration in East London and therefore the bidding costs have to be a significant factor.

Alan Keen

103. Could I come back again and ask a question I asked Craig Reedie when he was on his own, especially as we have got Steve who has had such experience as a competing athlete. The cost of hosting the Games would be dramatically reduced if it was spread throughout the country. I presume the footballers, even though they will be young, will be pretty rich competitors and the tennis players will be staying in hotels. How many of the 16,000 others will care so much about being in one village, as it were? If the Games are held throughout the country in venues that already exist and would not have to be built afresh, the athletes could still be together for the Opening Ceremony, as the shooters from Bisley were able to go to Manchester for the Opening Ceremony if they wished to, and that would reduce the cost immensely. Is it not just old-fashioned? Could I ask Steve, how much value do you put on actually being in a village with lots of other people, because you have got to train pretty hard, you cannot party every night unless your event is over on the first day?

(*Sir Steven Redgrave*) It is one of the biggest elements of the Olympic Games. We have world championships, most sports have world championships, every year apart from Olympic year and the focus is always on the Olympics. It is such a bigger and better event than any world championships you could go to. If the element is that you are sharing a village with top athletes from around the world, that is probably one of the biggest draws of the Olympics because, as Craig Reedie said earlier, it would be split into world championships quite easily if you spread it around the country. I am all for making a London bid and trying to make the bid that goes forward as much as possible an Olympic bid for the country, not just one area. That is quite important. If you start breaking up the elements from one area, not having a village but a series of villages, security-wise that becomes a huge issue but it also devalues from an athlete's point of view what the Olympic Games stands for and what you are trying to aim to go to.

Alan Keen: Thanks very much.

Derek Wyatt

104. Could I echo the Chairman's congratulations, Steve, for what you have done. I thought Al Oerter did pretty well with four lots of discus but yours was a sensational achievement. We watched, along with seven million people, but we went on the web the next day to find rowing in Kent and we found that there was not any. This was a huge disappointment for lots of kids who watched you who found the next day there was nothing for them. It is the legacy thing that gets more and more important in this bidding. I suppose one of the things that the bid might do is actually make sport more important politically. It might actually bring a Secretary of State, so I guess I ought to take more interest in this suddenly. That is what we have been arguing for. We have been arguing for a Sport and Health Department with its own Secretary of State. It will be quite interesting to see what the political ramifications are. Steve, what I want to ask you is do you really think that the Princess Royal will go out there and bang the drums quietly in the committee stages when she goes? Is she an asset to us in this bid? Will she fight tooth and nail for us?

(*Sir Steven Redgrave*) Certainly I cannot speak for the Princess Royal but knowing her very well over the years that I have been involved in sport, she does bang the drum very well in her own way. Obviously in the position that she holds it is very difficult to be extremely loud about it but she promotes sports, she promotes British sport tremendously well and obviously, it goes without saying, is a tremendous supporter of the British Olympic Association. I do not quite know what you want me to say.

105. I asked earlier about—

(*Sir Steven Redgrave*) We are not saying which person it should be who is banging the drum towards the London Olympic bid.

106. We had a football bid where we had Sir Bobby Charlton, Sir Geoff Hurst and Tony Banks eventually as the political correspondent, as it were, for the Games. I have asked before: are you the person then who should be our charismatic leader of the bid? Is it a sports person who will do this better, is it a group or is it a politician?

(*Sir Steven Redgrave*) I think that debate would go on much longer than the time that we have here to decide which person it should be. I would be extremely interested in pushing the London bid to the full amount to get the benefit that we can get out of it. I think it should not be just one person but a number of people but there has to be a figurehead put on it, people like to have a figurehead. I do not see myself as being that person but I see myself as maybe being part of the team pushing towards it. The body would have to look at it once we decided that we go forward with a bid, should that be a political person or should that be a sporting person. At this stage I do not think it is an issue, the issue is are we going to put a bid forward or not.

(*Mr Reedie*) The answer is yes, all of them but at certain times and in certain circumstances.

Chairman

107. If I can just intervene before you go on, Derek. One of my major concerns is this: when the Arup people came before us they talked about a concordat of involved bodies. We had a kind of concordat after the Commonwealth Games were allocated to Manchester and, frankly, what we got was a shambles and a mess. Everybody was well-intentioned, everyone was doing their best, but there was no structure. Following the recommendation of this Select Committee the Prime Minister appointed Mr McCartney and Mr McCartney then created a structure which was extremely efficient and delivered a very successful games. Is it really possible in a major project like the Olympics, first of all in dealing with the bid and, secondly, if the bid were to be successful in preparing for the Games to do it in this way, to do it with an agglomeration of committees rather than

[Chairman *Cont*]

one person? When we went to Sydney what we found was there were two committees which were organising the Games. One, the Games themselves and the other the transport in Sydney. Both of them were under the Minister for Sport for New South Wales.

(*Mr Reedie*) The answer, Chairman, is in the bidding phase when you put together a committee, and I have outlined my dream committee, the time to make use of Steve's talents is with particular members who would like to speak to him. The time to use political talents is with members who would wish to conduct the debate on a political basis. The same with finance and the same with organisation. There is a slight difference between bidding and organising. When you come to organising, Sydney is a very good example. There was an Olympics Co-ordination Commission run by Michael Knight, who was the Minister for the Olympics. There was a Transport Commission, which was run by the public sector. There was a Security Commission, which was run by the public sector. There was the sports part which was run principally by the Australian Olympic Committee. They pulled it off. It is a very good model to follow. Sport will not be good at developing facilities. Sport will not be good at running transport. Sport will not necessarily be good at security, but it is better at sport. That is the way I would like to see it developed. I am certain that it can be done. One of the absolutely principal players in this, as happened in Australia, would be the political dimension and the political leadership involved. Latterly I became a director of the two Manchester companies maybe 18 months out from the Games and the structure which worked then, which eventually came into place with the funding agencies and the finance committee and good people all around the table, I am pleased to hear you say that it worked well.

Derek Wyatt

108. Simon, can I ask is it absolutely a given that the Games must be inside the M25? In other words, if I was to say that there was a formidable site just outside the M25 and that that would therefore give ownership to one county council and there would not be the GLA, the sub-boroughs, the transportation and so on, is it absolutely a given that you cannot look outside the M25?

(*Mr Clegg*) No, of course you can, but it also picks up the point that Mr Keen was making as well. The more you disperse the Games, the more you dilute the effectiveness of your bid and at the end of the day there is no silver medal in this race. If we are going to bid for the Olympic Games we have got to put together the most compact and the most attractive bid in the eyes of the voting constituency because at the end of the day if it is not acceptable to them then all the rest of the issues and work that has been done are purely academic.

109. Given that the Government is due to publish its university report next week, or at least before 31 January, there may be some reshuffling of what universities are, we may be going back to a three or four tier type university system, there will definitely be some shuffling around London, so here is an opportunity for the Government to allocate some

funds to move a university out physically, which is what is needed because you cannot get the accommodation for students, so here is a chance to look at something that would fit into an Olympic bid but it may not be inside the M25. If the Government said on the 30th, "We are quite interested in this but we would just like to look at some other sites", you would not be opposed to that?

(*Mr Clegg*) Of course we would not be opposed to it. We have entered into all the discussions with an open mind. If I turn to my Chairman and colleague here, within the eyes of the International Olympic Committee a London bid outside the M25 is doomed to failure in my opinion.

(*Mr Reedie*) It would be a much harder sell.

110. Because 12 events happen outside of London anyway? Because in Barcelona some participants were accommodated across borders in France and Italy. They were accommodated there and they missed their events.

(*Mr Clegg*) You could not sustain the level of facilities that you need outside the M25. One of the positive things about the area we are looking at at the moment is that there are already some existing facilities that can be creatively converted. Our vision for the future of the Olympic Games, and this is certainly shared by Dick Pound, the Chairman of the Olympic Games Commission, is that you will see a much better creative use of facilities in the future and a much greater use of temporary facilities in the future. Certainly in terms of the model, the specimen model that Arup worked up costings for, a lot of the facilities that we have identified are already in place and can be transformed to an Olympic configuration.

111. But one of the attractions of a university site, the legacy would be that it has the accommodation because that has to be built and it has the facilities, so it could be a great sports university, so there is a different view perhaps.

(*Mr Clegg*) To build 28 different sports facilities, including training facilities and warm-up facilities, I think that you would be seriously pushed to get those on one site outside the M25 and to be able to provide a sustainable legacy.

Derek Wyatt: Well, I think the jury is out until we have a look.

Miss Kirkbride

112. When the public are asked if they would like the Government to bid for the Olympics, they say yes and I am told that when they are reminded of what happened with the Dome, then public support falls quite dramatically because of the extra public money that went into such a big event. I am wondering really, and probably to Mr Reedie, what kind of reassurance you can give us that the costs of bidding for the Olympics and the subsequent costs of building the facilities are not going to be a massive burden on the taxpayer and will lose public support and credibility for the whole project. I am thinking of previous experiences of other countries where cost overruns have been a problem.

(*Mr Reedie*) I do not accept the premise that it is inevitable that any major project must be subject to cost overruns. I think if it is properly run and

[**Miss Kirkbride** *Cont*]
properly project-managed, then it can be delivered within whatever final budget is agreed. Now, I am aware of alternative figures which presumably will be brought to you tomorrow by the Secretary of State. Before we go ahead and if a decision is taken to go ahead, then the final budget will have to be agreed. Once it has been agreed, I see absolutely no reason why, with modern management and project management techniques, we cannot deliver it. I obviously cannot give you any absolute guarantees as I am not perhaps really in that business, but I think it is a rather depressing view that you have to start with the assumption that everything, but everything will be late and more expensive. I see no reason why the whole effort to build the infrastructure and to build the facilities should not be sufficient as a catalyst to get it done properly and on time.

Chairman

113. How does Athens measure up on that?

(*Mr Reedie*) Athens had many of the sports facilities, many more of the sports facilities in place when it was bidding than London would have. The Greek Government are taking the opportunity to improve in their ideas one or two of the existing facilities. For example, quite an expensive roof is being put on the main stadium and it is a very prestigious project for the Greek Government. As far as the sports facilities are concerned, I have no great concerns. They are building temporary facilities for those sports which are not popular in Greece and that seems to me to make much sense. What the Greek Government is doing is to improve the infrastructure of the city using the Olympic Games as a catalyst. The new road improvements, the light railway improvements, the metro improvements are all being funded deliberately by the city because the Games are there, not as a direct condition of hosting the Games. The sports side of it I am quite comfortable with from a cost and an organisational point of view. There is a lot of development work going on in Athens on the general infrastructure and it has also attracted very substantial European Union funding which has not been taken into account in any of the projections that have come before you.

Miss Kirkbride

114. Again going by the little list that you set out earlier of how the points are awarded, why do you feel you will get full marks and why do you feel that you will get less than full marks in terms of your pitch to the Secretary of State?

(*Mr Reedie*) If you take the specimen project prepared by Arup's, I think we will score quite highly on the general concept. I think we will score very highly on accommodation and this is the real issue. The reality is that Sydney, a city of four million people, was only just big enough. Athens is struggling, for example, building lots of media villages. We would not have to do that in London. We have enough beds for everybody who wants to come and enough beds for everybody who wants to come to support the Games and be a spectator. I think we would score quite highly on how we would

structure, build, convert and present our sports venues. One of the interesting concepts is the use of the Excel area down in that part of London which is an absolutely enormous exhibition complex. The Atlanta Games managed to get six sports inside their complex and we could get more inside Excel, and that is just taking the facility, turning it into sports stadia and then turning it back into an exhibition hall thereafter. I think we would score quite highly on those issues. I also think at the moment that we would actually score quite highly on public support.

115. And transport?

(*Mr Clegg*) Just on the public support, we very much look forward to receiving the Secretary of State's announcement this afternoon on the public polls which were commissioned through ICM and I think that will be very interesting and very indicative in terms of the level of public support. I also think we will score very heavily on government support because we have always said that unless we have the complete and utter support of the Government, then there will be no bid, so if we are running a bid, then we can count on a very high level of government support. As I am sure you are aware, we have secured cross-party support even from the Scottish National Party which surprised us and we very much look forward to working wholeheartedly with government in terms of driving this project forward.

(*Mr Reedie*) Julie mentioned transportation. There is a public perception that transport is difficult. You should speak to one of the gentlemen who is involved in the Vancouver bid who says that he thinks that the London Underground is wonderful because he can get around London on it at any given time. I think that was backed up a little bit by the Arup people this morning who said that there is a wide and diverse system of public transport here. Please make no mistake, every Olympic city manages its transport pretty firmly for the 16 to 18 days of the Games because that is the way that it has to be done. Sydney did it, Athens will do it, Beijing will do it, London would do it, New York would do it, Paris would do it and we are no different from any other, but it can be done and I think it is quite significant that the Arup study said that it could be done without the absolute necessity of finishing Crossrail, although that would help. The other issue, I have to say, where I think we would score quite highly is security because all of the security studies and investigations for Athens have been coordinated by the British Ambassador in Athens. The security consultant there is Peter Ryan who runs security in Sydney and who is also working for the IOC for Athens and for Beijing, so we would be well served in that area.

116. You say that one of the advantages would be investment in grassroots sport which will hopefully enable us to win medals at the Olympics. Bearing in mind that we will not have Steve around for 2012 to compete then and of course possibly not even the next Olympic Games either, why should we be putting that investment in? Why do we have the most chance of getting a bigger clutch of medals than we have so far seen for the UK, in your inspired guess?

(*Sir Steven Redgrave*) Since I have been involved in Olympic sport, the grassroots level is the key area and something that Australia did extremely well is that once they were awarded the Games, they

[Miss Kirkbride *Cont]*

focused on a programme to bring the emphasis up and that was not just youngsters that would be competing in their Games because it is very difficult to bring up ten-year-olds to 14-year-olds to be ready in six or four years' time to be competing in their own Games. They set up a lot of initiatives to promote sport using the Olympics as motivation for that for keeping their success onwards and we know how well they have done in that and how Australia are staying at the forefront of sport at the level of success they have got. It is initiatives like that that we have to follow. Coming back from the 1984 Olympics, from Los Angeles, having the Olympic gold medal, being able to pick it up and go to lots of schools, as I have done from that time, and dangle it in front of young kids you see them mesmerised by this medal as they put it around the room. From my own experience of having the world championships in Nottingham in 1986, a young kid came up to me who was just getting involved in the sport at that time, a few years later I was coaching him and then a few years on from that competing in a crew with him and winning a gold medal. That was James Cracknell, from the four. It is those experiences from athletes around the country at the time that motivate the people who will become the athletes of the future. Having something like the Olympic Games in Great Britain will be absolutely immense for the legacy that will not be seen and not really talked about very much, of going around to so many different schools, universities, business and industry as well. The feeling of what the Olympics could do for the British people, you just cannot put a price on it, it is absolutely amazing. There are very few people I have met since 1984 onwards—Lots of people have talked to me about hosting the Games: "When are we going to have a Games in this country? We are not going to see it in our lifetime". We have the opportunity of being able to go forward and push forward and win this bid that we could put forward.

Mr Doran

117. Just a couple of points. Following on from what Sir Steven Redgrave has said, I do not think there is any doubt whatsoever that what we would want to see and what the country would want to see would be a successful Olympic bid. There are still quite a number of hurdles to be got over and I am still concerned about a number of issues. I am not a London MP, for example, so the cost is a big issue for me. We have got quite a number of different costs floating around. We have got the Arup cost and one minister made a suggestion of a cost of £3.6 billion not so long ago and the figure of £5 billion floats around, although there is income from that, I understand that. As a Scottish MP, one major concern is the cost of the Games, not the Games itself but the infrastructure to support the Games, would act as a drain on resources in the rest of the country. That is not a territory that you will be able to deal with directly, I do not expect you to deal with that, but do you understand that that is a serious problem in the regions?

(*Sir Steven Redgrave*) Definitely. I remember speaking to Craig many years ago just after the Commonwealth Games in Edinburgh and I said "This is fantastic", and it is still one of the best sporting events I have ever been to in Edinburgh, I said "This would be a fantastic venue for an Olympic Games" and Craig, being a Scot, pointed out to me that there was no chance. Yes, it has the romance that the IOC could bid for it but the legacy of building up to it would not be able to sustain it. That is why I have said from the outset I would like to see this as much a British bid as a London bid as we can possibly make it. I do not know the answer as to how to bring the rest of the country involved in it but from my point of view I want to see it as a British bid, not just a London bid.

118. The legacy is important. I noted the point in your brief but I had not really appreciated it until you mentioned this morning the possibility of training facilities. I am interested to know how that would be pushed. Is that something that could be dealt with prior to the decision in 2005?

(*Mr Reedie*) The organising committee for any Summer Games will contact every one of the 199 national Olympic committees and give them a list of pre-Olympic training facilities. It is actually proactive. Let us assume for the sake of this discussion that a London bid goes ahead and it wins, the London organising committee would be telling the other 199 national Olympic committees "Here is where you can train". If we are short of 50 metre swimming pools, we are probably short of rowing courses as well, but please do not get into that debate. Strathclyde Park, for example, would be an ideal training facility for rowing courses.

119. Is that not going to be regarded as being too far away?

(*Mr Reedie*) Not at all. Strathclyde Park is closer to London than the Gold Coast was to Sydney, I can tell you.

(*Sir Steven Redgrave*) And Tallahassee to Atlanta.

(*Mr Reedie*) And Tallahassee to Atlanta. That business is there. What was significant on the Gold Coast was that it was not just other investment but the Queensland Government and the Brisbane City Council also invested in the facilities themselves because they used the fact that the British team was there as a means of promoting their city and also buying very mundane things like judo mats, which they did not have. They bought two and the judo team trained on them and they are still there. There is nationwide business to be done.

120. That is one of the difficulties. Another difficulty is our own track record in this area, particularly our recent track record with Wembley, with Pickett's Lock and the World Athletics Championship in 2005. Julie Kirkbride has already mentioned the Dome. Manchester itself, as the Chairman has said, was heading for difficulties before fairly severe action was taken. That surely cannot be of assistance to us.

(*Mr Reedie*) I hope, and rather believe, that memories are shorter rather than longer. By the time 2005 comes I would expect Wembley to be well under way as being the best football stadium in the world. By that stage we will be a bit further away from the Pickett's Lock decision. In Olympic sporting terms that was the damaging one. Although the Commonwealth Games were a struggle to bring to fruition they were a huge success and the rest of the

[Mr Doran *Cont*]

world saw that success. They were not hugely interested two years out in what committee problems were under way. The Manchester experience has done well. We are running the World Indoor Athletics Championships in Birmingham in March and I have every confidence in the capacity of UK Athletics, who are a first class governing body, to run a first class event there. I am sorry, I cannot just wait forever until people forget the names Wembley and Picketts Lock. I think there is a good enough sales pitch to be made because the opportunity is now and I think we should go for it.

Chairman

121. Thank you very much indeed. Last week I was in New York and saw Richard Rodgers' Oscar and today I have seen one of Sir Steven Redgrave's many gold medals; who says that it is not a treat chairing this committee. Thank you very much indeed. Yes, Mr Reedie?

(*Mr Reedie*) Am I allowed one last comment, Chairman. I hope you would accept that the criticism of some of the other projects has been that they were not worked on and thought through. This whole exercise has been done over many years to make sure that all of the information is on the table before the decision is taken, which I think has been an argument on many occasions brought to sport by your committee.

Chairman: I am happy to leave you with the last word, Mr Reedie. Thank you.

WEDNESDAY 15 JANUARY 2003

Members present:

Mr Gerald Kaufman, in the Chair

Mr Chris Bryant   Miss Julie Kirkbride
Mr Frank Doran   John Thurso
Mr Adrian Flook   Derek Wyatt
Alan Keen

Examination of Witnesses

RT HON TESSA JOWELL, a Member of the House, Secretary of State for Culture, Media and Sport, RT HON
RICHARD CABORN, a Member of the House, Minister for Sport, and MR ROBERT RAINE, Head of
Commonwealth Games Division, Department for Culture, Media and Sport, examined.

Chairman

122. Secretary of State, Minister, Mr Raine, we would like to welcome you to this meeting this morning. We are particularly grateful that you found time to be here in your own very limited timetable in consideration of these matters and we are grateful to you for the material that we have had supplied to us, which is of considerable use. May I take it, Secretary of State, that we can take your speech yesterday as your introductory statement?

(*Tessa Jowell*) I think so. This is like a debate in continuous session!

Chairman: On that basis we will go straight into questioning.

Mr Doran

123. Good morning. You were very careful in your speech yesterday, Secretary of State, to distinguish between the very powerful sporting case which you referred to and, obviously, the financial cost. Which will weigh the most heavy in the Government's decision?

(*Tessa Jowell*) Both will, to some extent, and I think we are at the stage in this debate, and it is one of the many reasons that we welcome the Select Committee's inquiry at this point, of moving beyond the sense of euphoria and can-do, the excitement that comes with the Games, which I think has often driven these kinds of big, bold decisions in the past. What we are trying to ensure is that if we decide to bid for the Games we do so in full recognition of the sporting case and the opportunity to showcase the UK and London in particular, but we do so in full recognition of the hard choices for sport and right across all the other areas of key Government investment and that we make those hard choices clear before the decision is made and not after. Your Committee has scrutinised so many of these decisions and too often we have made these decisions and then wondered afterwards why they cost so much and why public priorities have had to be distorted in order to pick up a cost that should have been anticipated at the outset. That is what we want to avoid and this is a decision which has got to be driven by hard realism about what it would cost in terms of cash, money, effort and

Government commitment, because the other bit is easy—the sense of feel good, national pride and so forth.

124. If we can move on to costs, then, even before we have put in a bid the estimates seem to be rising, and the Arup paper and a number of witnesses yesterday seemed to think it was very low. Yesterday in your speech you came out with a figure of about £4.5 billion and I have heard figures even higher than that and all the evidence shows, not just from our own experience of Wembley, and even the Manchester Games which were so successful but were more expensive than anticipated, that in previous Olympics costs rose inexorably. What confidence does the Government have that it can control these costs?

(*Tessa Jowell*) We are investing a lot of effort at the moment in getting the very best estimate of costs that we can, and I will ask Robert Raine who has been heavily engaged in this over the last few weeks to deal with any detailed questions that you may have. You will understand that making judgments now about costs in 10 years' time is difficult, but we have recruited additional help from PricewaterhouseCoopers to assist in that, and I have to say that the exhaustive scrutiny of the costs does mean that the extent of cost is rising. Now none of this is a reason for saying no, but the exercise itself is important in order to give us much greater confidence that the figure we sign up to at the end of this process is a figure that we can be pretty confident will face not just the country as a whole but the Government of the day if we bid for and win the Games in 2012. However, I would just add as a postscript that the experience of the Commonwealth Games in Manchester, which more than doubled in cost, has given us in relation to an event of a much smaller scale a very clear indication of where underestimates can seriously distort the budget, so that experience has been very much applied and we have commissioned the Office for Government Commerce to undertake a risk assessment which I think will cover both the assessment of the costs as well as the ability to deliver the organisational capacity that an event of this scale would require.

[Mr Doran *Cont]*

(*Mr Raine*) We have approached costs over the past few weeks in two ways: first of all, by a direct examination of some of the elements which have built up the costs put forward in the Arup report, and we have had some dialogue with people within Whitehall, with the other stakeholders, and those who would be responsible for delivery about risks and contingencies around those costs. We also, as the Secretary of State mentioned, took some help from PricewaterhouseCoopers to look at probabilities around those costs and they have indicated that, at this stage of the planning, there is a very wide range in which costs could fall a billion pounds of difference for an 80% range of confidence. There is nothing particularly surprising about that, given the complexity—

125. It may not be surprising, but it would be worrying.

(*Mr Raine*) Obviously, as the Secretary of State has said, what is important for Government is to identify the figure at the high end of that range within which, with the confidence that we need, the Games could be delivered if the event goes ahead.

126. If the Government makes the decision to go ahead, the way in which it works with the Olympic Association, etc, will be extremely important but it will also be extremely important that the Government gets its own organisation right, and we are well aware on this Committee that the Manchester Games was in trouble until the Prime Minister took the decision to appoint Ian McCartney and to give him special responsibility—and I think Mr Raine came on at that time—and managed to turn things round. That is an important lesson, I think, that seems to have been learned. Will there be a dedicated Minister appointed who will be responsible for seeing all of this process through, particularly given the level of costs which we are obviously talking about?

(*Tessa Jowell*) We are obviously in discussion, both within Government and outside Government, with the key agencies that would form the critical partnerships to deliver the bid for the period between now and 2005 when the decision is taken and particularly if we were to win after 2005, and we would very much draw on your Committee's recommendation and the success of appointing Ian McCartney in that dedicated way in doing that. We have to settle the issue of the departmental responsibility for this within Government. I am confident, however, that if we decide to bid, a short time after that decision has been announced we will be in a position to announce the way in which the organisation of the bid will be handled. We would expect, as we have indicated, that the Government will reach a decision at the end of this month and that will be followed some weeks after by an announcement of the organisation of the bid team.

(*Mr Caborn*) On the financing, one point that was interesting on our visits to cities that have already run Olympics was that in broad terms, on the cost, every one of them has doubled from the first figure that was given, but what was more important I think was that then creates all sorts of problems trying to raise the additional money. It saps the strength of the organisation like for instance, in Manchester which then diverts resources trying to raise money, and very

importantly you then start getting bad press because it is costing more than was said. We are very mindful, therefore, of the experience we had in Manchester which this Committee put out very clearly indeed. It is not just about the money but about the confidence and the culture that is around that at the time, which can be very sapping indeed.

Chairman

127. Could I follow up on one or two of the questions and answers that Frank Doran has initiated? Secretary of State, you talked about the various assessments and elements of costs but what you did not mention, and I am sure it is something you have taken into account, is displacement cost, that is what you could do with the money if you were not spending it on Olympic infrastructure both within sport and in terms of other Government expenditure—health, education, law and order, etc. I take it that in the assessments of expenditure those displacement costs have been taken into account?

(*Tessa Jowell*) Yes, certainly, and it is precisely that point which is the dimension that we are looking at in assessing the likely level of tourist income. Some people will come to London, or hundreds of thousands of people will come to London for the Olympics but there will be others who would otherwise come to London who will stay away because of the Olympics. We estimate that during the Olympic month an additional 600,000 people will be in London each day because of the Games—a net increase in August of about 300,000 per day—so yes, we are looking at the displacement effect in relation to tourism, and I would say in relation to this and all the figures that this is very fast moving work and I would be very happy for my Department to share further figures with you as the work is completed, which will obviously be over the next week to 10 days. Secondly, we estimate that if you were going out to buy the benefits that Olympic development will create, aside from the levels of tourism income and so forth, for the £2.5 billion upper range of underwriting that we believe would be required from the public sector, if you were simply going out to buy those 4,000 homes accommodating 16,000 athletes, 400 permanent jobs and the facilities, you would have to spend about £300 million in order to get that gain. Now, that would not buy you an Olympic-sized stadium but I think that gives you a measure, if you like, of the opportunity cost, the £2 billion which is required on Olympic infrastructure which will not form part of the legacy that will be available to the people of East London after the Olympics are over.

128. When you talk about upper ranges of costs, in the material that you very kindly supplied to the Committee you talk about 2002 costs and London 2012 as £2,614 million: you also then go on to say that if you use London prices for comparing the Sydney costs, then the Sydney Games would have cost £3.24 billion in Australian Government expenditure. Now yesterday when I asked Mr Craig Reedie about how Athens was getting on he said, obviously entirely honestly and straightforwardly, that in terms of construction of infrastructure Athens was on course. On the other hand, the information that you have provided for us shows that, when you

[Chairman Cont]

talk about upper range of costs, in Sydney costs as estimated doubled in outturn and in Athens, which is 18 months away from the Games, costs have already doubled. When you talk about the upper range, therefore, I am assuming that what you mean is the upper range now, not allowing for any increase in costs of the kind that we have seen in the last Games and the next Games has taken place?

(Tessa Jowell) You are right, but the counter argument would be that had perhaps Sydney and Athens undertaken a rigorous assessment of cost rather like we have done in revising the figures that were devised by Arup, then perhaps the estimate of the final cost would have been closer to the actual final cost. I will ask Robert Raine to take you through the methodology on this but I think there are just a couple of other important points. First of all, Sydney costs are 80% of the costs in London—I think that is important to bear in mind: secondly, it is difficult to capture all the cost which is directly attributable to the Olympics. Richard will want to say something about Athens because he has visited Athens and discussed the development of the Olympics with the people there, but Athens is undertaking an enormous programme of infrastructure renewal—roads, airports, telecommunications and so forth—and Beijing is doing the same. The total expenditure by Beijing is likely to be in the region of £20 billion. That is part of the transformation of the city which is driven by the Olympics but a fraction of that cost is directly attributable to the Olympics. It was exactly the same in Barcelona, where I think in the final costs of the regeneration of Barcelona which coincided with the Olympics the Olympic facilities themselves represented about 9 or 10% of the total cost.

(Mr Raine) We are trying to estimate now that high figure, so I think it would not be reasonable to take the figures that the Secretary of State is quoting, the £2.5 billion potential public subsidy, and double that as the expected outturn based on historical experience elsewhere. In the memorandum we did give the Sydney outturn cost at 2002 prices, and allowing for the price comparisons the Sydney cost is around £3.2 billion at 2002 prices. That is exactly the same as the cost level which has come up at the 60% probability level in the work done by PricewaterhouseCoopers, so whilst we say in the memorandum we cannot rule out all kinds of exceptional events which could bite us over the next 10 years at the high levels which the Secretary of State is now quoting, that is intended to guard against the kind of cost escalation which we have seen elsewhere.

129. Could I ask you one other question before passing on the questioning and that is this: there are two kinds of costs or benefits being assessed. If one looks at the tables you provide about what happened in other Olympic Games cities, there are all kinds of figures given there about economic benefit, financial benefit, etc, and all of those are assessments which may or may not be accurate—and in some ways we will never know. On the other hand, what the Chancellor of the Exchequer would have to spend is very clear and would come out of his spending plans and would not balance against the rest of this insofar as there were tax revenues accruing which it is very difficult to work out. I remember in the very worst days of the Labour Party in opposition we used to go around saying how much we were going to spend on increased expenditure on all kinds of worthy causes and I remember being asked by a lady in Nelson Market Place how we were going to pay for it and I said, "Oh, it will all be paid for out of increased production", and the look on her face was, "Tell me another one". Actual expenditure is clear and the Chancellor and you, working with him, know exactly what you would have to spend now, even though it may go up. All the rest of it is notional and not directly balanceable against expenditures by the Treasury. Would I be right in saying that?

(Tessa Jowell) I think we are trying, as Robert has said—and this is why the work with PricewaterhouseCoopers is extending the upper range and not reducing the upper end of the range—to anticipate every eventuality which can be anticipated in order to build those costs in now, but I would just underline that the purpose of this exercise is in order to avoid what has been the fate of Olympic cities which is that they have ended up with a bill twice the size of the one they anticipated.

Mr Bryant

130. I just wanted to pursue the same kind of area, and I should apologise that it is Welsh Questions at 11.30 so I shall have to disappear before the end of this session. You have listed one potential benefit which is the regeneration of East London and you have now put a figure on that which I have not seen before if you were buying that on the open market, as it were, of some £300 million. Yesterday we heard from the BOA that one other cost and potential benefit would be £160 million worth of money being spent on elite sport over the next 10 years basically designed to get more Olympic medals at those Olympics. You have been talking about the possible economic benefits of additional tourism to London, and then there is this unquantifiable, incontrovertible feelgood factor which comes from running an excellent Olympic Games, although I think Atlanta probably had a feelbad factor as well from running a rather poor Games where people could not get to the events unless they had the Princess Royal to drive them there. How do you assess, then, the full package of those benefits and whether it really stacks up as opposed to spending that money on the Health Service in London or on economic regeneration or education?

(Tessa Jowell) Let me deal, first of all, with the sporting benefits. A number of these were set out in the recent strategy report that we published just before Christmas. The evidence shows that when athletes compete in their home country they are likely to win more medals so we could certainly expect that if we were to host the Olympics our athletes would win more medals. The Olympics would also come at the end of what will be a close to 15-year period of investment subject to our Government remaining in office, a 15-year period of investment in not just school sport but grass root sport, talent development and ailing sport—all of which improve medal performance. What hosting the Olympics does not provide any hard evidence of is boosting participation which is the second major objective of

[Mr Bryant Cont]

our sports strategy. We want to see more success at the elite level, more participation by children and more participation by the general public, and it does not appear to have a lasting effect in relation to that. The medal performance effect does appear to be sustained, although at a lower level.

131. Just for that one Olympics or for subsequent Olympics as well?

(Tessa Jowell) That is the point and again, if you look at the performance of the Spaniards, the Australians and the Americans, medal performance peaks when the Games are held in the home country and is sustained but at a lower level in subsequent Olympics, so that is something I think we could be pretty optimistic on. But you are quite right to say that the associated feel good, the sense of excitement that was generated by the Commonwealth Games in Manchester in the summer, is dependent on the event being a success. Nobody is going to get a great sense of euphoria if the performance of the Games is being panned in the newspapers around the world every day that they run. So the sporting benefits are those, and this is the clinical analysis of the sporting benefits. This is not presenting you with a gold medal and the exquisite excitement for our athletes that winning a gold medal brings and the excitement that their presence in schools around the country and so forth subsequently generates, as Steve Redgrave I know showed to you yesterday. But then there are the other benefits, and we are looking very hard at the regeneration gain in East London. I think it is fair to say that East London is in a slightly different position from Beijing or Athens or even from Sydney in that regeneration is planned for East London anyway and arguably the Olympics would add some value to that regeneration is planned for East London anyway and that regeneration to take place. There is, of course, the question of what would happen to the Olympic stadium after the event because every Olympic country shows that there is no week in/week out market for an 80,000 capacity stadium, so that is why we are looking at what the legacy use of a stadium might be. The obvious one is that it would be, as with the case with the athletic stadium in Manchester, that it would be taken over by one of the football clubs, and those discussions are currently taking place.

132. But the Arup report suggests that a legacy of it going to a football club would be more expensive than a legacy of it going to athletics?

(Mr Raine) Yes. Clearly the Arup assessment is that the conversion costs would be greater. The issue that Government has primarily in mind is the sustainability of the stadium long term, and football is frankly a much more promising prospect than athletics for that.

(Mr Caborn) I think one of the interesting features you see as you go round the other cities is there is a price which you have obviously focused on, and rightly, but there is also the value and we need to try and quantify the price and the value, and I think it depends how we approach that. Obviously the Secretary of State has outlined some ways but if you look at Barcelona which transformed itself, and Sydney, there was a very clear purpose of repositioning itself in the country, and if you look at what happened in Munich immediately after the war that was done for a specific reason, and mostly you

can say there were reasons for doing it and to a large extent they achieved what they set out to do. If you look at the wider value both to London and the UK you are looking at trying to, as it were, refresh the image of London. When I was on Trade it was amazing how people perceived London and the UK—it was an image of Big Ben, the red bus, and soldiers wearing busbies and what-have-you, and we were trying to change that with the Millennium Exhibition that we took round the world to show that Britain and the UK was actually at the forefront of technology, and there are all sorts of things you can quantify that you can get with the world exposure you can get from an Olympic Games, and you can use that in many and varied ways and to some extent how you use that is about political decision-making. For instance, Beijing has gone in very clearly as to why it is investing in the Olympics—it is not just the Olympics but what you are going to get out of it.

133. You mentioned red buses. As far as I can see at the moment the only means of getting to the Olympic site would be the No 38 bus which is pretty full at the moment, and route masters are being taken off over the next two to three years so it will be difficult to get out there. There was talk in the past of a Hackney to Chelsea line and Mrs Thatcher always said that the people of Chelsea had no need to go to Hackney and they certainly did not want the people of Hackney going to Chelsea! We heard yesterday that, if London Olympics is to be a serious proposal in the East End, London Transport will have to be managed to an "unprecedented degree". Are you confident that that is achievable, and what does that management to an "unprecedented degree" mean?

(Tessa Jowell) We are of the view that transport is not an obstacle to a bid, and I think it is very important to be clear about that. There would be in relation to your earlier question legacy benefits from the investment that would be made in improving transport—a new station at Stratford and a new station at Bromley-by-Bow in order to build the capacity to deal with the 60,000 people an hour that the Olympics would require—and detailed discussions again are continuing with the Department of Transport about how traffic would be managed during that period, but I think it is also important to be clear that we recognise that it is possible to manage the traffic and the demand of traffic during the Olympic period without Crossrail. As you know, discussions about Crossrail are continuing within Government.

134. Would your assumption be that Crossrail is part of this equation or not?

(Tessa Jowell) No. You cannot assume that Crossrail is part of the transport infrastructure for the Olympics.

Chairman

135. So why do both the Mayor of London and the Arup report factor Crossrail into the transport structure?

(Mr Raine) Arup considers both scenarios—with Crossrail and without.

136. We asked them about it yesterday.

[Chairman *Cont]*

(*Tessa Jowell*) I think even if a decision on Crossrail were taken in the next few weeks it would not be completed until 2011, so on the basis that all our assumptions are at the top end of caution we cannot possibly assume that Crossrail, subject to all those conditions, would be ready for the Olympics. Could we assume, even if it was given the go ahead today or tomorrow, it would be ready by 2011 in one of the biggest public transport infrastructure projects ever? So we are not planning on the assumption that Crossrail would be available. Were it to become available, then that would be a bonus.

137. When you talk about the top end of caution, the top end of caution of the opening of the Jubilee line extension in time for the Dome was that it would be in operation at least two years before the Dome was due to open. It opened a few days before the Dome and today, on St John's Wood station, literally hundreds of people were waiting on the platform because of breakdowns in signalling on the Jubilee line, so I recognise—
(*Tessa Jowell*) That is precisely my point.

138. So the top end of caution is sometimes not really the top end of caution.
(*Tessa Jowell*) I will go on that, wherever the top end of caution directs!

Mr Bryant

139. Finally from me, undoubtedly this process at the moment of the Select Committee hearing, the debate in the Commons yesterday and obviously the very substantial work that the Department has quite evidently done with the Treasury throughout the whole process and so on seems a good process and much more reliable than any other process we have seen before but in the end, if we decide to go for it, the question that most sporting organisations and people in Britain will be asking is, "Are we going to do this with a full heart?", because as somebody once said, "Equivocation will undo us"?
(*Tessa Jowell*) I have made that perfectly clear. The reason we are going through this rigorous exercise at this stage is to be as clear as we possibly can be, 10 years out, about the consequences. I have said that all the evidence shows that transport would not be an obstacle. If we decide we are going to go for it we will go hell for leather to win and all the commitment of Government will be deployed, but we are at the moment at the stage of examining the level of public sector underwriting of the costs of this and the very heavy choices and trade-offs that are involved in that.

Mr Wyatt

140. Good morning. I wonder if I could look at the cost side and discuss the Treasury's input here? With the Treasury, has there been an analysis of what is required for the East End of London in terms of the regeneration, and a costing of what that is irrespective of an Olympic bid, and if so what are the figures?
(*Tessa Jowell*) Yes. Mr Wyatt, you will be aware of the discussions within Government which are being chaired by the Prime Minister to consider the proposal for the development of the Thames Gateway of which the Olympic site is a small part, so yes, the discussions are within that broader context.

141. Do we know the figures yet?
(*Tessa Jowell*) The figures are in the process of development, and clearly the conclusion on the figures will be one of the factors in determining whether to proceed.

142. I raised this in the House yesterday but the Chancellor of the Exchequer had a Doomsday Book created in July 1997 of all the assets that the UK owns, and if we are concerned as a Government that we do not want to foist a London bid on the taxpayer what analysis has been done on what we do own in the Doomsday Book? For instance, taking one particular example, we talked and then put back and then opened the privatisation of Channel 4, which in today's terms might be worth between £750 million and £1 billion, and presumably there are 10, 12, 15 jewels like that in the Doomsday book. What analysis have we done of what that Doomsday Book has in it so that, if we have to find £5 billion or £7 billion, we could at least look at that Book.
(*Tessa Jowell*) Let me begin by saying that we have had an enormous amount of help from the Treasury in the work we are doing on the figures in relation to this and a Treasury official was an observer on the Arup group which developed the first figures and we have had a lot of Treasury assistance in helping refine and develop those figures. On your question about Channel 4, let me make absolutely clear that we have as a Government a manifesto commitment that we will not sell Channel 4 and we are not looking to sell existing assets in order to finance an Olympic Games. We are looking at the available sources of public income in the broadest possible sense. However, we have to accept that at the end of the day the provider of last resort is the taxpayer and that is why we are looking at this very much in the context of this underwriting of an Olympic bid and as being potentially a major public expenditure commitment that would have to be set alongside the commitment to building new hospitals, new schools and so forth, all the priorities that our Government was elected to deliver.

143. I understand on Friday you will be visiting the President of the IOC and having a discussion with him. I wonder if you could let us know what sorts of things you will be discussing. Let me try and tease some things from you. Some of us believe that the Olympics has been a fairly corrupt organisation. I remember making a film of David Jenkins and the drug abuse that existed in the American and British teams in 1988 for Channel 4, so I have some personal experience of the corruption that existed at the time in the IOC. To what extent do you feel that the IOC is now clean and there is no disruption, and to what extent do you feel the bidding process is clean and there is no corruption?
(*Tessa Jowell*) I think Jacques Rogge has seen it as his priority as President of the IOC to address directly all those allegations and facts about corrupt behaviour in the past and he has made that very clearly his mission as President and I know that Richard, who has had a number of discussions with him, has made that absolutely clear. When I see him

[Mr Wyatt *Cont*]

on Friday I want to establish the degree of transparency in the bidding process. It will never be, as I have said before, an exact science, but I want to get a better assessment than I currently have at the moment about the standing of the UK, the standing of London in Olympic circles and what probability we could put on actually winning a bid. I think at the moment the collective assessment within Government and in consultation with the key sporting bodies would be put at one in three or one in four. That is very simple. We expect that Paris, a German city and a Spanish city, Madrid or Seville, are likely to bid, so that gives us a one in three or one in four chance. There appears to be no overriding obstacle to a London bid. I think the feeling is that a London bid would be a technically strong bid. We know the judgments about Olympic winners are not made only on the technical strength of the bid, it is to elaborate the context in which those decisions will be taken and the factors that will be taken into account that I want to discuss with the President on Friday.

144. Can I take up some of Frank Doran's questioning. If the Cabinet agrees to going forward, is there any mad rush for this 30 January deadline? In other words, is the gun to your head so that you have to make this decision or could the Government say there are some problems with the figures, we have not had enough time between now and the thirtieth, we would like to look at another bid, say in North Kent, but we actually need more time? Could we say on the thirtieth we are going to tick it, we understand the public are behind it, but, to be honest, we need a little bit more time? Could we tick it in January and then decide not to formally apply in June? Secondly, you gave some thought about what you might be saying after the decision, if it was a tick. Is there going to be an Olympic Department? Is there going to be a Minister for the Olympics in the Cabinet Office? What is your current thinking on that?

(*Tessa Jowell*) Perhaps I could take the third question in your list of questions, Mr Wyatt. An Olympic bid will be a bid to host the Olympics in London rather than North Kent or anywhere else in the country and I think that that is absolutely clear. The end of January is an important deadline because the British Olympic Association have made clear that they will need time to prepare a bid, that they will be the bidding organisation, but as Jacques Rogge and everybody recognises, a bid can only proceed if it has the wholehearted support of the Government. We have made clear that we will do it by then. As you know, there is a tremendous amount of work to be done and the work is still in progress in order to meet that deadline, but no, I do not think it would be right to say we need more time. We have said for a long time that we will give a decision by the end of January and it is my intention that we meet that deadline. In relation to if we decide to bid, what then happens: I really do not have anything further to add to my answer to Frank Doran's question, which is that we would make an announcement a few weeks after about how the process of bidding would be organised within and beyond Government.

John Thurso

145. Can I first of all ask a simple factual question regarding accommodation. I think you said there would be a net increase in visitors of 300,000, which I presume is visitors and not visitor nights. Do we have that accommodation and, if not, how much needs to be built?

(*Tessa Jowell*) Yes, we do and it is because of London's hotel capacity and particularly its upper end of the range hotel capacity that London is in fact the only city that the BOA considers to be credible to host the Games.

146. So we do not need to build any more accommodation in hotel terms other than the village?

(*Tessa Jowell*) No, although I think if you have been out to Stratford lately you will see that there are a lot of hotel developments going on there. We do not need more hotel development. That does not mean to say there will not be more hotel development.

147. Can I come back to the question of costs and benefits and I must commend you on the work that has been done on the costs. It does seem to me that there were rather wobbly costs which the Arup Report started with, but you have probably flushed out many of the problems that might have come in the future, so the £2.6 billion is probably a pretty robust figure. The other thing is the table comparative to the other Games which is very useful. What have you done to compare the benefits that past Games have been able to have in the same way and what assessment have you made of the quality of those benefits?

(*Mr Caborn*) We have done that from the visits we have made. It is very difficult to compare like with like here. We are talking about the Sydney Games and there was a major motorway built from the airport to the Games village which was not costed into the cost of the Games. I think there are several benefits that we will look at. First of all, you want to make sure that you use the bidding stage very effectively, but you must have an exit strategy in the event of you not winning the bid. You can actually gain quite a lot out of that. If one looks at what Manchester and Birmingham did on their bids, they actually gained out of the bidding process. I think it is an approach that you can have to the whole bidding process. Beyond that then obviously there is delivering. Again, everybody stressed to us very clearly that we will want to make sure the bidding process time is actually used as a potential part of delivery as well. I think the problem that Athens has now is they lost out for three years in the bidding process and it has now cost them very dearly indeed because to some extent they are in crisis management and therefore they are paying premiums on much of the construction. In terms of the legacy, then what has been stressed to us is to make sure you use the facilities that you have already to the maximum and Sydney wish they had done that because there are now two areas competing with each other. The very important point is to make sure that your strategy is actually in place before you start and that is part of the bidding process as well, so you know what you are going to do with your facilities. For example, Sydney are paying £10 million a year in revenue charges, that is revenue not capital, for keeping their

[John Thurso *Cont*]

facilities going. You have hockey and tennis, which are massively under-utilized, which they believe and wish they had got an alternative use for, which could have been done as a strategy when they were designing the building. We have learned a lot from that. Therefore, I believe if we did bid then our exit strategy would be as cost-effective as possible, in fact probably better than any other Olympics before. I think the Manchester one was an experience in terms of being able to have a reasonable exit strategy and how you would bring Manchester City into that stadium. They were criticised immediately after the Games when they were going to rip up the track and dig six foot deeper to get 10,000 more seats in there. When you lift the revenue implications off the back of a city or a country it is worth considering. Bayern Munich are now coming out of the Munich stadium after many years of playing there because of a dispute with the architect and it is going to cost Munich city £6 million a year revenue to keep that stadium as it is now. Bayern Munich will move out in about the next six months.

148. It seems to me from the evidence we received yesterday that it is an absolute prerequisite of any attempt to make a bid that the Government is totally behind it, not just ticking the boxes but absolutely full-bloodedly behind it and I think from the evidence you have given you have indicated that that will be the Government's position. There was also clearly very strong public support probably based on the feel good factor. The mood of music over the last 24 hours has been very much about costs and is it worth it and could not we get it all in a different way. Putting it into perspective, the cost is about three-quarters of the costs of, for example, decommissioning a nuclear reactor. So it depends on how up choose to look at it. Do we not really need to say that this should not be about puritanical cost management, this really should be about Britain going out for a flagship event and just standing up and saying we are going to do this, we have made the best estimate of cost, it is pretty robust, it is worth it, let us get on with it?

(*Tessa Jowell*) That may well be the conclusion that we reach, but it has to be a conclusion which is rooted in an understanding of the choices, that it is a choice between doing this and putting more money into hospitals, putting more money into schools, putting more money into transport, putting more money into more grass-roots sport, putting more money into getting more children playing more sport at school. You cannot ever retreat from the choices that you have to make and this is precisely the purpose of the debate that we have tried to create. In a sense let us go for it and let us go for it because we are a proud nation and we are going to showcase London and our athletes are going to win more medals than ever before. That is why you do it, but that is the easy bit. The hard bit, as the experience of the Commonwealth Games has shown, the experience of Picketts Lock has shown, the experience of Wembley has shown, is that it is very easy to be driven by euphoria alone and then the hard reckoning follows afterwards and that is what we want to avoid, so that we say to people, if we decide to bid, yes, we have decided because, in full understanding of the consequences, this is such a great thing for Britain and if we do not bid it will be because we have decided after rigorous examination that the costs are just too great and other very precious priorities, not just of the Government but of people up and down the country, would have to suffer if we were to do this. I think the poll, which I hope you got in good time, that we commissioned showed some very interesting conclusions. Yes, people are overwhelmingly in favour of our making a bid. The numbers fall when people are pressed in committing themselves to that alongside the consequences. There is one very interesting chart in the polling evidence which shows that, from memory, if you tell somebody they have £100, overwhelmingly what the sample showed was that you spend the largest slug of your money on more schools, the next largest slug on more hospitals, the next largest slug on increasing the value of pensions and then, interestingly, above reducing taxes, you spend money on an Olympic bid. I think the public's priorities are very clear indeed, but nobody should believe that hosting the Olympics would be somehow a free good, that we can just decide to do it as a decision that is divorced from the costs, the costs for sport, the costs for transport and all our commitments to public service renewal.

149. So ultimately the Chancellor will decide?

(*Tessa Jowell*) No, the Chancellor will not decide, the Government will decide and the Government will decide because right across Government there is a passion for sport and investment in sport which the Chancellor shares. Look at the money that we won for sport in the last spending round, building on investment in sport in the previous spending round. The investment in sport from the Exchequer has more than doubled in the last five years, so across Government there is a passion about sport, the good that it can bring and the sense of national pride that it can generate, but that is very realistically set alongside our commitments to other areas of public service investment as well.

Alan Keen

150. Can I just ask about one issue and say a few words to put it into context. I asked Steve Redgrave yesterday about the value of the Olympic village and he said that it is everything. He said it means such a lot to the athletes to live in one village. On the other hand, the alternative to that, I reckon, and maybe you can help, that it must cost £½ billion in order to have 18,000 athletes living in a village for three weeks, the alternative is to spread it around the country. Steve said you could have what would be like a world championships where it is spread around the country rather than have 18,000 athletes living in one village. Because we want them all to live in one village for three weeks and to build a stadium, it is going to cost what, £300 million at least, and then it would be handed over or given to a football club which maybe does not even want it. We perhaps could save £½ billion, and as you are going to see the IOC on Friday, it is an ideal time to talk about it, but we could save £½ billion by having the events spread around the country and we would not then have to build the stadium because we could have the athletics in Wembley Stadium, for instance, and £18 million is

[**Alan Keen** *Cont*]
the last estimate we have had to put in the metal framing to reduce the seating and make an area big enough for athletics. We have already given £20 million to the FA which you cannot take back from them now. We have given £20 million in order to make it compatible for athletics, and events could also be held around the whole country and we would save £½ billion. If you said to the athletes, "Look, instead of living in a village, we could give you £27,000 each", that would still come to £½ billion, which is a lot of money, so it is costing every nation every four years and it is costing taxpayers and kids who would get that money for sports equipment and facilities, and I reckon it is at least £½ billion we would save by spreading it around the country and this is every four years. Because the IOC is such an undemocratic organisation, nobody can put these points and they do not have to answer to anybody. You are going to see them on Friday and you are not in a position to say, "Look, I think you should do this", because if you take a hard line, they are going to say, "Right, you might as well not even bid because you are not getting the Games". It is an undemocratic organisation, so it is hard to get these changes put forward, so I think you have a job, but I hope you will try to convince me that it is not costing us £½ billion.

(*Tessa Jowell*) Let me deal, first of all, with the costs of the Olympic village which Arup estimate to be at about £62 million and obviously there would have to be some conversion of the accommodation from single-person accommodation for the athletes to family housing which would provide the 4,000 homes legacy afterwards. I think you have asked an interesting question, Mr Keen, but it is in direct conflict with the IOC's own standards and obviously touches on our assessment of whether or not we could win. I think it would be highly desirable to disperse facilities in different parts of the country in order that the country as a whole could benefit from what will otherwise be an event which will largely benefit, particularly in relation to tourist numbers, the economy of London. There are ways in which we would expect to be able to do that through the development of training facilities in different parts of the country, for instance, before the Olympics themselves start. The athletes will come well ahead of time in order to acclimatise and to train and certainly it would be possible, it would be a requirement to have training camps in different parts of the country and some of the facilities will be dispersed. Shooting will be at Bisley as it was for the Commonwealth Games and so forth, and football would be held in stadia around the country. The IOC are quite clear that it is a city that bids to host the Games and they do not create the degree of latitude that you might want or that we might think is also desirable.

151. That is why I said as part of the question that it is difficult for us, the UK, to go to the IOC and say, "Why don't you do this?", but if we do not do it now, if things are going to be perpetuated over another century, and you mentioned straightaway in your answer about the cost of the village, though it is not the accommodation of the village that I am talking about, but having to build a major stadium which is not going to be needed afterwards and having to put swimming pools in places and then having to

dismantle them again afterwards, the overall cost of having to build a stadium and all the associated accommodation and everything else that goes with it. What I am saying is that I would like you to calculate how much cheaper it would be if we used stadia that are already around the country because I think it is something which, even if we do not put it to the IOC on Friday, which might damage our ability to win the bid, we should put it to them at some point. With an undemocratic organisation like it is, it is very hard for anybody to bring about any changes. As I said in the debate, I love the Olympics, so I am not criticising the Olympics, but it is just that it must cost £½ billion at least to get all of that stuff in one area and it just seems an awful lot to pay when it could be spread around the country and more people could enjoy it. That £½ billion at least, or £27,000 per athlete, seems an awful lot just to get the athletes together in one village for three weeks when one billion people or more are going to watch it on television and enjoy it. That is the real question I am asking.

(*Mr Caborn*) I think that Rogge is very mindful of the point that you make and he has discussed with a number of people how you can actually contain and indeed to some extent downsize the Olympics because it is growing at a rate and has been, some would say, over-commercialised and indeed it has taken it out of the price tag for many nations to run now and I think the IOC and particularly Rogge are mindful of that and are looking at how they can bring it into manageable proportions so that other nations can actually run that. I think, therefore, that any of those suggestions which are put forward, he would be exploring those. The debate a few weeks ago in the IOC was about the number of events and there was obviously a bit of consternation from those who are not likely to be in the bid for the Games in 2012. I think on the question of the village, it is an important one. It is one that we had a lot of discussion about when we ran the Commonwealth Games. There is a question of security, first of all, which we all know from Munich and that has to be a consideration. Secondly, I think there is a desire of the athletes to actually live together and the camaraderie of the Olympics, I think, is an important part and if you have ever been into one of these villages, they are fantastic. I have had the opportunity of visiting two or three of them. Also it can be used very effectively in the exit strategy. If you look at what has happened, for example, in Sydney, half of that is now a campus and they use it very creatively. They use the press, which was again a very big construction in Sydney for the Games there, they have actually used that facility to turn it over now into the sports science and medicine part of the university and they use the housing as part of the campus, so they knew exactly what they were going to do with that and you can see that in a number of other areas. Universities in London are short of both accommodation and facilities, so there are ways that we can look at that. Again in Manchester, we coupled with the university there to look at the swimming complex, so there are lots of crossovers here that you can use. It is obviously an expenditure, but it can also be a major asset in the exit strategy if it is used creatively.

Miss Kirkbride

152. Secretary of State, listening to you yesterday and this morning, I think most people would all agree that some big baths of cold water have been poured over Britain's Olympic aspirations really. I wonder if you could put more of a case as to why it might be a good idea. First of all, it was in the Labour Party Manifesto in 1997 that you would bring the Olympics to Britain, so what has changed?

(*Tessa Jowell*) Well, I am not pouring a bath of cold water over this at all, but I am doing what I think it is my job to do. The Secretary of State's job to do is not to walk the country into an unfunded commitment or into a huge commitment, the funding of which would reduce our ability to meet our commitments in other areas of public spending. I think that, as I have said, the polling that we have published today shows very clearly where the public are on this. Making the case for the Olympics is the easy bit. Of course there is a case for sport which has been made by ministers across government, but this also comes with very heavy costs and I would say to you that this Select Committee has taken a very trenchant view of the handling of big projects by Government, including projects by my Department, and you have been highly critical in the past about the failure to take account of the true cost and the true burden on government. I take that very seriously indeed. The Minister for Sport takes that very seriously indeed. My Permanent Secretary and the officials of my Department take that very seriously indeed. Therefore, in exposing the costs of an Olympic bid and the choices that are involved in deciding to go ahead with an Olympic bid, I am doing my job not just for sport, but for the other investments that we in this Government hold very dear indeed on behalf of the people of this country who have elected us to deliver them.

153. But other countries which are known to us who have had the Olympics, with the exception of America, have a smaller GNP than we have. They also have the same priorities for their populations, Australia and Spain both have the same priorities for their populations, yet they can afford them. We are the fourth largest economy in the world and you are very much giving the impression that we cannot afford them.

(*Tessa Jowell*) No, I am not saying that. The Games are affordable. They are affordable if we decide we are not going to do other things. Those who are directly involved in sport have made it very clear that they would not, for instance, want the price of the Olympics to be reducing our commitment to grassroots sport, reducing our commitment to sport in schools, reducing our commitment to elite sport, so you have to accept that there are choices. There is not a cache of money which is available cost-free from any of these choices and available to spend on the Olympics. It is money from the taxpayer or certainly it is money which is underwritten by the taxpayer. We will obviously look, we are looking at the extent that we might be able to use Lottery income in order to contribute to this and a number of other options are currently being explored, but at the end of the day, taking the most cautious scenario, we have to be prepared to say that we want this so much that we are prepared for the taxpayer to underwrite it

and we want it so much that we are prepared to make choices between other priorities. Otherwise, it is simply not a decision that has been taken in the real world and in relation to your—

154. I am sorry, Chairman, but we do not have very long and if the Secretary of State makes very long answers, then we do not get a chance to put other questions to her. One cannot help but wonder, though, when talking about schools and hospitals, that it is just a good way of warming up the general public to the disappointment of the Government saying, "No, we are not having the courage and the aspiration for an Olympic bid". The truth is that the Government spends something like £400 billion every year and we are talking about a project 10 years away and yes, I do accept that £4.5 billion, at the top end of what it might be, is a lot of money, but, goodness me, we are going to earn a lot of money in the meantime and if we want to go to the theatre, we have to pay for the ticket, do we not? If Britain wants to host the Olympics, if we want to let our domestic population come here and see the Olympics, then there is a price to be paid, but are you really saying that there are so many schools and hospitals which are not going to be built as a result of that? It does not seem credible when we spend £400 billion every year under your Government.

(*Tessa Jowell*) The facts are there. If we spend £2.5 billion from public money on the Olympics for all the reasons that we have been discussing this morning, all the positive reasons, then that is £2.5 billion that will not be spent on other competing projects. That is a matter of fact. In relation to your point about other cities, I think it is also important to be clear that Barcelona, Beijing, Sydney and Athens all bid for and wanted the Olympics because it would drive regeneration in their cities. As I said in answer to, I think, Mr Wyatt's question, the judgment is that the part of East London which would be the Olympic site is currently planned for regeneration and the regeneration of that part of London is not dependent on the Olympics. The Olympics would add some value.

155. Taking that point up, you made it yesterday, and you have inferred it this morning, that only London could possibly be considered for a credible Olympic bid. Bearing in mind that London is incredibly built up, is it not the case this is the only opportunity we have left to credibly go to the IOC and say we would like to host the Olympics, because once that redevelopment has taken place in the East End there is simply not another site left in London, which is the only city that can bid for this bid, that can possibly take a case. The moment for the United Kingdom to actually put forward an Olympic bid is now because of that redevelopment opportunity. That closes and that is it, the UK is not going to have an Olympic bid.

(*Tessa Jowell*) In looking at the balance sheet for and against, the argument for the bidding, the aspirational balance sheet, the actual costs in the balance sheet, the opportunity costs in the balance sheet, the legacy benefits in the balance sheet that is obviously a factor.

156. Once this goes that is it.

[**Miss Kirkbride** *Cont*]

(*Tessa Jowell*) It is a judgment rather than a fact. The judgment is that it is in East London that you get the synergy between the space required for Olympic development and the planned regeneration, so that is correct, yes. It is also likely that after 2012 if those sites are not used for Olympic facilities will have been developed for other purposes. There is a third element, which again is more art than science, there is a feeling, a belief dependent on decisions like where the 2010 Winter Olympics will be held, that 2012 will be at the European Games and after that the IOC will move to another continent. You are not categorically right in what you say but there are certainly judgments that would support your view.

Miss Kirkbride: Thank you, Mr Chairman.

Mr Flook

157. If the Commonwealth Games in Manchester had not been a success would we be sitting here now? To put it another way around, are you not a victim of your own success?

(*Tessa Jowell*) I think that is a very interesting question. Obviously the consideration about whether or not to bid for the Olympics preceded the Commonwealth Games and I think we commissioned the Arup Report at the beginning of 2002. The Arup Report, which has heavily informed judgments about the costs, was commissioned long before the Commonwealth Games. I think there are two things that the Commonwealth Games have changed, one is—and I think there are those in the international sporting community who have been quite explicit about this—the Commonwealth Games demonstrated that the United Kingdom could host and could deliver a fantastically successful sporting event on that scale. Remember, the Olympics are 10 times the size of the Commonwealth Games—it depends what measures you use—the Olympics by a factor of more than two are much bigger, somewhere between a factor of 4 to 8 bigger than the Commonwealth Games. I think it is also fair to say that the right decision to withdraw from hosting the 2005 World Athletics Championships did cost us in confidence in international sporting circles and that was confidence that was re-established with the success of the Commonwealth Games.

(*Mr Caborn*) I also think as a result of the IAAF indoor games we are to run here in Birmingham in 2003, we have the Commonwealth and the IAAF, and I am sure Birmingham will rise to the occasion and produce an extremely good indoor games.

158. The DCMS will be aware that the *Daily Telegraph* has been a big supporter of the notion of having the Olympic Games in London, in Britain in 2012. I was interested in today's *Telegraph* the honourable gentlemen, the member for West Ham said that everyone has to get behind this—this was reported from yesterday's Chamber—and almost sign up for it in blood, a classic over-exaggeration on his part. The *Telegraph* also says that the winability of the four, affordability, deliverability, legacy and winability is about the only given, which of course it is not. As a decision by the IOC is very likely to be after the next General Election, because I believe that

it is in July 2005, and it is likely there could be an election in May 2005, what would be the most important piece of advice you would give your likely successor on how to take forward a successful decision by the IOC to give London the 2012 Olympics?

(*Tessa Jowell*) I think that is a series of well phrased, hypothetical questions. I cannot possibly answer about the date of the next general election.

159. I appreciate that.

Chairman: Politically he is being totally uncontroversial.

Mr Flook

160. I do not wish to prejudge it either.

(*Tessa Jowell*) What I would hope is that if we do decide to bid that our friends in the press, who have been powerful advocates for the case for the bid will remain powerful advocates of the bid and also the Government and the BOA in the event that we win a bid and proceed to put in place the facilities for an Olympics.

161. What piece of advice on winning from all of the lessons you are likely to learn and all lessons you have learned, apart from the Dome, from Wembley, from Manchester, what piece of advice will you give the person who will be Secretary of State in August 2005?

(*Tessa Jowell*) There are two, and this may be a note to myself, for all I know. First of all, be absolutely clear what you are in for and go through the exercise of anticipation and be as confident as you possibly can be of the costs and the other operational issues which are involved before saying yes. If you then say yes you go hell for leather, you give it everything you have to make it the greatest possible success it can be.

(*Mr Caborn*) It will not be of any use because in August 2005 the decision will have been made in July.

Mr Flook: It would take a week to think about how you are going to put it into practice.

Chairman

162. Could I make the point which follows on what Adrian has said, if the Government were to decide on making a bid then it would appear to me that one of the strongest cases that it could put is that no government has ever gone through such a rigorous assessment of the process of making the bid and if the Government has come to the conclusion that it should make a bid it is because it is determined to win and that it has taken every conceivable factor into account. There you are, I have summed it up for you. Maybe I will be the next secretary of state.

(*Mr Caborn*) Thanks to your Committee, quite honestly, because it is after your Committee the PIU Report came and the process we followed is very much what was recommended by your Committee.

Chairman: Thank you very much indeed. Thank you, Secretary of State and your associates. Thank you very much.

WEDNESDAY 15 JANUARY 2003

Members present:

Mr Gerald Kaufman, in the Chair

Mr Frank Doran	Rosemary McKenna
Mr Adrian Flook	Ms Debra Shipley
Alan Keen	John Thurso
Miss Julie Kirkbride	Derek Wyatt

Examination of Witnesses

MR RICHARD SUMRAY, Mayor's representative on 2012 Olympic Bid Stakeholders Group, Greater London Authority, MR TONY WINTERBOTTOM, Director of Strategy Implementation and Project Development, MR MICHAEL WARD, Chief Executive, London Development Agency, MR JAY WALDER, Managing Director, Finance and Planning, and MR BARRY BROE, Director of Strategic Planning, Transport for London, examined.

Chairman: Gentlemen, thank you very much indeed for coming to see us this afternoon. We have got a very attenuated timescale for this report and we are grateful to you for co-operating in the timetable. Mr Wyatt?

Mr Wyatt

163. Good afternoon. We have had an interesting day and a half so far. What concerns us most is transport. What can you tell us that will put us out of our misery so we can give a tick for this Olympic Games? We have been told three separate stories on Crossrail. Can we just dismiss that? If you dismiss it, are you confident the alternatives will be there? Given that London comes to a halt every day somewhere, we do not want people to miss their heats as they did in Atlanta.

(*Mr Walder*) On behalf of the GLA group let me welcome the opportunity to appear before the Committee this afternoon. We understand the issues of transport, we have looked at it carefully in the initial stage. One of the great advantages here is the siting of the games. The siting of the Games in the Thames Gateway is both ideal from the interests of regeneration and transport, it is obviously one of the most deprived areas of the country and it has been highlighted in the London Plan as an opportunity area for London. It is also a very sensible location from a transport perspective. This area has good transport infrastructure and there are improvements underway right now that will make that transport infrastructure much better, such as a major increase in capacity on the Jubilee Line as part of the PPP effort and the Channel Tunnel Rail Link which are underway. What that says, along with our review of this, is that with some additional infrastructure and I think it is relatively modest in the scheme of things, and importantly, service enhancements and demand management, we believe that London's transport system can accommodate the Games. While Crossrail is a critically important project for London and the Mayor and TfL are very supportive of it and continue to plan the project, we believe that a successful London Games can be delivered without

the Crossrail project. We believe that we can manage all of the issues, the planning, the building and operation, in order to be ready for the 2012 Olympic Games and we would urge to proceed on that basis. So I think the transport issues for the most part should not be a constraint within the overall scheme.

164. Let me come on to the management of big projects. Wherever you look in London, the Eye did not open on time, Portcullis overran by two years, the British Museum has had its problems, the British Library took 17 years, the Dome was on time, but, sadly, the Jubilee Line was only open two days before when it should have been open two years before. Have we really got the skill in management in this country to manage big projects because there is not much evidence that we have?

(*Mr Winterbottom*) Most of the projects that you have just referred to are projects in the public sector and a lot of those projects were projects where there perhaps was not the final definition which enabled a firm tight contract to be put together and I do agree that recent history is littered with those. However, there is also a number of projects in the country that are unsung but actually run to time and are built budget. And certainly as far as the London Development Agency is concerned, we have substantial experience of much smaller projects—I grant you, they are not as complex as the ones that you have just mentioned—where we have been able, working with the private sector particularly and making sure that we have really researched the project, to bring projects in on time and to budget. The only confidence that I can give you in relation to this project is perhaps the way that we have approached it. Contrary to any other project that I am aware of, when we first got involved with this project the Mayor insisted that we actually looked and did a pre-feasibility study as to whether or not this was something that we should go for, which is the Arup Report and I think at least that has given us a good baseline to look at the sort of complex issues that we have to deliver. We think that delivering the Games will be complex, will be difficult, but clearly it will need a very focused, very firm and very clear line

[**Mr Wyatt** Cont]
of delivery with people who understand delivery and it needs to be time critical, but we do have quite a lot of time.

165. Mark Bostock yesterday said kept saying it was a specimen contract. Is the difference of opinion between the Government and the Arup Report the fact that this is not fully a costing of the actual Games, this is a sort of model of what could be the Games? If it is actually the Games then why are they called specimen costings?

(Mr Winterbottom) This is where I would like to go into your first question also. It is very important we get the stages of this bidding process correct. We have not spent a great deal of money on the Arup Report, but what it has done is it gives us that specimen, these are the issues that have to be tackled, this is what we think those issues will cost. There is another piece of work that needs to be done and that needs to be done relatively quickly. If London and the Government decide that we should bid for those Games then the important thing is that each of those items need to be thoroughly investigated as part of the bidding process so that we are very clear as we go forward that we understand the issues, the costs, the difficulties, the challenges and in each sub-component of that bid we understand what the end date is, when we have to deliver it, what it is going to cost, who is going to deliver it and who is going to be responsible. That is the reason that we have gone down this route of getting a pre-feasibility piece of work.

166. The Chancellor is looking at this. That means that on the 30 January the Government is going to go okay, we have the full figures, it looks like £5 billion, we do not know but we will do it.

(Mr Sumray) What all the parties were agreed to, and this was a stakeholders group in which the Government and other parties were involved, was to get this cost benefit work done and in order to do that, as Arup expressed yesterday here, they developed the specimen proposal. The specimen proposal is not going to be exactly what the end result is and in fact if you look at the history of bids the end result is never quite what is even bid for. It is pretty well there or thereabouts and we believe that what Arup has come up with is actually sustainable and robust, but Arup have done this independently. The Government have had an independent review of that and there are discussions going on between Arup and the Government about this. That is right and proper and it is right and proper that as much work as possible can be done around costs. I think the other thing is that in our knowledge and certainly I think this has also been expressed here, no other event of this kind has ever had such detailed work done on it before any announcement has been made about whether or not to make a bid. We think that is absolutely right and proper given the history we have had of some of the projects that have gone wrong, but it will never be exact at this stage, it cannot be. What you can get is a scenario, and I know the Government are developing this, around the probability and risk and I think that is what one has to go with in the end.

167. The thing about the World Athletics Championship is nobody claimed it for London, no one owns it physically, no one claimed "This is ours".

People were attached to it but nobody owned it. Manchester City worked for the Commonwealth Games. Even if they got the figures wrong initially, they owned it and bullied it and it won. Here we are being asked as a Government to trust the GLA, a relatively new body, to work across four boroughs that are stretched at the moment to run their boroughs. Do you think that this should be run by a Minister being chairman of this so that there is a Minister inside the Cabinet Office, do you think it should be run in the Mayor's office with somebody full time there? Do you think the BOA should be chairman of running this from Wandsworth? What is your view of taking this forward?

(Mr Ward) First of all, it needs clear ministerial ownership. In a sense the start point is that no national bid can succeed without proper support from international government and that does mean the ministerial champion. The World Athletics Championship did not have an effective sponsor in London because we were in the period of no London government at that time, we relied on Government office and less formal structures. We now have a wide range of structures. While the GLA is a new organisation, Transport for London draws upon 70 years experience of London transport as an organisation. The London Development Agency draws upon the very substantial project management experience of English Partnerships which in turn draws on the experience of London Docklands Development Corporation as major players in East London. I took my colleagues to talk to people in Manchester who had worked both on the Commonwealth Games and on the Olympic bid earlier this year. The Manchester experience is it needs to be very firmly rooted in the local authority. There they had an organisation to run the Commonwealth Games but the local authority itself procuring the stadium as a capital project. We think, and there is more work to do on the detail, you will need at least one special delivery vehicle to do the Olympics and that will need to be sponsored both by Government and by ourselves. You will probably need an organisation to run and market the Games. You will certainly need an organisation to build the stadium. Some of the international experience suggests you need a dedicated authority with transport and highways powers.

Chairman

168. Mr Ward, you have just offered a recipe which if it had been followed in Manchester would have led to a disastrous Commonwealth Games. Although Mr Wyatt is absolutely right in saying that Manchester owned the Commonwealth Games, Manchester City Council very wisely and readily accepted that they had to be under a Minister and that the Minister had to create the structure, control the structure and take responsibility for it. This is not a question of Government support. In New South Wales the Minister for Sport was in control both of organising the Games and organising the transport. Anything else and we are headed for, in my view, a catastrophe. A Minister in charge as in Manchester is a huge success. In a moment I would like you to respond to that, but I want to put a couple of other

[**Chairman** *Cont*]

points consequent upon what Mr Wyatt has been asking. Firstly, Mr Walder said he is confident that the Jubilee Line will be able to cope. I do not know if Mr Walder was on the Jubilee Line this morning—I was. The Jubilee Line was practically inoperable. There were two separate signal break downs in two separate places, hundreds of people were fighting to get on the trains at every station when these trains actually arrived. The argument is that after the botch of the way in which the signalling system was originally produced for the Jubilee Line Extension the whole signalling system needs to be replaced. How after day after day experience when I travel on the Jubilee Line Mr Walder can be confident that in eight and a half years it will be ready, I fail to understand and I would be grateful for clarification. Thirdly, I heard no answer to the question put by Mr Wyatt about Crossrail. Transport for London sends us in a document which says we are not factoring in Crossrail. Okay, that creates problems about getting to the new stadium, but nevertheless that is clear. The Secretary of State yesterday says no factoring in of Crossrail. In a statement published in the Evening Standard yesterday the Mayor says Crossrail will be running by 2011 and will be a great boost to getting to the Olympic Games stadium. Arup says the delivery date for Crossrail is by 2016 but some of it should be in place in time for the Games. I really would like to know which, if any, of these statements is accurate.

(*Mr Walder*) If I can take each in turn. I shared the use of the Jubilee Line this morning and I do use it on a regular basis. You are correct to say that there are very serious signalling difficulties on the Jubilee Line as it stands right now. You are correct to say that the Jubilee Line needs an entirely new signalling system on that line, I have no argument with either of those two statements. The point I was making was that that is actually contracted for now. In the contract that the Government let in December of last year for the JNP portion of the PPP the specification includes a complete new signal system on the Jubilee Line by 2009, so it is fair to accept that the situation as it sits today would not be adequate to do it, but I think the project is both funded and moving forward and in place to be able to do it well before 2012. That enhancement to the Jubilee Line is quite significant. In terms of the trains, it would add a seventh carriage to the train which is an increase of 15% on each train that goes through. In addition, it would increase the peak capacity of the system from about 22 trains an hour running currently to about 30 trains per hour as it would run with the new signal system. In aggregate you would get about a 45% increase in capacity on the Jubilee Line which is the equivalent of a very major enhancement as a result of that. In regard to Crossrail, the Crossrail project is proceeding. It is the expectation, with Government support, that Crossrail would come as part of a hybrid Bill before Parliament later this year, but the most optimistic schedule for Crossrail has the project being completed around the end of 2011. This is a project of a magnitude greater than the projects that you identified before. It is a project that at this point is only in the preliminary design stage. We have not gone through achieving Parliamentary powers, we have not gone through the process of bidding out and structuring the project and completing that work.

You would be hard pressed as we sit here today to say that the largest public works project that has been undertaken will be brought in spot on from a schedule developed before preliminary design is completed. It would be inappropriate to plan on that basis.

169. Could you or Mr Sumray explain why the Mayor yesterday said it will be ready for use in time for the Commonwealth Games in 2012?

(*Mr Sumray*) It is a question for the Mayor. I think the point that Tessa Jowell made to you this morning to you is right, that the Olympic Games can be delivered without Crossrail being there and at this stage I think, as she put it, it is a risk in relation to being completed in time. The key thing is, and this was dealt with in the Arup Report, can it be delivered without Crossrail. The Arup Report indicated and Transport for London are in agreement that it can be delivered without Crossrail. Even more to the point, talking about breakdowns, Sydney in its Olympic Games relied upon one particular loop in the railway system to get 70% of the spectators to it. Had that broken down during the Olympic Games there would have been real problems and it did break down when that system was first launched about 18 months beforehand. It did not, but in fact in the London context here we have many more routes into East London than Sydney actually had so there is less risk with the London situation than there was with the Sydney situation.

(*Mr Walder*) The other major significant infrastructure investment that would be made on the transport side is the Channel Tunnel Rail Link. That project is scheduled for completion by 2007. In both the case of the Jubilee Line and the case of CTRL you are not putting yourself in a position where you are backed up against the wall in terms of completing those projects on time to be ready for the Olympic Games. The site that has been selected benefits from four tube lines, two national rail lines and the Docklands Light Railway. That is a very very significant transport capacity. Overall, when you look at the entire system, the Olympic Games would add about 1% to the daily transport flows that we deal with in London, a range, as you point out this morning, that the system has to accommodate on a fairly regular basis. The real issue in terms of transport is not the delivery of these major projects, the real issue is the concentration of activity in a very small area. That will likely necessitate some improvements, like station improvements at Stratford station, but that is nowhere near the complexity of the other items that you have mentioned.

170. Okay. What you say, Mr Ward, is very persuasive, but I would still like to hear from Mr Sumray, who is here as the Mayor's representative, why the Mayor is quoted within quotation marks in yesterday's Evening Standard as saying that Crossrail should be running by 2011 and will be a great boost to transport in time for the Olympic Games.

(*Mr Sumray*) That is the timetable that is there at the moment. It is desirable, the Mayor has expressed it in this way, for it to be completed in time.

[**Chairman** *Cont*]

171. He did not say desirable, he said it would be there.

(*Mr Sumray*) That is the plan at the moment. If it was there it would be a significant boost to the Games.

172. He did not say that, he did not hypothesise. He said that provided Government approval is given, which he expects shortly, Crossrail will be in operation by 2011 and will be a great boost to the Olympic Games.

(*Mr Sumray*) The last part of that is absolutely right. The first part is the Mayor working on the expectations under the current plans that it would be, but the fact is that, as we know with any of these really major projects, there are risks and the point about this particular risk is that in relation to the Olympic Games, it is not one that we should be taking about its deliverability. We do not absolutely need Crossrail for the Olympic Games. As the Arup Report put it and I am sure the Mayor would agree with this, it would be a significant boost to the Olympic Games but it is not an absolute necessity for it.

Mr Flook

173. It is now not much more than about a year since the fiasco of the bid for the World Athletics Championship. Do you each in turn believe the Government will back this bid when they look at it at the end of this month?

(*Mr Sumray*) I do not know whether the Government will back it at the moment and indeed the Secretary of State—

174. Mr Winterbottom?

(*Mr Sumray*) Just to say, if the Government do back it, I think the point that others have made which we need to reiterate is that there has to be wholehearted and absolute support from all government departments to make sure that it works, it requires that, otherwise there is no point in bidding. All the stakeholders say it has to have full and unequivocal support. It cannot work with half-hearted support and we saw that in the sense of what happened at Picketts Lock. It has to have full support from the Government in order to make it work.

175. Mr Sumray, you may not have had the chance yet to read the transcript of Tessa Jowell's words in the House of Commons yesterday, but did you get the sense that there was that full backing from what she was saying?

(*Mr Sumray*) I was there yesterday so I heard the speech. What I think that she was doing, which is what she said this morning, was creating a balance sheet and that balance sheet was to say this is actually what is required in order to make a bid. We have to understand what the costs are. I think there has been a little bit too much concentration on the costs and potentially not enough concentration on some of the benefits that accrue in making a bid. I think the benefits as far as regeneration is concerned, the benefits for the local community, the legacy done properly, all of those things are huge benefits plus the factors which cannot be costed, the feel good factors and all of those things are significant benefits. It is also not just about costs and benefits, it is also about a range of other things which in a way cannot be costed. What I got from her yesterday was the need, an understandable need, from the Treasury and other government departments to try and provide what the worst-case scenario is. I hope at the end of the day that she and other ministers will support it. We cannot be sure that obviously will be the case.

(*Mr Winterbottom*) I think we will bid.

(*Mr Ward*) I think we should, but they must take the proper decision on all the facts and the investigations they are doing, what any government must do.

176. Do you think the Treasury are doing their own analysis in the way that Arup have done it?

(*Mr Ward*) They must do, they must do, and I think that most of what we see in the papers are different versions of different documents which are circulating in government departments, some giving an upside, some giving a downside, and that must be part of the process of taking a decision.

(*Mr Walder*) I believe the Government will bid, I hope the Government does bid. One point I would make about it is that we are talking about it as a London bid and if it is a bid here, if it is a London bid, that is a UK bid and it has to be thought of as a UK bid.

(*Mr Broe*) I think the Government should bid.

177. The reason for asking all that is that losing the IAAF Games really meant no athletics stadium. What will not happen if we do not bid? If there is no bid, what will not happen in the way that you all want it to happen?

(*Mr Sumray*) The opportunity for very significant developments, regeneration opportunities, particularly for the people of that part of East London, but actually opportunities for the country as a whole, and I agree wholeheartedly with the point being made that it is the country that will benefit as a whole, not just London and not just that part of London. The boroughs described yesterday, and I think absolutely appropriately, what the nature is of that population of that part of East London. It is a very young population with a high ethnic minority proportion there, very deprived, and there will be real opportunities missed to support that population, to get them involved, to get them engaged and really to get them engaged in sport and other things and to improve people's health. All of those sorts of issues are things which would be missed if the Games was not bid for, and the speeded-up regeneration of that part of London is very important. Legacy in sport is again something which would not happen in the same way. I have figures here about swimming pools and it was raised yesterday where Amsterdam has three 50-metre swimming pools, Barcelona six, Berlin 19, Paris 18—

178. To save you reading the report, there are more in the basin of Paris than there are in the whole of the United Kingdom.

(*Mr Sumray*) Precisely, and I think here we have opportunities which quite frankly would not occur if we did not have the bid.

179. What will happen transport-wise or what would not happen?

[**Mr Flook** *Cont*]

(*Mr Walder*) Transport is actually interesting in this regard. For the most part, we are not relying on new infrastructure to be able to accommodate the Games, so you are not able to point to a piece of infrastructure, for the most part, which would not be there. On the other hand, I think there is experience from similar situations that residents change their travel behaviour during times of major events for a large part because demand management measures have to be put in place because people see it as no choice, but it also exposes them to other travel patterns than the ones they have been accustomed to. Interestingly, some of the experience is that when people are actually exposed to different travel patterns, they sometimes retain those travel patterns. The use of public transportation rises, people who use public transportation move to walking, cycling, other modes of travel, and that actually is a legacy benefit that you do not often think of from games of this nature. It gives an opportunity to try things in terms of demand management regarding our streets and the like that perhaps the day-to-day experience in London does not provide. That is really an opportunity.

180. The LDA?

(*Mr Ward*) I have two answers to your question. The first is the direct sporting legacy projects, the facilities, the stadia, *et cetera*, which clearly would not happen without a bid. The second is that the broader regeneration of the area identified around the Lee Valley I think would happen quicker if there was an Olympic bid and possibly the bid would be a catalyst for a more successful regeneration.

Ms Shipley

181. Actually this follows on really well because I think that was a very interesting question that Adrian Flook rose with you. He asked you about the positive and I would like to ask each of the witnesses about the negative and what your major reservation is. What major problem has to be solved, otherwise you can see a bad outcome? This is your moment to put on record that they have got to get X right, and if they do not get X right, what?

(*Mr Sumray*) We have to get the management—

182. No, just one major reservation, not the generalisation of what one has to get right, but is there any major problem sitting in there ready to bite? Is anybody willing to answer?

(*Mr Winterbottom*) I will have a go. Diffuse decision-taking.

183. Enough said. Next person please.

(*Mr Broe*) I think one of the most critical issues from a transport perspective is the actual event timetabling and scheduling because one of the key issues for transport is making sure that normal commuting movements and people trying to get to work on a normal day can do so, so we would like to see events scheduled at a time that minimises the conflict between people moving to the Games and people trying to get to work and go about their normal activity, so having events that are before the peak or after the peak would be critical for transport and that is an area where we have an opportunity to make sure that both ends can be achieved.

(*Mr Ward*) I agree with what Tony has said.

(*Mr Sumray*) My answer is still what we have to do rather than the negative and what we have to do is get the right bid team and organisation in place led by a minister. We have to try and minimise all the risks that there are and we have to be entrepreneurial in our approach to both bidding for and then organising the Games. I actually fundamentally believe that we can do it.

(*Mr Walder*) The basic question, I think, is the fear of failing to get focus early on in what we are doing. The year 2012 seems a long way away, but the reality of planning major works, as somebody asked about before, is that they require focus at a point. That seems like it is a very, very long way away and one of the things which has to happen now is a very active and appropriate debate which is taking place, so if the decision is made, as I hope it is, to go forward, then all parties have to get behind that and get focus because you start doing that work in 2003, not later.

184. Mr Ward, final chance?

(*Mr Ward*) I do not want to add to what my colleagues have said.

Miss Kirkbride

185. I have just a few points. First of all, the Secretary of State told us this morning that redevelopment of the East End could take place at a much cheaper price of £300 million rather than at a cost of £4.5 billion which is what the Olympics might cost us if things go awry. Would you like to comment on that?

(*Mr Winterbottom*) We are, the London Development Agency, at the moment spearheading, with the Office of the Deputy Prime Minister, the Thames Gateway as a major area to relieve pressure and tensions in the South-East and we are doing comprehensive regeneration investigations. I believe that a figure of £300 million as a total public sector involvement in the Lee Valley in terms of regeneration is a useful guesstimate and a figure that was plucked from somewhere, but, to me, it is going to need more than that.

(*Mr Ward*) Just to add to that, our annual revenue and capital budget for the whole of London at the moment is £300 million. I do not know whether the two figures are a coincidence, but that is a resource that we have to allocate across the whole City.

(*Mr Winterbottom*) This is very complex and the overall regeneration will take some time. The whole area will take much longer than the Olympics and I think £300 million is very light. I think that just underlines the need for very careful investigatory work.

186. One of the other flaws in the potential for the Government to go ahead with the bid is the use of the stadium subsequently and perhaps one of the areas that those of you who are very keen to pursue the bid are missing is in giving the Government sight of an end game there which is not going to be a great white elephant of an embarrassment to rival the Dome. Can you give us any thoughts on that?

(*Mr Sumray*) I think there are huge lessons to be learned from most previous Olympic Games. Seeing the Barcelona Stadium empty for six years, big issues

[Miss Kirkbride *Cont*]

around the Sydney Stadium now and so on are things that we have to learn. In my view, all new construction, whatever its nature, has to have its legacy sorted out before a brick is laid, before a sod is turned because that is absolutely essential and I think that is the real lesson to be learned.

187. Before the Cabinet takes its decision perhaps?

(*Mr Sumray*) Not before the Cabinet takes a decision. I do not think that is necessary, but certainly it has to be sorted out before we get into the specifics. I first had a meeting with the Chairman of West Ham a year and a half ago to discuss the possibility of moving into a stadium. It does not have to be that solution, but certainly a solution which is sustainable in the long term is right and I happen to think that what happened in Manchester with the stadium is absolutely spot on. I know there was some criticism, as the Sports Minister said today, but the fact is that that stadium has an enduring and sustainable legacy. That is what has to happen, it seems to me, with everything that is built for the Olympics and I think all the work we have done so far actually is aimed towards that happening.

188. At the moment you are in a position of wanting the go-ahead without giving sight of what that end game is and that is quite a weakness in your case, is it not?

(*Mr Sumray*) No, because I think it is a question of the stage one has reached. We need a go-ahead now in order to negotiate that. You cannot negotiate before anybody knows what is happening, so I think it is a chicken-and-egg situation there. Until there is some certainty about a bid and about siting it and everything else, you have nothing to negotiate with. I think the key thing is for us to recognise, for all of the team working on it to recognise that it is that legacy which needs to be sorted out in advance and the Olympic village is the same. You do not build the Olympic village for the Olympics, but you build the village for what it is going to be used for 60 or 80 years afterwards.

189. As one final point, planning and who decides often bogs down various projects, or it has done in my part of the world with getting hold of the football stadium because Solihull was not prepared to let the land go for such a stadium. What reassurance can you give that you would acquire the relevant planning powers so that it would not get bogged down in local council rivalry, *et cetera*?

(*Mr Ward*) This comes back to the question about delivery organisations which in a sense is left over from the Chairman's previous question. You have to have a development organisation with planning powers.

190. Well, would that be done through a Bill here in the House of Commons, an Olympic Bill, which would give you those powers, or do they already exist?

(*Mr Ward*) You could do a Bill. I can see three ways in which you could do this. First of all, you could have specific legislation and that might be the most straightforward way to do it. Secondly, you could use the powers of English Partnerships, the national government regeneration agency, which can declare urban development areas and can take the powers of planning authorities there. In contrast both to the East Manchester site where the Commonwealth Games took place and the site to the west of the city where the first Olympic bid was centred, the pattern of land ownership is much more complex in the Lee Valley with many relatively small owners of small parcels of land, and the river itself dividing two planning authorities, so whilst Tower Hamlets and Newham are the main ones, there are also interests in both Waltham Forest and Hackney, so a special-purpose vehicle which took the planning powers with the consent of the local authorities in the area would, I think, be essential to get the planning right. It would be sensible for that vehicle also to be the one that did any compulsory purchase which was necessary, first a planning framework and then a CPO, and whether it is something created by special legislation or EP or the third option, which is to use the Urban Development Corporation legislation, I cannot see that you can do it without a vehicle of that nature. That goes back to the Chairman's previous question. Of course you will need a minister in charge, but it is in the end a city and not a country that bids. What you have to do, and I think this mirrors what Richard Sumray said in answer to an earlier question, is get the governance right. There may well be one thing that does those land-use issues in the early part of the process, giving way to an organisation and management body later. The identity of the vehicle within that overall structure that builds the stadium may be partly determined by the end use of the stadium. You have to have one structure with different elements drawing on different statutory powers.

Chairman

191. I am particularly grateful to you, Mr Ward, for coming back to that question—

(*Mr Ward*) I did write it down.

Chairman: —so that you rendered my intervention otiose. Do any other colleagues want to put questions? There you are, you see, how easily satisfied this Committee is! Thank you very much indeed.

Examination of Witnesses

SIR RODNEY WALKER KT, Chairman, and MR JOHN SCOTT, Director, International Relations and Major Events, UK Sport; and MR ROGER DRAPER, Acting Chief Executive, and MR IAN FYTCHE, Director of Strategy, Sport England, examined.

Chairman

192. Sir Rodney, we are always pleased to see you and we are grateful to you and your colleagues for coming before us today. Could I begin myself by asking you a question, an answer to which I would dearly like to have. You, Sir Rodney, among others, have been an observer of the Wembley saga over the years. We, in this Committee, championed Wembley as a dual-use stadium to which Sport England provided £120 million in Lottery money for dual use so that it should be available for the 2012 Olympic Games should Britain be successful in a bid for those Games. We were told yesterday when we had an evidence session that all that Wembley would be used for if we got the 2012 Olympic Games was football, so I would be very grateful to you indeed for explaining the situation to me because clearly the Government would have been very misguided to approve the go-ahead of £20 million it is giving as a subsidy if in fact Wembley is not going to be one of the locations of the 2012 Games should we get them.

(*Sir Rodney Walker*) Thank you, Chairman. What an interesting question! I think my involvement with Wembley has been more than merely as an observer. I seem to remember starting this project off in 1995 when I was then Chairman of Sport England and you are quite right in your recollection that the £120 million Lottery grant was given for a national stadium, a national multi-sports stadium. I then left the project in 1998 as I moved to UK Sport, at which time the Football Association became more directly involved in its ownership and management. I then rejoined it back in 2000 when the Football Association asked me to become Chairman of Wembley National Stadium Ltd, at which stage, you will recall, athletics, having been removed from Wembley, was brought back in by way of a design option through a platform. Then, due to circumstances beyond my control, I left the Wembley project again in March of last year and what the arrangements are that exist now between Sport England and the Football Association and the use of a stadium for athletics are not clear to me.

Derek Wyatt

193. Forgive me for going over some older ground, but I thought the whole basis of when Chris Smith announced Wembley in that magnificent presentation was that there had been an intervention by the British Olympic Association to ensure that this could be the foundation of an Olympic bid. We heard this morning the Sports Minister say that you could not get the track in for practice, that there is not enough accommodation and that the transport is terrible, but I think we have known that for a long time, so are you saying that the BOA has changed its mind?

(*Sir Rodney Walker*) My understanding is, you are quite right, that there was a point when the British Olympic Association said that a stadium that could not provide 80,000 seats and an athletics track would be inadequate for an Olympic bid. I think subsequently the IOC have made it clear that is not any longer a consideration and that a stadium with smaller capacity would suffice. I think Roger from Sport England, who now have ownership or always have had ownership of this perhaps, ought to be afforded the opportunity to bring you up to date.

(*Mr Draper*) I think the first thing to say is that Wembley does have the capability not only to be the centrepiece of the Olympic Games, but also the track and field athletics events.

194. It will not be. They told us that it will not be. They told us that the opening ceremony would be in the new stadium and that all Wembley will do is football and a bit of equestrian.

(*Mr Draper*) I think the Chief Executive of Wembley National Stadium has in fact written to the Committee actually outlining their thoughts in terms of offering the stadium for not just athletics, but also for being the centrepiece of the Olympic stadium. Now, obviously it is down to the Olympic Bid Committee to make that decision. I think it is a wider issue than just the stadium itself. It is linked with infrastructure, it is linked with regeneration and it is linked with transport, hence the rationale behind the East London site.

Chairman

195. Mr Draper, I realise that you come before us absolutely pure. You are not implicated in any of this whatsoever. That being so, you have the advantage of being able to be absolutely open with us because you are not involved in any personal confession of any kind. We have done, how many, Derek, three inquiries, maybe more, five, I have lost track, into Wembley Stadium. The view of this Committee from day one was clear, on the basis that Sport England gave £120 million to the FA/WNSL so that it could be dual use and available for the Olympic Games of 2012. In view of the fact that we were told yesterday that if we were to get the 2012 Olympic Games only football would take place there, what have we been going on about at Wembley for all of these years? I really would like to know. I would like to get it out of my mind and think about something else, but it keeps coming back.

(*Mr Draper*) You are quite correct in fact, that in the bid document football and the final of the football event is to be held at Wembley, but the fact is that Wembley has got the capability to host international athletics and also, if necessary, be the centrepiece of an Olympic bid. Now the Olympic Bid Committee have chosen another site, but it is actually written into the agreement with Wembley Stadium that it should host Olympic events.

196. Well, Mr Draper, in that case, let me ask you this question: does London need two athletics stadia? If London does not need two athletics stadia and will have one in the dual-use Wembley, what would

[Chairman *Cont*]

happen, what should happen to this projected stadium to be built in the East End once its function of housing the Olympics for a few days nine and a half years from now is over?

(*Mr Draper*) Again it comes down to the legacy which Mr Sumray outlined earlier on today. You are quite right that there is not the necessity to have a permanent athletics stadium in London. There is no sustainability with that route whatsoever, but what we have learnt, and lessons of course have been learnt from Wembley and Picketts Lock and other events, mistakes have been made, is that the big issue with Manchester was this legacy and the anchor tenant. Obviously if a Premiership football club were to take on the stadium, then that would be the most viable option in terms of the future of the stadium and the legacy.

Derek Wyatt

197. No board of directors of any Premier League club, even West Ham given its position, could risk its shareholder value now for something in 2012 where it may or may not be a Premiership club, so the anchor tenant is a rubbish argument. No one is going to commit. No professional organisation is ever going to say, "Until 2010, okay, we'll go for it". Do you agree with that?

(*Mr Draper*) Obviously that is down to negotiations with individual clubs. I think the key thing with any stadium is that it is open to the community. The one lesson we learned with Manchester was that with the City of Manchester stadium it is built into the agreement that there is 100 days of community use for that stadium and also that profits over 32,500 capacity crowd go back to—

Derek Wyatt: If you were the Spurs board of directors now you would look at Wembley. You would not wait for 2012. You would want to build your own stadium: shareholder value.

Chairman: What is community use? Our stadium for the Commonwealth Games in Manchester, a beautiful stadium, is much smaller and is going to be taken over after conversion by Manchester City Football Club which is currently climbing steadily up the Premier League and will soon overtake Arsenal.

Derek Wyatt: You wish!

Chairman

198. It is axiomatic, Derek. But if Manchester City Football Club were not taking over that Commonwealth Games stadium what would it be used for? What community use would anybody in Manchester have for a structure that large except that the stadium projected for East London will be very much larger than the one in Eastlands in Manchester because it would be constructed for the opening and closing ceremonies of the Olympic Games and therefore need to accommodate 80,000. What community use or what legacy would it be there for? I would really like to know and you are the appropriate body to ask because somehow or other I think you are going to be dragged into it.

(*Mr Fytche*) The issues you are outlining, Mr Chairman, are exactly the right issues. It is about viability. It is about legacy and the Arup report sets out two broad options for the stadium and clearly those challenges, as Mr Winterbottom said earlier, are ones that are still to be faced. If the bid were to go forward then clearly issues about legacy, sustainability, the centrepiece for every generation project within that part of London would have to be satisfactorily answered. I am sure those are the questions that are exercising minds at the moment in terms of the decision that has to be taken at the end of January and the scoping of works beyond that should the bid move forward.

Derek Wyatt

199. I have a small suggestion and that is that you ask Spurs or West Ham or somebody to actually take on the legacy now and get building in two years' time for the stadium that would then be there ready and waiting, because I cannot see how else you will get the legacy that you want. Listen: we want to talk about the Olympic bid as well.

(*Sir Rodney Walker*) I think it is worth reminding ourselves so that we do not get into rewriting history that the Sport England decision to grant the initial £112 million to Manchester was conditional upon the stadium having an anchor tenant before the money was spent.

200. Indeed; good point. There is lots of discussion. I suppose if I am honest we would like to see a London bid but we also have some deep reservations which you can get the flavour of even though it is 10 years to go and all that. What reservations do you have, Sir Rodney especially, in terms of the fact that we have got changes coming to the way sport is going to be organised in Britain? In a sense people off the record said to us that Sport England got in the way in the Manchester bid but they would not put it on record. They said that they did not like it because they did not like the success that Manchester was enjoying. They wanted to claim it because, after all, they were paying for it. We are concerned that GLA is a young body and is going to take on the largest—if Crossrail is the largest project ever, the Olympics is not far short, or probably bigger, GLA is going to take on two big projects simultaneously running where we are not sure we have got the management expertise in the country. Are you confident about the structure of the way in which the bid would work so that on 1 February or whatever it is when the Prime Minister says we are doing it, now that you know who the minister is, you know who the board will be that will run it; you are confident that the structures underneath—you cannot say that they are going to be working but are you confident about this?

(*Sir Rodney Walker*) I hardly think I am the appropriate person to pass judgement on this but, as always, I am happy to give you a view. You asked the questions of the previous witnesses and the fact is that this project can succeed providing you get the ownership right. The ownership has to be with government, absolutely no question. It seems to me that it is unlikely that Crossrail could be relied upon to be ready in time. I think there would need to be very convincing arguments put forward as to how the transport can be organised so as to make traffic movements around London acceptable to those who

[Derek Wyatt *Cont]*

go about their work and those who come to London to attend the Olympic Games. This is a very personal view. I do not think it is necessarily helpful that at this stage two expert groups using the same base data on what the underwriting costs of the Olympic Games might be managed to come up with figures about a billion pounds apart, although I heard today that those numbers are still being worked upon. I accept the Chairman's point that Manchester worked because there was in the end clear ownership. Wembley became difficult because at several stages there was no clear ownership of the project. If there is clear ministerial-led ownership of this project and if all the right bodies work together, if vested interests are set aside, there is absolutely no reason why this country is not capable of both bidding for and succeeding in securing the Olympic Games, and indeed organising a successful event.

Alan Keen

201. As the two bodies responsible for the only channel for funding for sport I would like to ask the same question I asked this morning. I said that I asked Steve Redgrave yesterday about the importance of the village, everybody being together, and he said it had massive importance to the competitors. I agree with that and I say again the same words: I love the Olympics but I reckon that because we have to fit everything, apart from Bisley and yachting and canoeing and rowing, into a small area so that all the competitors can travel a short distance to the events, it must be costing us at the minimum half a billion pounds. I do not mean the cost of the village; that is possibly a whole billion. The cost really is having to construct stadia that will have no use in the future. If I can come back to West Ham or Spurs, they are both making losses at the moment so how can they come along in 10 years' time and fund or convince financiers that their profits can fund a stadium that is going to cost £350 million?

(*Sir Rodney Walker*) The truth is that, as someone who until the beginning of last year was chairman of a Premier League soccer club that went on to be relegated, I know only too well the problems of the economics of whether or not you are in the Premier League or in the First Division. My crystal ball cannot tell me what is going to be happening in nine months, let alone in nine years. The whole legacy issue is critical, not just to the stadium but to the after use of the whole facilities that are developed as part of any successful Olympic bid. John, you might like to have a word, but I know that the whole of the Sports Council—Sport England are here to speak for themselves but I have the authority to speak for Sport Scotland and the Sports Council for Wales and indeed the Sports Council for Northern Ireland—are wholeheartedly behind this bid but it is not at any price. It must not under any circumstance prejudice their existing funding, our existing funding. We have to have a very carefully thought through legacy programme today and not start to think how we deal with that at some point in the future.

The Committee suspended from 4.09 pm to 4.23 pm for a division in the House

Alan Keen

202. I did not get to the end of the question at the beginning but the point I am making is that because we have to have a village and all the events have to be in that area it adds costs to hosting the Olympics, I reckon at least half a billion and probably a billion. If we could spread them round the country—and I went to Japan for the World Cup and the atmosphere was brilliant. We went to different places—more people could get to see it. If we could do that with the Olympics, the point I am really asking you is that it is difficult for the Government. The Minister and the Secretary of State are going to see the President of the IOC on Friday. It will not do our bid any good if they go there telling them how they should organise the Olympic Games in the future. I am really asking you as the main channellers of funding in sport in this country, will you make these representations that the Olympics, just for the sake of having 18,000 athletes in one village, which is very nice, although it is not so nice for those whose event comes on the last day and they want a party—we could save somewhere between half a billion and a billion pounds by using facilities we have got around the country now. The athletics could be at Wembley as they were supposed to be. The football could be at the main stadium and spread around the country as it is going to be in fact. What I am saying is that instead of having the athletes all together in one village for the three weeks of the Olympics, we could put a party on for them and they could stay for a week after the Olympics when they could all get drunk if that is what they do. I think somebody needs to go to the IOC and put this point to them. We have been taking evidence from people in the last couple of days and there are tremendous difficulties. There would hardly be a difficulty if we could use stadia around the country and we did not have to have the village. It is the village that causes all the problems that we are facing now.

(*Mr Scott*) The point you make has been put to the IOC on a number of occasions but the reality is that whilst they are in the privileged position of having a number of cities very prepared to come forward with bids that offer a very coherent, a very focused, a very centralised approach to the delivery of the Games, that is the location they will choose in preference. The preference there of course is many-fold. It offers logistical, organisational and, most critically, security advantages. One of the key things, as we know, with the Olympics is the high risk they offer in terms of a terrorist target. Having a single athletes village enables you to control much more access and all the issues that we saw unfortunately in 1972 in Munich. The other point I would make is that whilst there is a cost we have to look at what the return is afterwards. You say yes, there is a cost to build the village, but what you then have is the opportunity to put on to the market place the infrastructure you have put in place: quality housing, well served, good transport links. There is an enhanced value to it. You will actually sell the village after the Games. It will have been developed through public investment but there will be a return to the public purse once you do sell it. The final point I would make about the opportunity that we have with the current proposal that Arup have worked up, which has rightly been

[Alan Keen Cont]

described as a specimen proposal, is that the key part of the Arup work was to see whether London could actually put together a bid that could be internationally competitive. That was the first key thing we had to do; otherwise there was no point even moving to the next stage. I think that was shown to be feasible. What it has shown as well, however, is that we are able to use a large number of existing facilities through the use of Excel, through the use of the Dome. We are actually not needing to put in place expensive permanent facilities that would not have an ongoing use. The key legacy facilities are the swimming complex, and we have already heard that London as a capital city is appallingly provided with swimming facilities, and of course the stadium where we do have to look at what the legacy uses are. There are options and we obviously have to work those up, but at this point in time, as Mr Wyatt has picked up, we are not in a position to say categorically what it will be. Those are significant improvements to the infrastructure of this capital city and something I believe we should be striving to achieve if we want to stand up to international comparison and offer opportunities to the residents of London and Greater London.

203. I do not disagree with anything you have said but the real question is: should we not be able (not just us, but other nations as well) to exert pressure on the IOC so that we do not have to operate int his wasteful way? Do you agree it is wasteful?

(Mr Scott) No.

204. We do not know what the stadium is going to be used for as a legacy. You do not need two penn'orth of brains to know that nobody can afford to buy it. A football club certainly cannot afford to buy it and finance it. It just does not work. We have already got Wembley that can be adapted for athletics. If we do not waste anything else we are wasting a stadium that is going to cost somewhere near £400 million.

(Mr Scott) What we are doing is, we are looking—

Chairman

205. Before you respond to Mr Keen's question, I would like to put a supplement to it so that you can answer Mr Keen and perhaps answer the supplement and if Mr Draper would like to add to that then I would value that too. I was somewhat bewildered, I have to say, after this Committee has gone through so many examinations of the Wembley project, suddenly to find that there was to be factored in a new stadium in East London. We have a letter from Mr Cunnah, the Chief Executive of Wembley National Stadium, sent to me and dated January 10, in which he says that Wembley Stadium will be available for the Olympics for whatever uses were deemed appropriate, whether as a secondary venue or as the centerpiece stadium "as per our obligations under the terms of our funding agreement with Sport England"; very straightforward. It confirms what Mr Keen has been assuming. It confirms what I think the other members of the Committee have been assuming. Mr Cunnah goes on to say that the IOC has confirmed that the Wembley capacity, 68,400 for athletic events, which could be increased to more

than 70,000, would be perfectly satisfactory to the IOC as the Olympic stadium. So, we are having built, with £120 million worth of Lottery money by courtesy of Sport England, plus £20 million from Her Majesty's Government, plus another £20 million from London, this stadium which Mr Cunnah says—and I have got absolutely no reason to question his statement—is going to be absolutely state of the art, the best stadium in the world, offering fans, participants, officials from broadcasters, unparalleled facilities. What exactly then will be the purpose of another stadium in East London?

(Mr Scott) May I answer first Mr Keen's points and then come on to yours, Mr Chairman? The requirements of the IOC are laid out very specifically and each bidding city is required to answer an extremely exhaustive and very technical submission before they are even considered to go forward as candidate cities. As you know, it is now a two-stage process. If we wish to secure the Games it is clearly in our interests to satisfy those requirements. If we do not satisfy those requirements we will not move forward and there will have been no point even putting ourselves up for the prospect of hosting the Games. As currently written the requirements are that you provide a coherent village with all the security and services for the reasons I have already elaborated. The issue of the stadium is obviously of great concern to the IOC and, as Sir Rodney has already mentioned, it has never been a requirement of the IOC that a specific number of seats be provided. They have always said that it should be suitable to the requirements of the host nation, so 68,000–72,000, if that is what we wish to put forward, would be acceptable to the IOC. If we look at the comments you made, Mr Chairman, about Wembley playing a part in the delivery of the Olympics, it is absolutely correct. Wembley, as currently envisaged, would play a major role in the football tournament which is one of the premier events of the Olympic programme and would host the finals. To suggest that it could actually be the centrepiece stadium is, I would argue, a bit more difficult because in order to be competitive, and this comes back to this absolutely key issue as the Secretary of State mentioned yesterday, if we cannot win the bid there is absolutely no point going forward. The last thing we want to do is handicap ourselves with something that would be exploited by the opposition. One of the difficulties clearly is the amount of land needed to construct the village and all the ancillary services for that which at the moment are available at Bromley-by-Bow or Stratford. If we were to suggest that we have a village there and the additional facilities as currently envisaged down the Lee Valley but have the athletics at Wembley and therefore transport the athletes across London, that would be, I believe, a killer to our bid. It would not secure the backing of the IOC. Hence, if we wish to go for the Games we do have to provide a second stadium and that is when we come up against the challenge of what do we do with that stadium after the Games.

206. But this has only just come up, has it not? In all our enquiries into Wembley Stadium lasting over years the problem of the location of the village in relation to the stadium has never ever come up. Now we are told that we need a new stadium in East

[Chairman *Cont]*

London that is likely to be surplus to requirements as soon as the Olympics are over, should we get them, because of its juxtaposition to a village whose location has not been decided upon anyhow. I realise that distances in Manchester are not the same as distances in London but the village in Manchester was some considerable distance away from the stadium in Manchester and because, among other things, the structure created by Mr McCartney included an excellent transport system, there was no problem in getting there. I lament that we are having to put these questions to you but this was not a relevant issue yesterday when we had the IOC and the BOA in front of us. Why at this stage has this whole issue of the juxtaposition of the village to the stadium become critical to the likelihood of a successful bid and why have we only just heard about it now? Why, after all of these years, ever since 1996 when Sport England handed over £120 million for Wembley, is it, seven years later, that this has suddenly surfaced as a problem?

(*Mr Scott*) Mr Chairman, I believe it has always been understood that in order to deliver a winnable bid you had to get the closest match between the IOC requirements and your solution. The key requirement of the IOC is obviously the cohesiveness of the bid and the simplicity of the management and the security of the operation and that is why the solution that is being looked at now provides that best option. It is not unreasonable to suggest that attempting to transport athletes for an extremely hectic programme—the athletics programme, as you know, is of the longest duration during the Games and is considered the blue riband event of the Games—from either Stratford or Bromley-by-Bow to Wembley would be an almost impossible task and would be, as I have argued already, seen as an Achilles heel of our bid and would make it unwinnable.

(*Mr Fytche*) In 1999 when the key decisions were being taken surrounding the development of the Wembley project and the key decisions about the commitment of the Lottery funds to that project, the debate about the Olympics at that time was very much focused on two different models that could have been taken forward in a study such as this—a West London model and an East London model. At the time it is fair to say I think that BOA were evaluating which was the best option. They were looking at Wembley in the west and other options in the east and it was only later, once the GLA and the Mayor had come on board and other circumstances in terms of a regeneration framework for London had developed, that I think at the start of this study the focus to the Arup work has been very much on the East End and that obviously reflects the wider dimensions of the Olympic bid in the current policy circumstances in terms of regeneration, the transport developments and so on. We heard earlier about the CTRL developments and that sort of thing. I think the current context for the bid is obviously that much wider, city/region type of debate and the stadium proposals are being looked at in that wider context.

Chairman: Before we proceed, Mr Doran wants to do some questioning but I would like to ask a question of my fellow members of this Select Committee. Am I the only one to whom this comes as a great surprise and novelty? Am I the only one?

Mr Doran

207. If could follow that through, I spent many hours looking over the Wembley contract documents in all the various reports into Wembley. I have to express my concern because I am quite specific in my memory that in all of the discussions we had about the public money which was going into the Wembley project that it was tied to athletics, and then a certain proportion of it was removed and we had all the discussions about the £20 million or so which may or may not be going back to Sport England because the athletics platform had been removed, but it was specifically because Wembley was going to provide the base for an Olympic bid. We are hearing something quite different now on which Mr Fytche gave us evidence in the previous enquiries and I do not remember any discussions at all about two evaluation bids, an east bid and a west bid.

(*Mr Fytche*) The question of the Wembley project and its objectives was very clear at the outset, that it was a stadium for three sports, primarily obviously for football and rugby league, but with the capability of conversion to host these two major athletics events, and that is a critical distinction. The purpose of the project was to create that capability and therefore the option for the bidders of those events to use the stadium if at a subsequent time, if they chose to bid, it fitted in with the wider strategic context within which those bids would be put forward, and that is a decision that clearly the BOA and its key stakeholders and government and the GLA have to grapple with and that obviously relates to some of the key issues that you have been exploring over the past couple of days on transport and the wider regeneration agenda.

208. What we were concerned about in the Wembley inquiry, and I am sorry to go back to that, was that £120 million of money went into a project which had all sorts of vicissitudes and there were major problems throughout the whole process of that project, and Sport England throughout seemed to be standing on the side lines, having paid the money up-front to purchase land at what seemed at the time to be an extravagant cost- it certainly did to us—£108 million I think was the cost, from memory—

(*Mr Fytche*) £106 million.

209. I was not too far out. That is a huge amount of money. Certainly I am fairly clear in my mind, yes, football and rugby were going to be the main generators of income for the stadium, that we had the World Athletics Championships in 2005, the primary reason I accept for the athletics component, but it was going to be a launch pad for an Olympic bid, and now we are somewhere very different.

(*Mr Fytche*) I think Sport England's objectives for its investment in the project were always very clear. It was a stadium for three sports but, emphasising again, there was the capability of hosting athletics should it come to the stadium, and at the time the debate centred around whether or not there were proposals for a bid either for the World Athletics Championships or the Olympics. It was not founded on the premise those events were committed and therefore coming, it was always acknowledged there would be a wide-ranging analysis of the options for

[Mr Doran Cont]

both the World Athletics and indeed the Olympics in the context of the wider agenda. I would say those objectives which Sport England set out to achieve, despite the well-documented delays in the project which have largely been about making sure from our perspective we have this sustainable legacy and viability for the project in place, have been achieved. Clearly we have talked about Manchester a bit today and clearly within Manchester the same sort of issues arose but there was at that time the opportunity to have that wider city-region debate and to ensure the stadium fitted into the wider regeneration framework, and clearly that debate is now taking place within London to ensure the same thing happens here in the context of the wider Olympic bid as a whole, not just the stadium.

Chairman

210. Since you mention Manchester, I am afraid that was not the situation at all. Indeed with regard to the village in Manchester it was decided *ab initio* that the university halls of residence in Fallowfield should be the village—they are in my constituency, I know them extremely well. The only regenerative aspect of it was after it was decided and after the Commonwealth Games officials inspected the halls of residence and they found some of them, in their view and their view was paramount and decisive, were not adequate or suitable for accommodation of the athletes, and therefore a number of them were up-graded and refurbished, providing in the end better accommodation for the students who now use them. That was not in any way part of the regeneration programme or assumptions for Manchester. Eastlands, yes, certainly, no doubt about it, but in terms of the village it was a by-product, it was not a regenerative project. What we are being told now, and I have to say I feel as though I have been conned, is that we suddenly discover that we have to have a new stadium, surplus to requirements so far as one can tell, in East London, not because we need two stadia, because as Mr Cunnah points out, Wembley stadium as it will be built will be very, very satisfactory indeed, but because of the juxtaposition and location of the village. Please tell me if I am wrong, because if I am wrong I want to know.

(*Mr Fytche*) I think it is a much wider debate than that. The Arup Report talks widely about the transport and regeneration context as a whole rather than just the juxtaposition between the stadium and the village. Clearly back in 1999 when the Wembley decision was made, there were options for the Olympic bid should it go forward based on both East London and West London in terms of the mix of the facilities, the type of facilities, the potential for refurbishment and how it fitted into the wider city context. I am sure those issues are being taken account of now and that the bid is being fitted into the best context for the city as a whole. I am sure those considerations will be fully evaluated as part of this decision-making process.

211. I will come back to you in a moment, Frank, but I really want to tease this out because I want to understand the situation. When, in 1996, Sport England handed over £120 million for the reconstruction of Wembley as a dual use stadium, did they then consider the location of the village in relation to the stadium? If they did, may we know what the decision was? If they did not, why not?

(*Mr Fytche*) The decision on the Sport England Lottery grant to the project at Wembley was the 1999 decision, and the earlier decision you refer to related to simply the choice of location for the stadium. The key decisions were in 1999. At that stage, as I say, the BOA, who are after all responsible for the Olympic proposal, were evaluating, as I understand it, a wide range of options. As John Scott would know more than I, the options for villages and facilities were looked at in the context of both a West and an East London bid, and that was obviously a BOA-led project as it is now.

212. I am just not having that. Sport England decided to back the reconstruction of Wembley with £120 million of Lottery money and it stipulated it would only do that if it was dual use, and they wanted it dual use so if we got the 2012 Games the Games could be staged there and the whole argument, including the discussion in Mr Chris Smith's kitchen, about handing back £20 million if it was not dual use, was because it looked as though for whatever reason, including Mr Smith's pre-occupation with Picketts Lock, it did not look as though it was going to be dual use, and then it came back to dual use, and Tessa Jowell announced it was dual use and it was going to go ahead, she gave it her blessing, et cetera, et cetera. Not one word was ever said throughout this entire protracted proceeding about the need for a village to be juxtaposed to the athletics stadium which is Wembley. So now, as I say, it looks as though, if the Government are willing to go ahead, we would have a new stadium for which no legacy use whatever is specifically planned solely because it needs the juxtaposition of the village. Please tell me if I am right or wrong. If I am wrong, do not hesitate to tell me.

(*Mr Scott*) If I could refer to my earlier comments, the village is one of the key factors but it is also to do with the total organisation of the Games, and that does include things like proximity to the media centre. I have to restress the importance of the security issue—security now is one of the most important factors that the IOC consider. I am sure you have seen the increasing cost there has been in recent Games. Having facilities very close together which minimise the need to transport key people—athletes, VIPs, et cetera—is something which gives you a competitive edge when you are bidding. I have not been privy to many of the earlier discussions but our role in this was to particularly advise on if London wishes to be in the game of staging Olympics what gives us the competitive edge. That is where we have been coming from. We are saying, what do we, a bidding city, need to provide if we aspire to host these Games? That is going through the technical requirements, looking at what can be provided in London and then assessing what benefits would flow from the provision of those facilities in that part of London. That is why the work which was undertaken by Arup focused on the East London option.

Mr Doran

213. The difficulty I have with that is that all of this was known in 1996. There are three particular problems I have, particularly with the position set out by Mr Fytche. One is the letter which the Chairman read out from Michael Cunnah from Wembley, which is clearly if you like a lobbying letter, saying, "Why do you need another stadium, we have Wembley". Within that letter he is pointing to the contract. I do not have the contract in front of me so I do not know whether the statement is accurate but clearly when the contract was written between Sport England and WNSL or its predecessor according to Mr Cunnah there was a specific obligation placed on WNSL to host the Olympics, as he says, either as a secondary venue or the centrepiece, so you have obviously covered your options there. But the clear understanding at WNSL is that they will be considered as the location. That is why he has written this letter. The third is your own submission to the Committee, and I appreciate there are other reasons for this, but you make it quite clear that you are only giving qualified support for a London Olympics, and one of the qualifications is that the bid is not reliant on Sport England Lottery funding. Would I be careless in speculating that you have already invested your money in the Olympic stadium, we just happen to be going for another Olympic stadium? One is enough to invest in.

(*Mr Draper*) I think the key issue with Wembley is we have provided the opportunity not just to host football, rugby league and athletics, but to utilise the stadium in other ways, whether that be World Championships, Olympic bids and so on. So that was built into the funding agreement. The second issue is the Lottery landscape has changed significantly. We certainly would not be in the position these days to be funding projects of the scale of Wembley. Lottery revenue coming into sport in 1998 were £270 million, our financial forecasts for Lottery revenue coming into sport next year are £170 million, that is £100 million lower than we were four or five years ago. Out of the Strategy Unit Report which has recently been published on Game Plan it is clear that our role as we reform and modernise the organisation is very much about driving up participation rates in this country in sport, making England a healthier nation, as well as getting successful athletes. Obviously what we are keen to do is make sure we have a balanced strategy across the board and we do not just build wonderful stadia and have wonderful events but we have wonderful athletes to fill them.

214. I understand all of that, Mr Draper, but it gets us away from the point. I am sorry to say it but the point now is the question mark over once again Sport England's contribution to Wembley Stadium and the circumstances in which it was made. Do you accept the decision, which we have gone over many times, is now back under question?

(*Mr Fytche*) No, I do not accept that. As I said earlier, Sport England had a very clear objective, for instance, investment in the Wembley project, and that was to create a stadium for three sports, primarily football and rugby league but with the capability of conversion to athletics should that be needed by the people who make those decisions, whether it is the World Athletics or an Olympic bid

process. That has always been extremely clear. Despite all the diversions and financing issues, Sport England has been consistent in its objectives for the project and has seen those through. The project which is now moving ahead on site is precisely the project which delivered the objectives set out in the funding agreement in 1999. So I think that Sport England and its Council have been very consistent in pursuing that, despite all of the delays and all of the issues we know about and have gone over many times. The issues which relate to whether or not Wembley forms the centrepiece of an Olympic bid again have always been very widely known and I am sure have been evaluated very clearly, but those are questions for the BOA and its partners as it looks for the best bid, if you like, the bid which puts London in the best light in terms of the IOC criteria. As John Scott has outlined, they extend beyond the realms of the stadium and the sports facilities into the much wider debate about transport, regeneration and security issues. It is perfectly legitimate therefore for the Bid Committee and for the partners looking at those issues to take that much wider view at this moment in time.

215. Do you accept that is contradicted by the letter from WNSL and what they believe their position to be and the contract between yourselves and WNSL?

(*Mr Fytche*) I think Michael Cunnah is emphasising the position as it stands, that he is under an obligation to make that stadium available for athletics as and when required, and if required, by Bid Committees who may put the bids forward. He has an obligation to provide that and he has reiterated that in his letter to the Committee.

Chairman

216. This just will not do. It really will not do. Mr Cunnah's letter is a clear, helpful letter, totally credible as far as I can see. I would not fault a word of it. What I want to be clear about on behalf of the Committee is this: when Sport England gave £120 million to FA/WNSL to build a dual use stadium on the Wembley site with the intention of its being the centrepiece stadium—because that was the basis upon which it was given and why the decision was made and why all the arguments about dual use and Picketts Lock and Mr Chris Smith's kitchen and all the rest of it came up—to house the 2012 Olympic Games should we get them, did Sport England at that time know that there would be a problem with the location of the village? If it did not know, it is culpable. If it did know, it is culpable. But I would like to know one way or the other what the position was.

(*Mr Fytche*) The position was that Sport England invested in a project, as I said before, to create the opportunity for it to form the centrepiece of the bid should the Bid Committee consider that to be the best option. You will find, going back to those days in 1999 and the launch of the project which you mentioned, the BOA themselves were talking about the potential for Wembley to be the centrepiece of the bid. All parties involved in the debate at that time acknowledged Wembley could be the centrepiece of the bid. It was later that the issues relating to athletics

[Chairman *Cont*]

and Picketts Lock arose but at the time the decisions were taken around Wembley it was clear that all parties felt that Wembley could be the centrepiece and therefore no issues relating to the position of the village *vis-a-vis* Wembley were problematic to it going forward at that stage.

Rosemary Mckenna

217. I agree with you, this has completely changed the whole debate and discussion that we have been having up to now because certainly my view was that you should never be building single purpose stadia in this country ever again and that we should always be looking to provide stadia which were multi-purpose, which could attract as many different kinds of events as possible and on that basis we supported the Wembley construction and the multi-purpose nature of that and that was premised on the fact that it would be the basis of the Olympic bid. We all felt that it was exactly the right thing to do. I cannot understand why this is coming up now. You have to put other things into the picture as well. If it was always going to be based in the East End, we had a site at the East End which would have been absolutely perfect. Nobody wanted to touch it because it was called the Dome. All of that should have been part of this debate at that time, not now. It seems to me that there has been absolutely no joined- up discussion whatsoever between all the various organisations who are going to have to be involved in a successful bid and I just feel at this stage in the whole debate it has been completely thrown in the air and we have got a whole new agenda in front of us.

(*Sir Rodney Walker*) Would it be helpful, Chairman, if I tried to draw some of these strands together?

Chairman

218. You are always helpful, Sir Rodney, that is why we invite you.

(*Sir Rodney Walker*) You remember that at the outset Wembley Stadium was to be on a configuration similar to that of the Stade de France and certainly my last involvement with it at that time was whether or not we were going to have demountable seats or retractable seats. When I returned to it it had moved on and the Football Association were in the lead, the project was much bigger, more ambitious and a decision had been taken that athletics would not be accommodated inside Wembley and it would be accommodated in a purpose-built stadium elsewhere. When I became re-engaged they sought to find a design solution to re-introduce the ability to stage athletics in the new Wembley and that is the situation that exists today. Where I think there is a danger of us mixing apples with pears is there is no doubt that Wembley as it was originally conceived, as Michael Cunnah has confirmed in his letter to you today, has the facilities to provide the athletics venue for an Olympic bid if that were the wish of those who are responsible for mounting the bid to the IOC. About two years ago I think the Mayor of London became involved in discussions with the BOA and at that stage, as Ian

has quite rightly confirmed to you, an analysis of a West London bid with Wembley as a centrepiece was examined and we began to explore for the first time— I did not but it began to be explored—the East London option which looked at the present site and all the regeneration benefits that that would bring to the area and the legacy that would result, and it was at that time that a quite deliberate and conscious decision was taken that if we had to bid for the Olympic Games then the bid would be based upon a location in East London and not in West London. I can confirm that I am aware that considerations were given to village accommodation in the West London area. I do not think it ever got to an advanced stage because by that time people's attention had turned to East London. So I think the honest answer is the West London options were looked at but never became fully developed because whilst that was being examined the attractions of East London became known and people's attention turned in that direction.

Chairman: Sir Rodney, you have been totally honest and straightforward, as one would always expect from you. Nevertheless, it has to be said that it astounds me and so far as I can gather it astounds colleagues in this Committee that at five o'clock, at the tail end of an inquiry, this suddenly emerges into the light of day as an issue about which none of us was aware and I am not for an instant saying that anybody deliberately concealed it, no, it was worse than that, it was a sin of omission. In the last Parliament Mr David Faber put a huge amount of work into this but none of this emerged. In this Parliament, if I may say so, among the rest of us, Frank Doran has put a huge amount of work into this and if any member of the Committee were to have been aware of this above the rest of us it would have been Frank Doran. So far as I can see it has come as as much a surprise to him as indeed to anybody else. So far as I can tell but please correct me if I am wrong, I believe Rosemary McKenna is right, this new issue of a fundamental new turn in this inquiry of the emergence of the need for a new stadium simply because of its juxtaposition with the need for a village is a stipulation not of Sport England, not of the Government, but of the British Olympic Association who will not be putting a penny into the construction of any of this but will be giving a wish-list which we then have to obey.

Alan Keen: I was aware and Ian Fytche is right, it is not Sport England who were at fault with Wembley. I am a West London MP so I was aware straightaway. As soon as I saw the decision was taken to hold it in East London I knew there was going to be the need to build a stadium and I say it again just to make sure, West Ham and Spurs are losing money now, there is no way they can finance a stadium unless it is gifted to them and in a way Manchester City has been a bit of a gift. When the decision was taken to move to East London I do not know whether people took account of the fact that a duplicate stadium had to be built and it would be of use to somebody, but you would have to give it to them, that is when the decision was taken that went against what Sport England envisaged when they put the money into Wembley Stadium. That is about it. I was aware from the moment it moved to East London. In fact, during this Committee hearing earlier on I said to people I

[Chairman *Cont*]

would put money on the fact that the Olympics will be held at Wembley Stadium, whatever you say about Picketts Lock. Obviously that has changed. So I was aware that we were duplicating the scene.

Derek Wyatt

219. Can I ask one question about the costs of this thing. How much will a new stadium cost?

(*Sir Rodney Walker*) I have not been part of the debate, although I may have views about how it might be constructed and how you might organise the event. Clearly it is difficult at this moment to trade those with you.

(*Mr Draper*) I am afraid we have not got those figures.

220. Is it £300 million or £700 million, what is it?

(*Mr Fytche*) I have not got the figures in front of me, but I think the Arup Report gives a range of costs for the options they have put forward and I am sure that they are doing further work on that with the Government at the moment. We would be happy to furnish you with any information we have on the stadium costs.

Chairman: I think we have taken this as far as we can with our witnesses. We are very, very grateful to you. Thank you, gentlemen. We much appreciate your time.

APPENDICES TO THE MINUTES OF EVIDENCE

Asterisks below denote the deletion of written evidence submitted to the Committee in confidence.

APPENDIX 1

Memorandum submitted by the Department for Culture, Media and Sport

INTRODUCTION

1. The Government has to decide by the end of January whether to support a bid by the British Olympic Association (BOA) for the 2012 Olympic Games and Paralympics. The BOA would make the bid but would not make a bid without the explicit support of the Government.

2. The BOA are required to inform the International Olympic Committee (IOC) of the name of the bidding city by July 2003. This means that the Government would have to inform the BOA of its intentions shortly, so that the BOA can put together a prospectus for the July deadline.

3. Full bids are required by the IOC by November 2004. The host city for the 2012 Olympic Games will be chosen in July 2005.

4. The Government has been considering the case for the Games since before January 2002, when the Arup consultancy was commissioned to undertake a Cost Benefit Analysis on staging the Games in London.

5. The experience of hosting the Commonwealth Games has enabled us to focus on assessing and mitigating potential liabilities. To come to a collective view by the end of this month, Government has been concentrating on four key areas in our assessment. They are:

— *Affordability* (What is the cost of providing the facilities and infrastructure necessary to stage the Games and would it represent good value for money?)

— *Deliverability* (How confident can we be that the proposals can be delivered effectively?)

— *Legacy* (Will the games leave a legacy of facilities and other benefits which is of long term value to the citizens of the United Kingdom?)

— *Winnability* (What would we have to do to produce a credible bid, and what are the chances of it succeeding?)

6. To supplement work on these criteria, we have also undertaken work on two other areas:

— visits to and an assessment of the experience of six cities in hosting or bidding for the Olympics; and

— an assessment of public opinion on bidding for the Games.

FOUR CRITERIA

Affordability

7. Clarity on costs will be needed. The Government as funder of last resort will be the underwriter for the Games. For example, significant cost overruns occurred in Montreal and its citizens will be paying for the 1976 Games until 2006. Sydney also experienced considerable increases in costs after the decision to bid, as has Athens. In both cases, the costs approximately doubled from the original estimates. Our own experience in hosting the Commonwealth Games emphasised the importance of prudent budgeting and the need for a considerable contingency.

8. Arup costed the Games at approximately £3.6 billion with revenues likely to be £2.5 billion leading to a public subsidy of £1.1 billion (all figures are at outturn prices). These figures represent a good baseline.

9. Arup's costs included figures for:

(a) Bidding
(b) New and upgraded sports facilities including a new Olympic Stadium and pool
(c) Transports costs for the Olympic Family (no major transport infrastructure costs included)
(d) Elite sport development programme
(e) Land purchase
(f) Staging the Games, including contingency

10. Work has been undertaken with the assistance of PricewaterhouseCoopers and involving further discussions with Arup, other stakeholders and those who would be involved in delivery. Uncertainties around costs and revenue continue to be identified and we expect this to be the case until plans are further developed. We currently assess that there is an 80 per cent probability that public subsidy will be in the range £1.1 billion to £2.1 billion.

However until we are able to achieve greater certainty we must allow for a higher potential public subsidy of around £2.5 billion. There might always be exceptional circumstances which could make it even higher.

11. We also need to consider the possible diversion of funds from other schemes and projects to support the Olympics. This is to be balanced against the benefits which the Olympics may bring.

12. We have compared the costs with our best estimate of costs for other Games. These are set out at Annex 1.

Deliverability

13. We would not bid for the Games without being confident that we could stage them to good effect. This means we must look closely at the available infrastructure. We must be sure we know the right type of organisation to bid for and then deliver the Games. And we must be sure that this organisation has the right leadership.

14. One of the key elements of delivering the Games effectively is transport. Transport arrangements based on the existing plans for the infrastructure and involving traffic management are being further assessed and costed where possible.

15. Work on the structure of the organisation required for both the bid and staging is being undertaken. This will examine, amongst other things, whether the organisation should be run centrally by the Government, should be at arm's length from Government or should be set up according to another model.

Legacy

16. One of the aims of the Games should be to leave a positive impact, in sporting and economic terms.

17. The Secretary of State and the Minister of Sport have visited a number of past and future Olympic cities to see the legacy of the Olympic Games. Annex 3 sets out some findings from the sporting perspective of these visits. The two key issues emerging are the importance of a clear legacy strategy for facility use after the Games, and that timely planning procedures are in place.

18. There is a clear need to plan for the use of facilities after the Games. Arup considered a new purpose-built Olympic stadium with a legacy as either an athletics stadium (seating capacity 20,000 – 30,000) or as a football stadium (60,000). It is unlikely that there enough large athletic events to make the athletics option viable. Work is currently being undertaken to assess whether a football club would be interested in occupying this stadium as an anchor tenant.

19. Further work is also being undertaken on the legacy for both élite and grassroots sport as a result of the Games. Previous Games have shown that although the home nation always performs well, this is not a lasting trend, and that any increase in participation is not necessarily sustained.

20. Work is also being undertaken on the impact the Games will have on the current Thames Gateway Regeneration plan for the Stratford area, assessing whether the Games will help or hinder this Plan.

21. An assessment of the economic impact for the UK of staging the Games is also being done.

22. Details of the regeneration and economic legacy of all the Games from 1972 to 2008 are included at Annex 4.

Winnability

23. Assessing whether we can win the bid is a vital component of the review. The bidding process will be expensive and so we must make a realistic assessment of the likelihood of winning. This is as much a question of art as one of science. We have been gathering information on the plans of other cities and the attitudes of the IOC. A summary assessment is included at Annex 2.

Opinion Poll

24. Support of all stakeholders and the public would certainly help the bid. An ICM telephone opinion poll carried out on behalf of the DCMS indicated that four out of 5 people want the Government to bid, though this figure falls to 73 per cent when the cost implications are included. There was general support across the whole country. Six focus groups were also carried out and their results show consistency with the opinion polls.

25. Overall the work we are currently finalising will provide us with the information to make an informed decision on whether the four key criteria are satisfied and whether the Government should support a bid for the 2012 Games or not.

13 January 2002

Annex 1

COMPARISON OF OLYMPICS COSTS

The table below provides an approximation of the costs of previous and future Olympic Games in sterling 2002 prices.

The comparisons are therefore only approximate. Some cities have incorporated infrastructure costs in their Olympic expenditure and others have not. Exchange rates and purchasing price parity issues, also need to be taken into account. For example Sydney's price parity is approximately 80 per cent of that of London. If we used London prices for the Sydney Games, the Sydney Games would have cost approximately £3.248 billion.

Host City	£GBP 2002 prices £(m)
Munich 1972	1,430
Montreal 1976	2,436
Moscow 1980	2,622
Los Angeles 1984	567
Seoul 1988	3,746
Barcelona 1992	8,057
Atlanta 1996	1,481
Sydney 2000	2,534
Athens 2004	3,937
Beijing 2008	9,775
London 2012[1]	2,614

Annex 2

LONDON OLYMPIC BID — WINNABILITY

1. It is difficult to assess the prospects for success of any bid for the 2012 Olympics at this stage. There are many important factors about which we cannot be certain: we cannot be sure who else will bid; how strong their bids will be; how they and we would be regarded by the voting members of the IOC; or whether it will be Europe's turn to stage the Summer Olympics. However, the Government needs to make the best estimate it can of the prospects before deciding whether it should support a bid.

2. Any London Bid would be technically strong and with the attraction of London as a major world city would offer a strong proposition to the IOC. Any public controversy in putting the bid together would not go unnoticed in IOC circles, and would detract significantly from its strength. Widespread public support is necessary and we are in the process of assessing attitudes to a bid across the country.

3. Our assessment is that around 30 voting IOC members might be favourably disposed towards a bid from the United Kingdom. If that were translated into votes at the selection, it would be approximately half of the number likely to be required for victory. To secure those and the additional 30 or so which would be required to win would require a great deal of work in convincing IOC members that the bid is of high quality, that Britain deserves the Games and would deliver. Our representatives on the IOC and the governing bodies of the major Olympic sports would have an important role, as would the network of UK official representation overseas.

4. Wholehearted cross party support is critical to the prospects of any bid. Considerable input will be needed from a number of key departments across Whitehall. Promoting an Olympic Bid will require a large commitment of attention and resource from Government. The two and a half year process cannot therefore be undertaken lightly.

5. The structure put in place for the bid and that which is proposed for staging the games will be important in convincing the IOC that Britain can be relied on to deliver.

[1] Based on Arup analysis (21 May 2002) using Mills Mead and Athletics legacy scenario

6. There can be no clear favourite to win the games at this stage. London's bid will be technically strong. Our capacity to convince the voting members of the IOC that Britain deserves the games and will deliver a top class event will be critical. We continue to work to refine our assessment of the prospects of any bid for 2012.

Annex 3

SPORTING LEGACY

1. This paper looks at the sporting legacy of the Olympic Games using historical data, visits by Ministers to previous and future Olympic cities, the recent Strategy Unit Report (Game Plan) and the details contained in the Arup Report on the 2012 Olympics.

The three key areas of sporting legacy are:

(a) Facilities
(b) Elite Success
(c) Participation

FACILITIES

- Many of the host nations did not have a clear exit strategy for their facilities after the Games.

- Where large scale new facilities have been built legacies of under use have arisen. The NSW Government faces an annual bill of £10 million for under use of facilities in Sydney. Barcelona is also experiencing this problem.

- Refurbishment of existing venues has proved to be the most cost effective. Both in Los Angeles (1984) and Atlanta (1996) great use was made of existing facilities. This issue is not only tied into predominantly privately funded Games, Moscow (1980) also used a stadium built in 1956 as its Olympic Stadium. This Stadium is still in use today, having re-invented itself a number of times since.

- Mistakes were often made at the design stage with limited thought on what would be the legacy of the Games. Multi purpose use should have been the key requirement but often the Stadium was designed purely for prestigious architectural design and large capacity.

- All Games which have required large scale public funding have been left with a legacy of facilities for which the local or national government has had to fund, including Munich which left behind excellent, well-used sporting facilities. Munich City Council is currently funding the Olympic Complex to the tune of £4-£6 million per year.

- An anchor tenant for the main Olympic Stadium would encourage sustainable use post Games. Both Moscow and Munich had football clubs using their Stadiums after the Games, which have helped to offset the costs

ELITE SUCCESS

- The host nation normally performs well at the games. Research from previous Games has shown this. For example Spain received one Gold medal at the 1988 Games and yet at the Barcelona Games in 1992 they received 13 Golds.

- In virtually every Games the host Country has done considerably better than the Games previously and has carried this success into future Games albeit at a lower rate. However, it is not just the Games by themselves that lead to this success.

- Hosting the Games has advantages for home athletes through increased support, knowledge of conditions, increased motivation and the introduction of new sports favourable to the home country.

- Other factors are obviously the size of the population and crucially the GDP of the nations involved. The more funds that are available the easier it is to use some to support athletes. For example the USA whose population and GDP is larger than most countries is always in the top five of medal winners.

- Governments can influence élite success through carefully planned sporting strategies. Australia set in train an élite strategy after its poor results in Montreal in 1976 and from 1988 to 2000 invested approximately £20 million a year. The results can be seen in 2000 with its Gold Medal count reaching sixteen compared to none in 1976 and only three in 1988

- Similarly Korea did well at its host Games in 1988 as it had an élite sports programme specifically to ensure success at these Games. Since then South Korea's total medal tally has dropped from 33 to 28 in 2000 but still higher than the six achieved in 1976.

- But if we look at Britain's performance in 1996 where we received only one gold medal and Sydney 2000 where we received eleven the key determinant seems to have been the introduction of lottery money through the World Class Programme in 1997.

- The use of additional funds to improve élite success in 2012 is currently being assessed.

- Research has shown that hosting the Games will increase the hosts medal share by 1.5 per cent of the total medals available. There are approximately 900 medals available.

- This increase, however, is linked to all the factors mentioned above and often countries ensure that they will do well in the Games by having programmes specifically for that purpose. Spain and South Korea have shown this in their medal gains

- The Games can be a catalyst to have a strong élite programme, not dissimilar to the UK's World Class Programme, but this programme needs to continue after the Games for continued success.

PARTICIPATION

- The Games by themselves cannot be shown of themselves to increase long term participation. There may be a short-term effect as people watch but it does not last long.

- For example Australia who have a strong élite programme have low participation rates and along with a changing diet are having problems with high obesity rates amongst its population. The USA has staged the Olympics twice in the last twenty years yet it has extremely low participation rates and has the highest rates of childhood and adult overweight and obesity.

- However, the Games can be used as the impetus for sports participation policies as can be seen by the programme initiated by Spain and South Korea after hosting their respective Games.

- Beijing has already initiated a major increased participation programme, which they would not have done without winning the right to stage the 2008 Games. The program is looking to increase participation rates to 61 per cent and ensure that 75 per cent of those tested will meet the physical health standard for the average citizen by 2008.

- The recently published Strategy Unit Report on sport outlines the Government's intention to focus on increased participation alongside international success.

Annex 4

REGENERATION AND ECONOMIC IMPACT OF THE OLYMPIC GAMES

A summary of the economic and regeneration effects of the Olympic Games is listed below. There are limited independent assessments on the economic effects of the Games and many of the figures quoted below are either from government sources or from consultants hired by governments to review the Games.

MUNICH 1972

Costs

Publicly funded.

Regeneration

The Olympic Park with all the sports facilities, the Olympic Village and the media centre was built on a desolate 3km tract of land four kilometres from the city centre. Munich previously had no large sports arenas. The buildings were surrounded by extensive parklands and a man made lake. The Park is used extensively by the local community and has regenerated what used to be the neglected part of the City.

The funding was also used for major developments in roads and the building of a brand new subway system.

The Olympic Village was converted into private housing and other parts were handed over to the University whose campus is now on the site further regenerating this desolate brownfield site.

Munich is one of the few Olympic sites that has made further constructive use of its facilities. Since 1972 over 7500 cultural and commercial events have taken place in this area. These include world championships, European championships, German championships and a variety of cultural events attracting over 130 million visitors.

Economic Impact

There has been a significant economic impact after the Games. Munich is one of the most affluent cities in Germany with a significant tourist industry. The Games accelerated the rebuilding process in West Germany and led to many changes including the pedestrianisation of the City Centre which has increased consumer spending.

MONTREAL 1976

Costs

Publicly funded.

Regeneration Impact

A new stadium, a new velodrome and an Olympic Village used for housing after the Games. New roads and a new airport

Economic Impact

Montreal seems to have received little long term benefit. The financial deficit from the Games was approximately $1billion dollars, which its citizens are still paying for. The final payment for this debt will be in 2005–06.

MOSCOW 1980

Costs

Publicly funded.

Regeneration

The development of the four main areas were located in poor run down areas. The Olympic village was used for social housing and the metro was extended.

Economic Impact

No information available but of the 300,000 anticipated visitors only a quarter attended these Games. It does not seem that there was any significant impact on the Russian economy.

LOS ANGELES 1984

Costs

Privately funded.

Regeneration

Renovation of the airport and installation of telecommunications infrastructure were the main elements of the regeneration impact. There were only four new athletics facilities built as the Games relied on existing facilities.

Economic Impact

The Games made a $225 million surplus of which 40 per cent went to the Amateur Athletic Foundation of Los Angeles. Estimates on tourism increases in Southern California were approximately $9 billon with $145 million tax revenues going to the local and state government . There was a counter effect with lower visitors than normal at Disneyland, Universal Studios and Six Flags Magic Mountain.

SEOUL 1988

Costs

Forty six per cent publicly funded

Regeneration

The development of the Olympic village was a key part of the urban regeneration objectives of the Games. A full-scale urban centre was constructed including housing, retail and other community facilities. Apartments to house athletes, journalists and other personnel during the Olympics were constructed for use as residential units after the Games. These housing projects have helped to ease the housing shortage in Seoul and the village is now fully integrated within the city.

The Korean Government used the Seoul Games as the catalyst to undertake a number of long-term infrastructure improvements including the expansion of Kimpo International Airport, construction of new roads and underground stations and telecommunication improvements.

Economic Impact

The Koreans state that between 1982 and 1988 the production resulting from Olympic Projects amounted to 0.4 per cent of GNP and that 336,000 new jobs were created during this period. In 1988 the Korean economy achieved growth of 12 per cent.

Care needs to be taken with some of these figures, as they have been not been independently assessed.

The Seoul Olympics, however, did promote the Korean tourist, sports, leisure, electronics and telecommunications industries.

BARCELONA 1992

Costs

Thirty eight per cent publicly funded

Regeneration

These have been the most expensive Games so far mainly due to the total transformation of Barcelona. From 1989 to 1992 Barcelona increased its roads by 15 per cent, sewerage system by 17 per cent, green zones and beaches by 78 per cent, and ponds and fountains by 268 per cent . Redevelopment of the airport, new housing, new ring roads, a new Olympic Village and Stadium and transportation infrastructures for towns that were Olympic sub sites were other regeneration costs that made these Games so expensive.

Economic Impact

From October 1986 to July 1992 the general rate of unemployment in Barcelona fell from 18.4 per cent to 9.6 per cent, whereas in the rest of Spain in 1992 the rate was 15.5 per cent. In 1993 there were still 50,000 fewer people unemployed than in 1986. The longer term impact has not been estimated. It is calculated that the total impact of the 1992 Barcelona Games could be around $26 billion (1992 prices) over the period 1987-92.

Barcelona is now regarded as one of the most beautiful cities in Europe and is also one of the most visited by tourists.

ATLANTA 1996

Costs

Fifteen per cent publicly funded

Regeneration

There was limited urban redevelopment with a new Olympic Stadium and the regeneration of Centennial Olympic Park. Most sporting facilities were upgrades rather than new builds. Over $600m was spent on infrastructure projects. Hosting the Games helped land one of six federal empowerment zones designations. Overall the city's efforts to use the Olympics to revitalize urban neighbourhoods fell short

Economic Impact

The Games brought in two million tourists and a £5 billion tourism boost. However the Games left a legacy of ill will in the neighbourhoods that bore the brunt of lost housing and dislocation. The negative media on accommodation, transportation and the bomb blast in Centennial Olympic Park did not help Atlanta's image. Overall the games probably raised Atlanta's profile as a tourism destination in the longer term.

SYDNEY 2000

Costs

Approx 30 per cent publicly funded

Regeneration

The brand new Olympic Stadium was located in the run down area in the heart of Sydney. The 770 hectare site was previously an abattoir and light industrial area.

The Athletes village housed 11,000 competitors and a further 4000 team officials. The village is now a new suburb of Newington with 6000 residents. This part of Sydney was wasteland before the Games and the Olympics has clearly been very effective in the regeneration of the area, with the rail line giving easy access to the city.

There was clearly a need for the city to improve its central road and rail links and the Games gave the impetus for this to happen. The Games were seen as a vehicle for change in this respect and some of the changes brought in for the games have remained in place afterwards (eg limiting deliveries in the city centre at certain times).

Economic Impact

The following has been stated as being the economic impact of the 2000 Games:

- ▸ $3 billion in business outcomes
- ▸ over $6 billion invested in the NSW infrastructure
- ▸ $1.2 billion on convention business for NSW between 1993 and 2007
- ▸ over $6 billion in inbound tourism during 2001
- ▸ enhanced business profile for Sydney, NSW and Australia.

ATHENS 2004

Costs

Approx 73 per cent publicly funded

Regeneration

This is an important reason for staging the Games in Athens. The Department of Labour is using a public housing organisation to build the Olympic Village. After the Games these apartments/housing will be used for social housing and be sold off with low interest rate mortgages by the public housing organisation.

The same will apply to some of the media sites currently under construction. The main media village will be in the refurbished Ministry of Education building. After the Games it will be sold off as an office block.

Many of these Olympic sites, including sporting sites, are being located in poor areas and their redevelopment is intended to bring about their regeneration.

The Faliron Olympic Site is located on the coast in an area which was first reclaimed from the sea in 1972. It is a rundown area with a main road running separating the poor housing stock from the reclaimed land. The current programme is the largest regeneration programme in Europe and is aiming to leave a legacy of reduced flooding risk, new housing stock, environmental improvements, a water park and excellent sports facilities.

Economic Impact

Athens's view is that the Games will once again put them on the world map and as a result lead to increased tourism and increased investment.

BEIJING 2008

Costs

Approximately 90 per cent publicly funded at this moment in time.

Regeneration

This is one of the main aims of Beijing. £20 billion is available to make Beijing a world-class city to upgrade medical facilities, relocate people from central Beijing to the suburbs, build a new airport terminal and a high tech underground system.

Beijing has promised to reduce the severe pollution levels currently affecting the city and has set aside £5.7 billion for environment protection as part of its capital investment for the Olympics.

Economic Impact

Beijing's economy has been growing at over 17 per cent per year over the last decade and likely to increase once it joins the World Trade Organisation. With the added investment in the Olympics interest from outside is likely to increase and thereby increase the growth rate.

Other key aims beside increased business investment is to put China as a whole on the tourist map. Hotels rooms are being increased to deal with the Olympics with the aim that after the Games tourism will increase and use this excess hotel capacity.

Annex 5

SURVEY OF PUBLIC OPINION ON A LONDON 2012 OLYMPIC BID:
SUMMARY OF THE RESEARCH APPROACH AND FINDINGS

INTRODUCTION

1. In December 2002 the Department for Culture, Media and Sport commissioned ICM Research to conduct a survey of public opinion in relation to a potential London bid for the Olympics in 2012. This was part of the wider process of consultation on whether to bid for the Olympics in 2012.

2. More than 3,000 people were surveyed across the UK. The key findings are set out below. The full set of results are published on the ICM Research website (www.icmresearch.co.uk).

KEY RESEARCH FINDINGS

- Four in five (81 per cent) say that a bid should be made. Support is consistent across the regions, with Scottish and Northern Irish adults among the most supportive. Londoners' themselves want the Games to be held in their city, with 82 per cent backing a bid.

- Paradoxically, 56 per cent of people think the money would be better spent on grassroots sports facilities (but not on non-sporting projects). 51 per cent think that London will receive the majority of the investment, from which the rest of the UK will fail to receive any dividend.

- When prompted with cost implications, the level of support for a London bid falls to 73 per cent.

- Seventy per cent believe the Olympics will bring a 'feel good factor' and prestige to the UK; 71 per cent think that the Manchester Commonwealth Game proved that the UK can run a successful Olympics; 60 per cent think the Games will bring employment and investment opportunities, while providing a long-term legacy for the East End; 65 per cent feel hosting the Olympics will create more sporting opportunities for young people.

- More people (53 per cent) would prefer to bid for the Olympics than the World Cup. However, fieldwork did take place at a time of considerable media attention for the Olympic Bid.

- Overall, there has been a 12 per cent upward swing in the public's preference for a London bid since this question was last by ICM Research in June 2002. The broadly positive Olympic coverage in the run up to Christmas may have had much to do with this change.

METHODOLOGY

3. ICM Research interviewed a random sample of 3,267 people aged 18+ by telephone between 19-23 December 2002. Equal numbers of interviews were achieved in each Government Office region of the country thereby enabling statistical comparisons between the regions. London was boosted to 502 interviews. Data within each region was weighted to the profile of all adults in that area. To obtain data representative of the whole country, data was then weighted to reflect the actual proportion of the total population living in each area.

North East	252 interviews
North West	252 interviews
Yorks & the Humber	250 interviews
East Midlands	252 interviews
West Midlands	252 interviews
East of England	251 interviews
Greater London	502 interviews
South East	251 interviews
South West	250 interviews
Wales	253 interviews
Scotland	250 interviews
Northern Ireland	252 interviews
Total (UK)	3,267 interviews

The data on 3,267 interviews is correct to within +/- 1.7 per cent at the 95 per cent confidence level. The data at regional level (250 interviews) is correct to within +/- 6.2 per cent.

Statistically significant differences are observed at the following levels of response:

Sample size to be compared	Differences required to be statistically significant at or near		
	10% or 90% +/-	30% or 70% +/-	50% +/-
250 and 250	5.3%	8.0%	8.8%

Supplementary Memorandum submitted by the Department for Culture, Media and Sport

1. The Clerk to the Culture, Media and Sport Select Committee asked for information from the Department for Culture, Media and Sport supplementary to the evidence given by the Secretary of State for Culture, Media and Sport on 15 January 2003.

2. *Question: Evolution of cost estimates (consistent basis) from Arup Report to latest figures, with public sector subsidy identified:*

- *for the Olympic balance sheet*
- *for related infrastructure not directly attributable, ie*
  - *London security*
  - *transport infrastructure*
  - *off-zone site*

3. DCMS has considered the Olympic costs and revenues identified in the Arup Report and re-examined them as a basis for long term public expenditure planning. There have been three complementary approaches: a critical appraisal of risks and contingencies; a probability analysis; and benchmarking

4. Arup put forward four physical options for the Olympics. Officials have used the option of the Olympics village being situated at Mill Meads and a football legacy for the stadium as the basis for their work. This is because the Mill Meads option is held to be the best in regeneration terms and a long term football use for the stadium is more likely to be realisable than an athletics use. The Arup Report shows however that there are not significant differences between any of the four options for long term planning purposes.

CRITICAL APPRAISAL

5. Arup's report is based on constant 2002 prices and these were first inflated using an assumption of 2.5 per cent a year through to the end of the Olympic project period. Officials also followed the assumptions which Arup made of a five per cent staging contingency and a capital contingency of 30-50 per cent across the period 2009-12. This produced the assessment shown in Table 1 column A below.

Table 1

Cost Element	A	Arup (£m)	B	DCMS (£m)
Arup base case		3,558		3,558
Construction contingency				26
Staging contingency				225
Price parity				70
Look of London				40
Transport				500
Land				55
Venues				50
Administration				150
Revised cost estimate		3,558		4,674
Revenue				
Arup base case		2,450		2,450
Revenue risk				400
Revised revenue estimate		2,450		2,050
Subsidy		-1,108		-2,624

6. Officials then discussed with Arup, other stakeholders, other Government Departments and agencies who would be responsible for delivery, and those who had been involved in previous Games, including the Commonwealth Games in Manchester, the degree of certainty that there was around the Arup estimates. Based on these discussions officials believe that there is a risk of cost escalation in a number of areas. These are shown in Table 1 Column B. The concerns are:

Staging Contingency
Allowance is given for a 15 per cent staging contingency in line with assumptions made in the New York bid for the 2012 Olympics and reflecting the general concern about uncertainties in a complex 10-year project.

Price parity
Discussions with Arup identified that the costs in their assessment based on the Sydney Olympics would need to be increased to reflect the relative purchasing power parity of the pound and Australian dollar.

Look of London
An allowance is made for expenditure on improving the appearance of London (eg street dressing and cleaning) which is derived from spending on the Commonwealth Games in Manchester.

Transport
Discussions with transport agencies confirmed that it should be possible to meet Olympic spectator, officials and media transport requirements to a satisfactory level during the Games but that this would require additional investment in principally station capacity and service enhancements. The high end of the range of estimates is shown in the table. A low end estimate would be £200 million.

Land
Revised estimates from the London Development Agency for land acquisition are higher than the earlier assumptions used by Arup.

Venues
There is risk around the assumptions made that suitable indoor competition venues and training centres throughout East London will be available without significant additional expenditure.

Administration

Additional administration costs may be needed to attract from around the world the right number of top quality planners and Games' deliverers for a short term, high risk project.

7. Officials have also made an allowance for revenue shortfall of £400 million (16 per cent) on the Arup assumption. The revenues flowing from IOC contracts are not under the organisers' control and subject to international market pressures. Ticket price and sale estimates are relatively high and, despite the good sales, both at the Commonwealth Games in Manchester and the Sydney Olympics, there remains a risk of the estimate not being realised.

PROBABILITY ASSESSMENT

8. DCMS also commissioned work in conjunction with PricewaterhouseCoopers to assess the probability ranges around costs and revenues. This involved a debate on the key uncertainties and the quantification of probabilistic distribution of those uncertainties drawing on the judgement of the Department, those whom it had consulted and Arup. The table below shows the results of that discussion. The key figure is the assessment of a 90 per cent probability that the public subsidy would be no more than £2.1 billion. PricewaterhouseCoopers however went on to say that the range for the public subsidy appeared relatively small given the timeframe and nature of the bid decision, and added that they would expect that with further work the range for the public subsidy would initially broaden until appropriate management control could be introduced.

Table 2

2012 Olympics	80% Probability Range (£ billion)
Costs	3.40 to 4.20
Revenues	1.85 to 2.54
Public Subsidy	1.0 to 2.10

BENCHMARK

9. By way of benchmark officials have also examined the outturn cost of the Sydney Olympics. As the Department's earlier memorandum showed, the outturn cost of the Sydney Games, taking into account purchasing power parity between the United Kingdom and Australia, is £3.248 billion at 2002 prices. This is at about 60 per cent probability of being achieved according to the work done by PricewaterhouseCoopers.

RESPONSIBILITY FOR JUDGEMENTS

10. The Department stresses that though it has consulted widely, including outside Government and with those responsible for Arup's original report, the judgements about costs and benefits are its own. This reflects the responsibility on the Department for assessing uncertainties and risks which will bear on public finances.

11. *Question: What is known about the preparatory work undertaken by Sydney/Athens on cost estimates? Anything like Arup? Anything like the subsequent, PWC assisted, analysis? What has the DCMS tried to find out?*

SYDNEY

12. The Auditor General of NSW summed up the Sydney bid as being "primarily concerned with a successful bid outcome rather than a detailed planning for the delivery of the Games. In this sense the assumptions within the Bid Estimates, when measured against current understanding and knowledge, were superficial."

ATHENS

13. The Minister for Sport was told by the Greek Government that there was no detailed cost benefit analysis for the 2004 bid. Athens looked at their figures for the failed 1996 bid and used them as a starting point for 2004.

14. *Question: What is known about why precisely Sydney/Athens costs doubled against estimate? Any pattern? Any relation to the proportion of planned expenditure on facilities, wider infrastructure, relationship to the absolute size or number of projects?*

SYDNEY

15. Sydney's original bid costs were estimated at approx £1 billion of which £125 million were to be borne by the public sector.

16. In 1998 when the Auditor-General of NSW re-evaluated the position, his view was that the budget was considerably under estimated:

- The budget had excluded capital costs for facilities, infrastructure and security.
- Also excluded were costs arising after the Games—redundancy payments and the costs of disruption to public services.
- Included were indirect revenues but not indirect costs.

17. The Sydney Games ended up costing £2.3 billion (using nominal exchange rates and outturn prices) with public contributions of between £580 million and £830 million.

ATHENS

18. Athens originally estimated that the Games would cost £1 billion. Since then the Organising Committee budget has increased to £1.23 billion but this does not include the £2.75 billion of Government spending set aside to cover creating and refurbishing Olympic venues.

19. The Government has also recently taken out an Olympic loan from the EU of £1 billion to help finance the Olympic Games.

20. The rise in costs relates primarily to capital infrastructure costs.

21. *Question: The 'bar' was raised for Manchester in 2002 by Kuala Lumpur and Sydney—what are the prospects for Beijing doing the same for the host of 2012? What are the chances of the IOC lowering the bar, on the back of the Pound Commission's work, before 2012?*

22. The IOC carefully defines the technical specification for each Olympic Games. This is done to a far greater degree than for the Commonwealth Games. We are therefore less likely to see the same step-change in standards post Beijing that we saw between the Victoria 1994 and Kuala Lumpur 1998 Commonwealth Games.

23. However tightly the specification is defined by the IOC there still remains scope for each Organising committee and host Government (national or city) to determine the quality of the Games' experience for athletes, VIPs, the media and spectators. This was the case with Sydney. While the experience will depend on tangible things, for example the quality of food, transport, hotels, accommodation, it is also shaped by more intangible or less controllable elements like the atmosphere in the host city, the weather and defining sporting moments (the 'Cathy Freeman' effect): a Beijing Games is likely to be very different in style than a London Games and so is unlikely to bear direct comparison.

24. The advice we have received is that the IOC will attempt to constrain the growth in scope of the summer Olympics. This reflects current IOC concerns about the sustainability of the Olympics event as it stands (these are set out in the Interim Report of The Olympic Games Study Commission which was presented to an extraordinary Session of the IOC in Mexico on Thursday, 28 November 2002). We do not yet know if this is likely to influence the competitive requirements which will be faced in the selection of the 2012 host.

17 January 2003

APPENDIX 2

Memorandum submitted by Arup

1. The Clerk of the Culture, Media and Sport Select Committee asked for information from Arup, supplementary to the evidence given by Mark Bostock, Sam Higginson and Nick Banks on 14 January 2003.

Question: Can you explain the rationale for using a discounted cashflow approach?

2. Discounting is recommended by the Treasury (see the Treasury Green Book for more details) as the most appropriate way to appraise investment in a particular project. The rationale for using a discount rate approach is something called 'social time preference' i.e. Government would prefer to have its goods and services sooner rather than later so that costs and revenue flows in the distant future are valued less than costs and revenue flows in the near future. A discount rate of six per cent was the standard recommended Treasury discount rate when we did our work (May 2002). This week a new discount rate of 3.5 per cent in the revised Green Book has been introduced.

Question: Was your work based upon an exempler Games?

3. Our work was based upon a 'specimen' or 'exempler' Games for London. As you know, the Arup Summary Report concluded that there was a considerable potential to improve the financial profile of the 'specimen' proposal through further development.

Question: Were your costs a 'high' estimate as they were based upon Sydney outturn prices?

4. Our land and infrastructure cost and revenue projections were based upon current experience of the costs of construction of facilities in the UK, supported on land costs and revenues by the real estate market knowledge of Insignia Richard Ellis. Our staging cost and revenue estimates drew upon a range of sources including recent previous bids from European cities such as Paris for 2008 and the outturn cost and revenues from the Sydney 2000 Olympics. Where appropriate we based our staging cost and revenue projections upon Sydney. The advantage of using the Sydney cost and revenue profiles is that they are outturn costs rather than bid cost and revenue profiles which may be over optimistic. Overall our costs and revenues were our best professional estimates given the time (16 weeks in early 2002) and the resources available.

Question: If cost estimates are inflated to 2012 prices must revenues and benefits also be inflated?

5. A consistent methodology and approach to the appraisal of the project is required. If costs are inflated to 2012 prices, revenues and benefits must also be inflated.

Question: Are benefits which can't be and/or weren't captured by (i) your particular study, and (ii) cost/benefit methodologies in general (needing other appraisal techniques)?

6. There are benefits which it has not been possible to quantify and incorporate into the analysis. Examples of such benefits would include the 'feel good factor' a boost to 'image' of the country, or an increase in sports participation amongst the general population. It is fair to say that there could also be potential unquantifable risks for example a badly run Games could have a negative effect on 'image'. Currently it is not possible to quantify or monetarise these impacts. We have placed significant importance on the need to identify the benefits at the outset, because of their importance in off-setting the financial deficit that we have concluded will be incurred.

Question: There seems to be some debate over apportionment—the scope of the Government's term 'public subsidy' which may cover costs not within the scope of your study (i.e. wider security for London, accelerating or guaranteeing planned infrastructure projects to meet the Olympic timetable (bidding as well as staging), or even customs and immigration in 2012) i.e. there is debate over the recipe as well as the likely size of the resulting cake.

7. There is not only a debate over the recipe as well as the size of the cake but also the attribution of costs and benefits. An example is government agencies claim that additional capital works will be required at Stratford station. We would accept this but argue that not all of these costs are necessarily attributable to the Olympics. If they are included as costs, the benefit of such provision needs to be incorporated in the revenue/benefit assessment.

Question: What work Sydney/Athens did or didn't do and how their process compared to the work undertaken by Arup and subsequently the Government and PwC?

8. I'm afraid we don't have any information on this. As far as we are aware no other study of the type we did is available in the public domain. Certainly, previous recent British efforts were promoted by cities/local authorities/individuals, without a full analysis of the overall costs and benefits of going for a bid/staging.

Summary Question: Why is the Government's estimate different from Arup's?

9. The first point we must emphasise is that our commission was a high-level cost-benefit analysis of a possible 2012 London bid. It was not a formal budget, nor did it represent a bid document.

10. In the Arup Summary Report, which went into the public domain in November 2002, we presented the case for a Mill Meads Olympic Village and an athletics legacy for the stadium. Most of the Government evaluation has been based upon a Mill Meads Olympic Village with a football legacy—this means that there are some small discrepancies amongst the totals (athletics gives you a better financial result because of the smaller footprint required for the legacy stadium allowing more post Games development on adjacent sites). For consistency we have focused upon Mill Meads with a football legacy in the figures below.

11. The best place to start is where we started which is to establish the cost and revenues line items in 2002 prices.

- costs in 2002 prices were estimated to be: £2,820 million, revenues: £1,998 million, balance: £822 million;

- if you discount these figures using a 6 per cent discount rate you get costs £1,808 million, revenues: £1,260 million, balance: £548 million;

- if you inflate these figures you get costs £3,443 million, revenues £2,450 million, balance: £983 million.

12. If you then look at the table submitted in the DCMS written evidence you will see an Arup base case and a DCMS case of £3,558 million in costs (we would argue that there is a small discrepancy in methodology here and it should be £3,443 million).

13. Government has then factored in a number of additional cost items equivalent to £1,090 million in inflated prices. They have also included a revenue risk allowance of £400 million. This should give you a result of—£2,483 million.

14. Whichever methodology is adopted a full appraisal of the project also requires an allowance to be made for wider quantifiable economic benefits. To produce an initial estimate in inflated prices we have taken the Arup case tourism assumed benefits as well as the Arup base case fiscal and employment benefits and inflated these figures. We have also assumed, a boost to exports after the Games of £0.5 billion in 2002 prices. Finally we have assumed that investment in tourism would be zero. Wider benefits in inflated prices using this initial analysis indicate a figure of £2.24 billion.

15. An overall position in inflated prices is set out in the table below (we have assumed a similar level of anticipated wider benefits in the DCMS case as we have projected in the Arup case).

Table 1

SUMMARY ARUP AND DCMS FINANCIAL AND
ECONOMIC PROJECTIONS USING INFLATED PRICES

	Arup £ billion inflated prices	*DCMS £ billion inflated prices*
Costs	3.44	4.53
Revenues	2.45	2.05
Financial balance	-0.99	-2.48
Wider benefits	2.24	2.24
Economic balance	1.25	-0.24

Summary Question: Why did Sydney and Athens get it wrong by 100 per cent and what is the likelihood we won't?

16. We are not able to comment in detail upon the Sydney and Athens experience from bid to outturn. We stated it in our report and reiterated during our oral evidence that if this experience is not to be repeated in London any Olympic Games will require effective co-ordination and project management. We contend that a concordat between the key stakeholders must be agreed upon before any bid is submitted (ie to cover both bidding and staging). Our emphasis is a strong project managed delivery, incorporating private sector skills to deliver this major event and establishing a legacy thereafter.

20 January 2003

APPENDIX 3

Memorandum submitted by British Olympic Association

INTRODUCTION

1. Since 1997 the British Olympic Association (BOA) has been engaged in preparatory work assessing the requirements, strategic planning and viability of a future Olympic Games bid for London.

2. This culminated in a 395 page report which was delivered to officials in the Department for Culture, Media and Sport (DCMS) in December 2000. This report was subsequently presented to the then Secretary of State for Culture Media and Sport, Minister for Sport, Mayor of London, Greater London Authority (GLA), Opposition frontbench spokespersons, Sport England and UK Sport.

3. It has been the BOA's approach to this project to be thorough and methodical and to benefit from early preparation. This is to create an environment where decisions can be taken by all key stakeholders with a clear understanding of the issues involved, the requirements needed, the cost-implications and the potential benefits to all sections of the community in both sporting and social terms.

4. What is clear is that to have any chance of success, there must be unanimous, unambiguous and unequivocal support from all the key stakeholders in the process. The BOA believes that London can mount a bid that is technically viable when assessed against IOC criteria, and will be attractive internationally when put in a competitive bidding environment against other world cities.

KEY STAKEHOLDERS GROUP

5. The Key Stakeholders Group is comprised of representatives from BOA, GLA and Government and was convened in June 2001. The Olympic Charter states that the BOA is the only body with the remit to put forward a candidate city from the UK for consideration by the IOC.

6. The elected representatives of the bidding city must also be signatories to any proposed candidature. In addition both central and local government must provide guarantees in relation to a wide range of issues from planning legislation, customs and immigration, legal issues, security and financial arrangements.

ROLE OF NATIONAL OLYMPIC COMMITTEES IN THE BID PROCESS

7. Following the recommendations of the IOC 2000 Reform Commission, the role of the NOC has been strengthened within the bid process. The NOC is now required to be involved in any Olympic candidature as a full partner with the bid committee.

8. The IOC has stipulated that the NOC must take full responsibility for its Olympic bid

(a)   as the sole official entity authorised by the IOC to submit an application to bid;
(b)   to ensure that an application meets IOC requirements;
(c)   for the actions of the bid committee during the bid application and candidature processes.

WHY LONDON?

9. Following Manchester's bid for the 2000 Olympic Games, the views of the IOC and International Federations were sought as they comprise the voting constituency. This is a process constantly updated by those people within the BOA who operate regularly within the international Olympic environment.

10. The conclusion is that from an international perspective only London would have the status to be competitive against other leading world cities bidding for the Olympic Games. A bid based around any other British city would therefore be unlikely to succeed.

2012 OR 2016?

11. The cost-benefit report makes it clear that to delay a bid for 2016 would raise the serious threat of blighting much needed regeneration in East London making it 'politically unattractive'. The conclusion is that no other area in London has the necessary transport capability nor land availability to be able to be a viable alternative for a delayed bid.

12. The international desire for continental rotation means that if a European city were to win the nomination for 2012, it would be extremely doubtful whether the Games would return to this continent before 2024 at the earliest.

COST BENEFIT ANALYSIS

13. Recent reports have questioned the grounding of the Arup financial analysis which formed the basis of the independent cost-benefit analysis. The model used by Arup was one which was requested by Treasury, and which is the standard model used for investment appraisals of projects of this size. The figures quoted are 2002 Net Present Value figures discounted at the Treasury rate of six per cent. This form of Treasury model does not allow for the inclusion of inflation of figures.

14. Government is currently carrying out an exercise which aims to budget for a 'bad case' scenario with significantly reduced revenues and contingency monies associated with poor planning and execution of the Games. The figures related to this are using a model based upon overall outturn figures and including inflation – representing 'money of the day' values. The two economic models are different and any comparison of figures is inaccurate as it will not be an assessment of like-with-like. It should be noted that Government's inflated figures will also be reflected in revenues as well as costs.

SPECIMEN PROPOSAL

15. The Arup proposal is based around a specimen Olympic Games proposal with Village and venues located in the heart of East London. This is currently an area experiencing high levels of deprivation (for example the Borough of Hackney has an unemployment rate of nearly 17 per cent).

16. Much of the targeted area currently has Objective 2 regeneration status, although the potential positive impact of European Union funding was not included in the analysis. A point to note is that Greece was recently awarded 1.4 billion euros from the EU for Olympic related transport projects from the Structural Fund.

THE CULTURE, MEDIA AND SPORT COMMITTEE

TRANSPORT

17. The report shows that London's airports will 'easily' have sufficient capacity to cater for overseas visitors. The call for an Olympic transport agency with powers to manage the transport network for the duration of the Games is in keeping with the arrangements for all host cities.

18. Sydney implemented a well-publicised scheme to get people to take public transport to competition venues. In effect no public car-parking was provided and spectators made the journey via rail, bus or ferry. The long term impact has been that the Games are now credited with changing many preconceptions about travel by public transport.

19. Arup concluded that "projected flows can be accommodated without delays and without unacceptable disruption to normal travel in London".

ACCOMMODATION

20. The level of available accommodation in London will be comfortably able to cope with projections of visitor arrivals. This is even considering that the overseas ticket projections used in the cost-benefit model are greater than any other modern Games.

21. Accommodation in previous and future Games has been under scrutiny. The London region's stock of accommodation by 2012 will be at least 200,000 rooms - comparing very favourably with any other international city.

SECURITY

22. Security is now a concern at all major events, sporting or otherwise. The Metropolitan Police were extensively consulted as part of this report dovetailing with their work chairing the advisory group in Athens.

23. The Arup Report concludes that aside from US cities "no other bidding city will be able to offer the same level of security expertise without calling upon outside assistance".

THE KEY BENEFITS OF HOSTING THE OLYMPIC GAMES

24. *British sport.* There is a tremendous feel good factor associated with the staging of an Olympics. Korea, Spain and Australia all achieved their highest medal tallies on home soil. The associated investment would also act as a catalyst for development of other Olympic sports which the UK has traditionally not fielded teams - eg basketball and volleyball. The inspiration will drive many of our youngsters to take part in sport and pursue dreams of becoming an Olympian.

25. *Health, crime and education.* Increased participation in sport will in turn lead to a healthier society. Anecdotally, participation in sport has led to downturns in youth crime and is a stimulus for education. It is the BOA's view that staging an Olympic Games can be the driving force and stimulus for nationwide programmes to encourage wider participation from which these society benefits can accrue.

26. *Volunteers.* Both Sydney and Manchester showed the benefits of having a dedicated and enthusiastic pool of volunteers. The experience of Sydney has shown that this culture of volunteerism has been continued, with people becoming auxiliary police officers, community workers, teaching assistants or carers for the elderly.

27. *Social inclusion.* The Olympics would be a driving force for breaking down divisions whether they be age, gender, race, disability or religion. The Games should celebrate local communities and ensure that the socially excluded have every opportunity to engage with the event. The aim is that after the Olympics, a legacy in terms of improved community leadership, enhanced cultural networks and a close engagement with the education sector will remain. This diversity would be celebrated through the staging of the Olympic and Paralympic Games.

28. *Regeneration and new housing.* Improved infrastructure including the provision of 4,000 new and much-needed homes in East London will be delivered. It will also stimulate and bring forward the comprehensive upgrade of the East End environment by developing contaminated and under-used land. An environmental legacy both through the sustainable design of facilities, but more importantly through changing perceptions of sustainability— in its widest sense—can be a tangible lasting legacy for London of hosting the Olympic Games.

29. *Employment.* The cost-benefit analysis stated that staging a Games in London would create around 9,000 new full-time jobs, of which 3,000 would be in the local East End economy. Businesses would be encouraged to relocate to the area through improved technological and transport links.

30. *Legacy.* The Olympic Games will provide facilities for both élite and grass root sports with defined legacies. Up to 100 training venues will be required in the form of refurbished school and community facilities.

31. *Tourism*. An independent study has shown that there was over £2 billion in inbound tourism spending in Australia attributable to the staging of the Olympics in 2000. The Games give a country a unique opportunity to showcase itself to a huge global audience. The Sydney Games were the most watched event in history with an estimated 3.7 billion people tuning in at some point during the 16 days.

32. *UK investment*. The expertise and the raised profile of staging the Games would have a beneficial impact on UK exports. Hosting the Sydney Games has allowed Australian companies to win 10 per cent of the capital projects in Beijing bringing in £1.1 billion.

33. *Convention industry*. Staging the Games would provide a significant boost to the convention industry. The Premier of New South Wales reported that the Sydney Games created bookings for £233 million worth of international business conferences. Such opportunities will not be limited to London alone.

34. *Feel good factor*. The Commonwealth Games showed the level of interest that there is in attending major sporting events in this country. The effects of home support on improved performances from British competitors cannot be underestimated. As Manchester showed the feel good factor derives not only from improved performances, but also from the national and civic pride that comes from staging a major world event.

35. *British cities*. It is not only London that can gain, other British cities and regions would gain through the preparation and training camps for overseas teams and through the staging of the football and sailing competitions. An example of this is the Team GB camp which was set up on the Gold Coast of Australia in the run up to Sydney. This contributed over £1 million to the local economy over a 12 month period. Given that there are 199 international NOCs - there is considerable scope for all large towns and cities to attract this lucrative pre-Games business.

CONCLUSION

36. The independent cost-benefit report has identified that staging the Olympic Games in London is technically viable. The financial appraisal attributed to the specimen proposal indicates that many of the costs can be offset through guaranteed income - much of which will flow via the TV rights and worldwide sponsorships negotiated by the IOC.

37. The outlook of the Arup Report is upbeat when assessing the financial situation - "in our view it should be possible to develop the specimen proposal so that the quantified benefits exceed the costs".

38. The key to the development of this project lies with the Key Stakeholders Group which must be unequivocal and unambiguous in its commitment to bring the world's greatest sporting prize back to the United Kingdom. The cost-benefit analysis concludes that "if all levels of government and other agencies are committed to a common proposal, the potential advantages of a 2012 Games centred on the Lower Lee Valley can be developed into a world-beating bid".

39. The BOA endorses this view. Given the public enthusiasm that was engendered by the successful hosting of the Commonwealth Games, the BOA believes that hosting the Olympic Games can make a major contribution to the development of sport and society in the UK.

40. To be successful, the Games bid will need wholehearted support from all political institutions; the backing of the nation's media; and a groundswell of support from a sport-loving public. There are many challenges to overcome in mounting a bid for an event of this scale and there are no guarantees of success. But the Olympic Games would provide an opportunity for London to reinforce itself as a world city - fit for the 21st Century - at the heart of a confident, competitive and prosperous nation.

TIMETABLE OF BOA PROCESS TO DATE

Sep 1993	Manchester fails to secure nomination for 2000 Olympic Games in Monte Carlo. This represents the third consecutive unsuccessful bid from the UK (Birmingham 1992, Manchester 1996, Manchester 2000).
1994	Review of IOC members indicates that London is the only British city likely to attract enough votes to win a bid. These views are constantly monitored and updated through BOA and governing bodies.
1995	National Olympic Committee of BOA (representatives of the 35 Governing Bodies of Olympic Sports) decides that next bid will be from UK's capital.
Feb 1997	Work begins on a potential London bid with a review of 2004 bidding cities and IOC requirements for staging a Games.
Aug 1997	Olympic Village, Transport and Facilities working groups set up to address key issues related to bid work.

Jun 1998	Environment working group set up to underpin work of other groups. The group evolves into the Sustainability working group.
Dec 2000	BOA deliver 395 page report on a potential London Olympic Bid to officials in the Department for Culture, Media and Sport.
Feb 2001	Presentation to Secretary of State and Minister for Sport at DCMS.
Mar 2001	Presentation to Mayor of London.
Apr 2001	Presentation to Conservative frontbench spokesmen.
May 2001	Presentation to Mayor's advisory cabinet.
Jun 2001	Key Stakeholders Group (Government, GLA, BOA) is created.
Jul 2001	Presentation to Liberal Democrat frontbench spokesman
Nov 2001	Production of Insignia Richard Ellis report into land availability for Olympic Games.
May 2002	Arup complete cost-benefit analysis study.
Nov 2002	Publication of summary of cost-benefit analysis. Mayor and BOA hold joint press conference to respond to conclusions of report. Mayor confirms his support for a London bid. BOA present Olympic bid work to National Governing Bodies of 35 Olympic sports and receive unanimous support. Athletes' Commission gives enthusiastic backing to proposed bid. Liberal Democrats and Conservative parties back viable London bid. Local boroughs supportive or unopposed to Olympic bid.
Dec 2002	British Paralympic Association unanimously backs proposed bid. Briefings in the House for Members of Commons and Lords. London First, London CBI and London Chamber of Commerce and Industry jointly sign a letter to the Prime Minister supporting bid proposals.
Jan 2003	Government to decide by end of month whether to support London bid.
July 2003	Last date for formal nominations of potential host cities by NOCs to IOC.
Jan 2004	Applicant City questionnaire to be completed.
Jan-Jun 2004	IOC/experts to examine replies.
Jun 2004	IOC Executive Board to decide on acceptance of Candidate Cities.
Aug 2004	Athens Olympic Games
Nov 2004	Candidature files to be received by the IOC.
Feb-Apr 2005	Evaluation Commission visits.
May 2005	Evaluation Commission report.
Jul 2005	Election of Host City for 2012 at IOC Session in Singapore.

10 January 2003

Supplementary Memorandum submitted by the British Olympic Association

SYNOPSIS

1. The British Olympic Association (BOA) wish to clarify the situation regarding the potential usage of Wembley for a future London Olympic Games following comments made at the Select Committee hearing of 15 January 2003.

2. The decision to progress work on the basis of an East London bid was done according to:

— Stated wish of the Mayor of London to see the Games help bring forward regeneration in the deprived areas of East London.

— Conclusions of a report by Insignia Richard Ellis on behalf of the Government/GLA/BOA to investigate potential Olympic sites for Village and main stadium (IRE report of Nov 2001). It recommended 4 sites in East London.

— IOC requirements stating the need for the main stadium and Olympic Village to be in close proximity.

— No athletics provision being provided at Wembley. Athletics was removed in December 1999 and was only reviewed in April 2002 with substantial cost adjustments to the earlier proposals.

— Review of other potential sporting sites and transportation infrastructure in London. The options of both East and West London Games—with a main stadium location next to the respective Village proposal— were investigated in detail in the BOA report of Dec 2000 (provided to the CMS Select Committee confidentially in Feb 2001).

— Assessment by GLA/LDA alongside Insignia Richard Ellis of the regeneration and social legacy opportunities in East London.

— The ability to provide a compact and logistically attractive Games concept to the IOC by provision of a main stadium, Olympic Village, media centre, and a number of sports located close to one another and also close to public transport nodes to facilitate access.

WEMBLEY BACKGROUND

3. The BOA had no involvement in the decision to locate the new national stadium at Wembley leading up to that decision being taken in 1996.

4. The BOA did not have any input into, or indeed any knowledge of, the contents of the Lottery Funding Agreement that was put in place between the English Sports Council, the Football Association and the English National Stadium Development Company Ltd. Until the BOA was able to view a copy of this in late 2000, we were unsure as to what was specifically included in the contractual obligations for the new Wembley Stadium - especially with regard to Olympic use.

5. From 1997–1999 Wembley formed the proposed focal point of the Olympic feasibility work that was taking place. The BOA was given assurances from the English Sports Council that the Olympic provision was being catered for, although we were not invited to have input into any issues concerning the stadium.

6. As documented in evidence submitted to the CMS Select Committee in January 2000, Simon Clegg wrote to Derek Casey (then Chief Executive of ESC) on three occasions about the lack of BOA involvement.

— *19 March 1998*
"Despite our offers of assistance to provide the Olympic dimension, this has not been sought. We have been left wondering who is providing this input and how much weight is being given to the requirements of the facility in the context of a future Olympic bid."

— *20 May 1998*
"If the Olympic dimension is not fully considered by the appropriate people at the design stage it will be irretrievable and any shortfall (in Olympic terms) in the main stadium will seriously devalue any future Olympic bid".

— *10 July 1998*
"I do not want to be presented with a *fait accompli* which will not meet the necessary future Olympic requirements and will necessitate our announcement that we are unable to mount a bid to stage a future Olympic Games."

7. Derek Casey submitted written evidence to the Committee in April 1999 stating that "The major conditions [of the Lottery Funding Agreement] are to: Develop a National Stadium in England…The minimum capacities are 80,000 seats for football and rugby league and 65,000 seats for athletics (capable of upgrade to a higher figure for the Olympic Games)" (section 19.1, p.3).

8. Having now viewed the Lottery Funding Agreement the bracketed words "capable of upgrade to a higher figure for the Olympic Games" do not exist, a view confirmed by Bob Stubbs (Chief Executive of ENSDC/WNSL) on 14 December 1999.

9. The Lottery Funding Agreement also erroneously details UK Athletics as the eventholder for the Olympic Games, rather than the British Olympic Association.

WEMBLEY EVIDENCE

10. For further background information, we would also refer to the BOA's written and oral submissions to the CMS Select Committee over Wembley from 1999-2001.

EAST AND WEST OPTIONS IN BOA REPORT

11. Following the decision to remove athletics from Wembley on 1 December 1999, the decision was taken to assess two options—a West London and an East London option.

12. The IOC requirements are laid out in the Manual for Candidate Cities, Olympic Charter and Host City Contract. IOC documentation is freely available on their website www.olympics.org. The Manual states that "proximity of [competition] sites to each other and to the nerve centres of the Games (Olympic Village, IBC, MPC, etc) and to the city centre is highly recommended. Site concentration if planned sensibly will certainly ease the running of the Games."

13. With regards to the Olympic Village—the IOC state in the IOC Olympic Village Guidelines that "the Olympic Village must be close to the main Olympic stadium or a nucleus of competition venues, in order to keep the athletes travelling time to a minimum". This situation is the same for the needs of the athletes taking part in the Paralympic Games.

14. In 2000, the IOC introduced the Candidature Acceptance Procedure which is a preliminary questionnaire designed to whittle down prospective candidate cities by means of a general evaluation of infrastructure. This is to prevent cities which do not possess the basic infrastructure from spending large amounts of money on a candidature.

15. The Olympic Village section (weighting 4) assesses:

— Location of Village (with particular emphasis on travel times to venues)
— Post Olympic use
— Overall Village concept
— Financing

16. Only the location of Village/travel time to venues are awarded a 'high weighting' within this section.

IOC AND INTERNATIONAL FEDERATION REQUIREMENTS

17. Sporting requirements at Olympic Games are governed by the relevant International Sports Federations. The requirements for Olympic athletics are based upon the model for the World Athletics Championships which has no seating capacity stipulation.

18. In 1999 the IOC had a requirement from the 2004 Manual for Candidate Cities that stated "The desired capacity of the stadium to be used for official ceremonies is approximately 75,000".

19. Despite the statement in Mr Cunnah's letter about correspondence from the IOC (dated 9 July 1998) this figure of 75,000 was confirmed via correspondence from the IOC's Manager for Candidate City Relations and separately from the NOC Relations Director (both 1 December 1999).

20. In 2001 the IOC brought out the 2008 Manual for Candidate Cities which states "In addition to spectators from the host country and from around the world, the proposed venue for the Opening and Closing ceremonies must be sufficient to accommodate accredited athletes, team officials and other entitled persons".

21. In terms of numbers, the Olympic Games now has to cater for up to 17,000 athletes and officials, 5,000 Olympic Family VIPs, 2,000 judges and referees, 20,000 members of the media, 7,000 sponsors, 45,000 volunteers and domestic and overseas spectators.

22. Recent Olympic Games and 2008 bid cities main stadia have the following capacities:

1996	Atlanta	85,000
2000	Sydney	115,000
2004	Athens	80,000
2008	Beijing	80,000
bidder Toronto		100,000
bidder Paris		75,700
bidder Osaka		80,000
bidder Istanbul		80,000

INSIGNIA RICHARD ELLIS REPORT

23. The Key Stakeholders Group decided in 2001 to endorse an East London bid following an independent evaluation of land availability conducted by Insignia Richard Ellis. After the Mayor's election in 2000, he stated clearly that he wished to see an Olympic Games used to help speed up the regeneration of the East End of London.

24. The Key Stakeholder's Group, via the London Development Agency, employed IRE to assess the land availability, costs and opportunities of sites across London. This was in order to identify the potential options available for a stadium, village and media centre. The executive summary of this report is also included as Appendix E in the full Arup report (which has been shown confidentially to the CMS Select Committee).

25. On the first page the report states:

"The Olympic Village, Media Centre and Indoor Arena need to be located within reasonable proximity of the Olympic Stadium. We interpret this as a maximum of 30 minutes". (1.2)

26. ***

27. ***

BOA REPORT ON HOSTING THE OLYMPIC GAMES

28. The full BOA report was delivered in confidence to the CMS Select Committee in February 2001.

29. The BOA report into the outline feasibility and requirements of staging the Games in London was delivered to officials in Government on 15 December 2000. It was presented to the then Secretary of State (Rt Hon Chris Smith MP) and the then Minister for Sport (Kate Hoey MP) on 1 Feb 2001. It was presented to the Mayor of London on 9 March 2001. Sport England and UK Sport have also had copies since 2001.

30. The report details the outline of the Facilities Working Group with the key requirements being:

"International Federation Requirements which have provided the necessary base-line criteria. A travelling time of 30 minutes to most competition venues from the Village. Location of suitable training facilities within a 45 minutes sector from the Village." (p.97)

31. The working group had representatives from BOA, London International Sport and Sport England.

32. The report details 3 Olympic options which are outlined on p.97

"With the uncertainty, then removal of athletics from Wembley, the focus of the group has now realigned itself to looking at main stadium sites at Northolt (west), Stratford (east) and Picketts Lock (east)."

33. On p.99 the report says:

"The most advantageous site for a stadium in East London is on the northern part of the railway lands at Stratford. The stadium would be next to one of the principal transport hubs in Europe and close by the most likely Olympic Village site."

34. Between pp.97 and 207 the options for sports are given predicated on either a West London Games based around a Village and Stadium at Northolt Aerodrome or an East London Games based upon a Village at Hackney Wick and a main stadium at either Stratford or Picketts Lock.

35. The proposed athletics options are on p.117 which details an East London (Stratford) scenario with a new stadium venue at Stratford.

36. On p.215 the text in the Village section reiterates the IOC's requirements about close proximity to the main stadium which is again noted on p.235.

37. On p. 236 the report states:

"The chief criterion is the ease of access to the main Olympic venue."

38. "In the West London option this is likely to be a new stadium located at, or close to, the site of the Village. In East London the accessibility of Stratford, in terms of public transport (enhanced by the CTRL link) means that this location is preferable for the siting of a new stadium in this sector of London." (p.236)

39. The issue of quality of the bid with regard to this is also discussed:

"The general locational criterion for the village is a thirty minute travelling time from an assembly point in the Village to the athletes' changing or warm-up facilities at the main stadium. Quicker journey times would enhance the bid."

40. Explicit references to the main stadium location in the East are also made in the transport chapter (19).

41. Village venues were sought initially according to the following criteria:

— At least 50 hectares
— Reasonably well located with the respect to the main Olympic stadium (initially using Wembley as the focal point in the West and Stratford in the East)
— Reasonable degree of certainty as to their availability. (p. 242)

42. In summary the BOA report of December 2000 states throughout that there are two location options (West and East). At the time of this report there was no athletics provision in Wembley and a notional new stadium development was considered as part of an Olympic Village development. In the East a Village development in Hackney Wick/Temple Mills was the primary option with a main stadium development either at Stratford, or at the newly conceived Picketts Lock (dependent on the outcome of discussions on this).

43. At no point in the report is there an option of an East London village and a main stadium at Wembley.

ATHLETICS POST-WEMBLEY

44. Following the decision to remove athletics from Wembley on 1 December 1999, the option of athletics at Wembley has not been an issue for discussion in Olympic terms as focus turned to Picketts Lock. Following the collapse of Picketts Lock, and a subsequent hiatus in proceedings, the BOA were asked to comment alongside UK Athletics on the new platform solutions being devised for Wembley.

45. The basis of this evaluation was a report by Citex/Sport Concepts which was prepared for Sport England on 30 April 2002. This was a review of the athletics provision in Wembley.

46. The report states on p.4:

"In light of the decision by the Mayor of London that any London Olympic bid should be focused on East London, for the purposes of this report and to more accurately compare like for like, the 1999 cost is based upon the 67,000 spectator seats illustrated in the design at that time without the additional temporary seats to deliver an 80,000 capacity Olympic facility."

47. On p.17 the report says:

"For the purposes of this report, the British Olympic Association have stated that sightlines are a compliance issue for UK Athletics, given that the study relates to the staging of the IAAF World Championships in Athletics."

TIMESCALES

48. Following the election of Athens as Host City for 2004 in Lausanne in 1997, the BOA made the decision that due to continental rotation (Athens 2004, Turin 2006) and Beijing's strong candidature then a bid for 2008 would be unlikely to succeed. 2012 therefore became the next opportunity to mount a viable and successful bid.

CONCLUSION

49. If we are to bid for the Olympic Games in 2012 then this must be a credible, technically viable and attractive proposal to the members of the IOC. The compactness of the Games is important as is the issue of legacy of facilities which the Stakeholders Group has always sought to address. We thank Mr Cunnah for the offer of Wembley as a potential venue for the Olympic Games, which is in line with the obligations set out in the Lottery Funding Agreement. We hope to see the finest football stadium in the world staging the final of the 2012 London Olympic football tournament.

50. However for all the reasons stated above the need to create a new stadium at the heart of a compact and viable Games concept is important to the development of a world-beating Olympic bid centred on the Lower Lee Valley. The potential benefits to this deprived area of London, and the UK as a whole, should not get snagged on the desire to reincorporate Wembley into an East London proposal that will therefore be destined for failure.

51. As the BOA said at the Select Committee on 14 January:

"The more you disperse the Games, the more you dilute the effectiveness of your bid and at the end of the day there is no silver medal in this race. If we are going to bid for the Olympic Games we have got to put together the most compact and the most attractive bid in the eyes of the voting constituency because at the end of the day if it is not acceptable to them then all the rest of the issues and work that has been done are purely academic."

16 January 2003

APPENDIX 4

Memorandum submitted by the British Paralympic Association

1. At a meeting of the National Paralympic Committee on 5 December 2002, held at the Queen's Club, the British Paralympic Association unanimously endorsed the British Olympic Association's bid for London as a venue for the 2012 Olympic and Paralympic Games.

2. As you will be aware, the current agreement between the International Olympic and Paralympic Committees provide for the host city the obligation to organise both Games. Following the outstanding success of the British Paralympic team in Sydney, where it finished second in the medal table, we have worked tirelessly to ensure that Great Britain remains at the forefront of Paralympic sport and a London Games would endorse this position. It is our belief that a London bid will enhance the growing reputation of Great Britain's élite disabled athletes and firmly demonstrate H.M. Government's commitment to their sporting success.

3. The present administration's current commitment to sport and the legacy it leaves through social inclusion, health, education and facilities can have few clearer illustrations than in supporting a Paralympic Games in London. The benefits that would accrue to Great Britain's disabled people through the demonstration of national commitment to their sports would be immense and tangible.

SOCIAL INCLUSION

4. The survey of sports participation by young people with a disability under the age of 16 conducted by Sport England, and indeed its parallel survey for adults, painted a depressing picture of lack of opportunity, encouragement, facilities and motivation. There is a desperate need for sporting heroes and cultural encouragement, particularly for young people with a disability. That Great Britain, through Stoke Mandeville, is also the birthplace of the Paralympic movement makes it all the more damning that disabled people in GB continue to find such barriers to participation. There is, therefore, a compelling practical purpose, as well as providing a uniquely symbolic reason, for supporting a London bid. A London Games would demonstrate an acceptance of the role of sport in enhancing the lives of people with a disability, and perhaps more fundamentally their right to participate in the ultimate sporting arena. That GB should at last, in the 21st Century, fully embrace and endorse the rights of disabled people to equality of opportunity and access in both sport and society in general would be a powerful message conveyed within the Olympic/Paralympic bid and one endorsed by concrete and practical outcomes.

HEALTH

5. The recent Strategy Unit Report 'Game Plan' highlighted very clearly the health, and by extrapolation economic, benefits of participation in sport. The costs of at least £2 billion a year of physical inactivity will be substantially contributed to by the needs of the c.8.5 million registered disabled people in GB. The benefit of using sport in medical rehabilitation was of course discovered and pioneered by Sir Ludwig Guttman and the benefits of sport to the further health of the general population are well evidenced. The current poor levels of participation in sporting activity by this significant minority grouping as well as the general population could begin to be addressed through the educational programme and sporting example that would be engendered by an Olympic/Paralympic bid.

6. Few better examples of the impact of sport on health could be found than through the Paralympics and would provide significant leverage in encouraging behavioural change to produce a sports and physical activity culture.

EDUCATION

7. The British Paralympic Association together with NASUWT and DfES has recently launched an awareness raising pack for schools on the Paralympics and disability sport. The motivation for this included the acknowledgement that awareness of disability and disability sport was very poor in our schools and a need to contribute to the implementation of SENDA[1995]. An Olympic/Paralympic bid would galvanise this work in schools and contribute significantly to the PSE/Citizenship agenda of the National Curriculum as well as highlighting the [lack of] provision in PE for children with a disability. Evidence of the impact on school children can be seen from the Sydney Paralympics where an innovative programme resulted in considerable support for the event and the widespread involvement of schools.

8. As in the case of health there needs to be a clear example set if we are to impact upon the culture of young people and a bid would offer a very focussed and explicit view of sport and physical activity that would be hard to ignore.

FACILITIES

9. Despite over 50 years of the Welfare State and the pioneering legislation of the Disability Discrimination Act 1995 [fully enacted October 2002] GB, and London in particular, can remain distinctly difficult to access for the disabled. These difficulties extend across all public facilities and transport and not merely in the sport arena. The creation of new/refurbished transport systems and the building and upgrading of facilities that are fully accessible

and would ensure that London begins to reflect the expectations of inhabitants and visitors of a modern capital city in the 21st century.

SPORT

10. Paralympic sport in GB has consistently been at the forefront of the movement and finished second in the medal table behind Australia in Sydney 2000. Despite hosting the early events in disability sport competition GB has never hosted a truly international multi-sport event for the Paralympic family. As is so often the case other nations have taken up the mantle once donned by GB and done so with great grace. The Olympic/Paralympic bid would go a long way to demonstrating that GB has not only the rhetoric but also the capability when it comes to organising major sporting events. This would be particularly apt in Paralympic sport where our representation and participation has not been matched by our delivery of major events.

11. Disability sport maintains a growing reputation and presence world-wide and once again there are perceptible differences developing across the world and between GB in the level of commitment and acceptance. The constant fight for credibility would be ended with a bid that committed itself to a Paralympics and the disabled sport movement in GB. Demonstrating an investment in the sustainability of British disability sport would not only immediately benefit the existing sportsmen and women but would also provide the infrastructure necessary to involve more and future generations in sport with all the benefits identified earlier. It would also demonstrate that GB is serious about sustaining its position as a leader in Paralympic sport and a major medal winner.

12. GB's reputation in Paralympic sport at present can be seen reflected in the appointment of Philip Craven as President of the International Paralympic Committee [and member of the IOC] and Bob Price as President of the European Paralympic Committee. In addition we have a significant number of representatives in senior positions in International Federations and organisations. These positions of influence are difficult to sustain when GB is consistently seen to be incapable of hosting major events.

GENERAL

13. It is our contention that an Olympic/Paralympic bid would deliver on the key policy issues identified by the Government and outlined above. These key areas of Government social policy could be quantified but it is in the qualitative not the quantitative impact that a more compelling reason can be made.

14. In economic terms we do not have detailed figures of our own that represent the impact of the Paralympic Games on the economy but we would endorse the findings that Arup has included in the report and which are based on the Sydney experience. We would, however, point out that the disabled community in GB is a very sophisticated economy that already generates a market in excess of £40 billion and we would therefore anticipate a significant consumer impact of a Paralympic Games.

15. Similarly it is difficult for us to put a value on the economic impact of developing fully accessible facilities and transport systems but it is not unreasonable to assume that it would be significant to GB, Londoners and overseas visitors. As a consequence the growing international disability market becomes a major factor to add to the economic equation.

16. A final area in which we believe significant social and economic value would be generated is in the areas of employment and volunteerism. The opportunity to encourage people with a disability to seek employment and/or to volunteer for the Games operation would be a significant signpost to the social values of GB. Further it would be a recognition of the ability of disabled people to contribute significantly to economic decisions around their own lives and to contribute to the wider economy.

17. BPA would be delighted to contribute further to your considerations if it is appropriate. Meanwhile, we would urge this committee to recognise the value of a London Olympic/Paralympic bid for Great Britain and to provide the support of H.M. Government and Parliament.

14 January 2003

APPENDIX 5

Memorandum submitted by the London Development Agency

1. The London Development Agency is London's economic development body, promoting economic renewal and development. Working for the Mayor and in partnership with business and others, it benefits all Londoners by delivering sustainable regeneration of London's economy. The LDA was set up in 2000 and is one of nine government-funded Regional Development Agencies in England.

2. We welcome the Committee's Inquiry into a potential London Bid for the Olympics as an important contribution to this debate. We very much welcome the opportunity to give evidence and look forward to hearing the Committee's recommendations.

BACKGROUND

3. The Mayor of London, Ken Livingstone agreed to meet the British Olympic Association two years ago. The British Olympic Association took the view that for Britain to mount a successful Olympic Bid it would have to be centred in London. In response the Mayor agreed to support a bid providing it satisfied the following criteria

- The bid should be centred in East London
- The bid should recognise the diversity of London
- The Government should underwrite the cost of the bid and the games

4. It was agreed that a committee would be formed, chaired by the British Olympic Association which would look into the efficacy and feasibility of bidding for the Olympic Games in 2012. The Mayor nominated three representatives to sit on that committee to represent London's interests. The Committee was set up and in addition to the mayoral nominees, included representatives from HM Treasury, PIU, Government Office for London, UK Sport, Sport England, DCMS and the British Olympic Association as a core membership.

5. Key issues raised at the first meeting of the Committee were Britain's credibility in relation to international sporting events. It was agreed by the Committee that a thorough piece of pre-feasibility work needed to be carried out in order to look in detail at the costs and benefits of taking forward any Olympic bid. The London Development Agency on behalf of the Committee jointly commissioned with DCMS and the British Olympic Association, an independent report to assess the feasibility of bidding for the Olympic Games. A rigorous procurement process was carried out which complied with European Procurement Regulations, a budget was agreed and Arup Associates were selected and formally appointed to undertake this piece of work.

6. The LDA believes that the Report provides an important first step in assessing the benefits associated with a bid. The process of assessing the feasibility has been professional, considered, cautious and realistic. It has been based on all the facts available and has drawn on the experience of experts from this country and abroad involved in similar projects. If the bid is going to progress, clearly more feasibility work will need to be undertaken to build on this important initial piece of work.

7. Arup's findings were presented to the Committee in June 2002 and subsequently were circulated more widely to interested parties. The East London boroughs affected by any Olympic bid were also consulted throughout the process.

8. The considerable benefit highlighted by the Arup Report, added to the success of the Commonwealth Games in Manchester and the resolution of the Wembley Stadium project add positive factors to the case for bidding.

COMMENTS AND RECOMMENDATIONS

9. Based on Arup's findings and an assessment of experiences in the UK and abroad, the LDA believes that an Olympic Games would have a positive impact on the economic and social development of London. The LDA would therefore support a bid.

10. The LDA believes that a bid would only have a chance of success with the Government's unequivocal backing. The LDA urges the Government to give a bid a clear commitment.

11. The LDA shares the Culture, Media and Sport Committee's own recommendation that the Government appoints a dedicated Minister to sponsor a bid, providing clear leadership and focus.

12. The LDA believes that a bid for the Games would create greater focus for the regeneration of one of the most deprived areas in the country, in East London. This area has already been identified by the Government and the LDA as a major priority for economic development, as much of it is derelict, underused and faces a number of other social and economic problems including social exclusion. A bid would provide focus and enable comprehensive development of this area.

13. Bid proposals are being developed in line with the objectives of the draft London Plan and the LDA's Corporate and Economic Development Strategy. Proposals will also be linked to local regeneration strategies promoted by the local authorities. The LDA will continue to liaise with the relevant local authorities, local regeneration agencies and major landowners in the area. A significant proportion of land required to construct the facilities is already in public ownership and a number of existing facilities in the Capital are likely to be utilised.

14. The LDA has been working closely with other parts of the GLA group in developing the proposals, most notably with Transport for London on transport issues and Metropolitan Police on security.

15. Since the publication of the Arup Report, the LDA has followed up some of the work identified, especially related to land ownership and assembly issues. Chartered Surveyors Insignia Richard Ellis and Solicitors Eversheds have undertaken further work on these issues, including exit strategies if London's bid is unsuccessful.

13 January 2003

APPENDIX 6

Memorandum submitted by Transport for London

INTRODUCTION

1. Transport for London (TfL) welcomes the opportunity to submit written evidence to the Committee's inquiry.

2. The following paper is based on the key transport issues and broad transport strategy needed to support a proposal to site the Olympics in the Stratford/Lower Lee Valley corridor. The following information is based on a strategic assessment only and TfL has yet to undertake detailed modelling and analysis.

Location

- The proposed siting in the Stratford/Lower Lee Valley corridor is sensible from a transport point of view as Stratford has very good public transport accessibility.

- The main Olympic zone would be served by the following public transport infrastructure:

  Docklands Light Railway (DLR), North London Line, Channel Tunnel Rail Link (CTRL) domestic services and mainline services via the Great Eastern route;

  London Underground Limited (LUL) services - the Jubilee Line provides a high capacity transit link along the corridor, while the Central Line is a direct route to Stratford from the City, West End and west London.

- However, the distance of the venues and facilities from Stratford station and the other stations in the Lower Lee Valley corridor is a constraint to efficient visitor movements within the Olympic zone. The proposed stadium location is around 1.5 km from Stratford regional station.

The Transport Task

- The magnitude of the Olympic demand, its timing during the day and its distribution across the network will all influence the extent to which Olympic demands congest the existing system. A key issue is the extent to which this Olympic travel would coincide with normal commuting.

- Initial TfL analysis indicates that the 'reference case' presented by Arup could be accommodated with some additional transport investment and demand management measures. TfL also agrees with the Arup report conclusion that the transport network, without enhancement and demand management measures, would be unable to cope with the 'worst case' scenario for Olympic transport demand presented in the Arup report.

Existing transport capacity

- London's transport network is already crowded and congested for large parts of the day. During the Olympics, capacity and crowding problems would be greatest where spectator flows coincide with normal commuter flows on links operating at or near capacity.

- However, travel demands are generally lower in August compared to the annual monthly average. In addition, with Stratford as the destination for the additional trips, journeys from central London in the morning peak period could utilise spare capacity in the contra-peak flow direction. However the extent of this would depend on the origins of trips. A risk would be that some reverse-flow trips could begin as additional with-flow trips, thus exacerbating crowding for part of the trip.

- Crowds travelling to the morning and (early) afternoon sessions could utilise spare capacity. However, crowds leaving the afternoon session could, depending upon the exact timings, coincide with the evening peak. Overall, careful event scheduling will be needed to ensure that any spare capacity in the transport network is used to the maximum extent possible.

Planned capacity increases

- Apart from the infrastructure already in place, additional investment in East London's transport network is planned to occur by 2012. This includes:

  a major upgrade of the Jubilee Line—adding around 45 per cent to existing capacity;

  an upgrade of the Central Line, providing improved service and increased peak capacity to the City, West End and west London;

a proposed extension of the DLR to Stratford International—this would provide a direct link between the Royals, Newham Arc of Opportunity, Stratford City and the Olympic zone; and

the CTRL between St Pancras and Stratford International— scheduled for completion in 2007, this will provide a new high capacity link.

- Although part of this proposed new capacity will have been utilised by 2012 by the forecast growth in jobs and population, the investments would assist in supporting Olympic travel demands.

Transport Strategy

- An integrated transport strategy will be needed that effectively combines the contribution of each mode—National Rail, the Underground, DLR, London Buses, coaches, park and ride and river transport. The transport strategy must be based on providing reliable and acceptable journey times, with tolerable travel conditions for all users.

- The strategy would be based on trying to use spare capacity where possible, for example off-peak periods and contra-peak services. The strategy should also be designed to minimise disruption and inconvenience to everyday travel in London. An effective strategy would not be based on just meeting the demands if all goes well. Appropriate contingency plans and risk management strategies need to be built in.

- To achieve this will require actions on the demand and supply side. On the supply side, investment will be needed in service enhancements to the public transport network, interchange improvements, bus priority and significant traffic management to create a bus priority corridor from central London to the Olympic zone.

- On the demand side, measures to manage and reduce overall travel demands would be essential. This includes event scheduling to avoid normal commuting peaks. The demand management strategy should also involve measures to reduce normal commuting into central London. Typical actions to achieve these outcomes could include more flexible working arrangements, advanced publicity, additional public holidays and fare incentives.

Rail

- Rail should be the primary focus of the transport strategy because of its high capacity to move large numbers of people. The National Rail, Underground and DLR networks need to support the majority of the transport demand. Service enhancements and additional rolling stock for rail, LUL and DLR will be needed to cater for the Olympic timetable. An example would be more late trains to cater for evening events. In addition, the North London Line could play an enhanced role with service upgrades.

- The existing layout of Stratford regional station would be inadequate to deal with the extra demand. LUL has undertaken an initial appraisal which indicates the need for a new ticket hall on the northern side of the station, along with other measures to increase capacity. Options for increasing the capacity of Stratford station will need further analysis.

- The transport strategy described in this paper assumes that Crossrail is not in place for the Games. The provision of Crossrail would provide significant additional capacity across central London to meet a sizeable proportion of the spectator demand. However, the transport strategy should not be made contingent on the successful delivery of Crossrail by 2012. A feasible strategy without Crossrail that combines investment and demand management measures can be implemented.

Road transport

- Although the transport strategy should be heavily focussed on rail, the highway network can play an important role in transporting officials, participants and spectators. It also offers flexibility as coaches can be provided within shorter lead times than rail upgrades.

- The fleet proposed by Arup of 3,000 coaches and minibuses for the Games represents around half of the existing London bus fleet. Sourcing and accommodating the fleet and the 4,500 drivers would be a significant task and require early planning. Sufficient terminal facilities in central London will also have to be planned and secured.

- A priority bus corridor between central London and Stratford would be essential to providing reliable quick journey times by road-based public transport to the games. This will require innovative and extensive traffic management measures. Without this, the risk is that more people will try to drive close to the site. Achieving this priority running will inevitably cause some disruption to normal traffic. However, traffic levels in August are historically lower than the annual average and normal traffic flows may also be further reduced in response to the Games. TfL and the London Boroughs would need to look at the following measures to deliver the level of priority needed:

- ▸ Priority lanes
- ▸ Intersection priorities and junction closures
- ▸ Parking restrictions
- ▸ Traffic management
- ▸ Bypasses routes and diversions

- Park and ride would be part of the strategy with the objective of getting people onto public transport as far away from the venues as possible to minimise traffic congestion near the venues. Remote park and ride facilities should be provided far away from the congested parts of London's network.

Additional investment needed

- The main investments needed to support the transport strategy will be:

  - ▸ National Rail and LUL services
  - ▸ DLR infrastructure and services
  - ▸ Stations, terminals and park and ride facilities
  - ▸ Bus priority and traffic management
  - ▸ Development costs — eg organisation, planning, contingency, information

- The investment strategy would be based on providing facilities that have a legacy benefit, such as contributing to regeneration or transport congestion relief. Where significant investment would be needed purely to support the temporary demands of the Games, opportunities to change the underlying demands should be fully considered before committing to investment. A large part of the proposed transport investment for the Games will have a legacy benefit in serving East London and the Thames Gateway regeneration.

- The transport element of the Games' costs as given in the Arup Report is too low and should allow for a larger contingency. The costs should include greater allowance for extensive traffic management measures, additional train rolling stock, train service enhancements, public transport information, improvements to key interchanges and rail terminals, and bus priority measures. Further work is needed to provide cost estimates of these enhancements.

FURTHER WORK

- Detailed work in partnership with the other transport agencies (London Underground, Strategic Rail Authority and Highways Agency) will be necessary to develop and refine the transport strategy. This will draw on the existing extensive experience of major event planning and transport impact assessment. The planning and implementation of the transport proposals will have to begin in advance of the proposed date for the setting up of the proposed Olympic Transport Agency. TfL intends to initiate modelling and analysis work to investigate in more detail the demand and capacity issues.

- The Olympic Transport Agency should be closely integrated with TfL and not a separate body. Additional executive powers may be necessary and the Agency will require significant and dedicated resources. The Olympic Transport Agency should be established at or around the date when the appointment of London is confirmed in 2005.

SUMMARY

- An effective integrated transport strategy can be produced to support the Olympics in London. The proposed location is good from a transport perspective as Stratford is well served by public transport.

- The strategy would be based on providing reliable fast public transport services, with a heavy focus on rail. Bus and coach services with high priority in the road network, and remote park and ride facilities would also be required. Demand management measures will be needed to reduce the risk of peak flows to the stadium coinciding with normal commuting flows.

- Additional investment in transport infrastructure and services will be needed to ensure that the transport strategy is implemented. Further work is now needed to analyse the transport requirements in more detail and confirm demands, the required infrastructure and services, and costs.

10 January 2003

APPENDIX 7

Memorandum submitted by Crossrail

CROSSRAIL LINE 1

1. Following on from your Select Committee's recent evidence sessions into an Olympic bid, and the House of Commons debate on the same subject, I am writing to clarify the planned timetable for the Crossrail project.

2. Crossrail expects the application for statutory consent for Crossrail Line 1 to be ready in November. It is hoped that this is the beginning of a programme and timetable that will lead to a construction completion date that is time for 2011, subject to obtaining powers, finance and procurement. The Line 1 train service itself would be in place by May 2012.

3. During the recent Select Committee sessions and the Commons debate, many MPs stated that they understood that 2016 was the proposed completion date. This is in fact two years after the scheduled completion of Crossrail Line 2; this is the route commonly known as 'Chelsea-Hackney line' which Chris Bryant MP discussed during the Select Committee hearing. Line 2 could be operational by 2014 at the earliest, and may even be catalysed further by the Line 1 process.

4. Discussion with Government has been taking place over many months, ensuring that Crossrail Line 1 meets all strategic consideration and requirement.

5. We have a project involving 200 people from across industry to carry out this task and a considerable amount of research is being applied towards submitting Crossrail for statutory approval. Once this is granted, we will be ready and able to make this scheme a reality.

6. As indicated by the Transport Secretary in Parliament before Christmas, we will be presenting our detailed plans for Crossrail Line 1 to him towards the end of February. This will include an economic and transport case for the scheme. Given the forthcoming public information and consultation stages, we will be continuing to meet key stakeholders.

7. I hope that this information helps clarify the current status and projected timetables of Crossrail Lines 1 and 2.

8. As Transport for London make clear in their evidence, Crossrail is a project vital to the future of London—it will transform London's transport infrastructure providing many regenerative, economic and social benefits.

9. I am confident that we have in place a robust scheme that will meet these challenges and we would be delighted to provide your Committee with more evidence if that would be helpful.

17 January 2003

APPENDIX 8

Memorandum submitted by Mr Max Caller,
Chief Executive of the London Borough of Hackney

10. Thank you for inviting me here to give evidence on behalf of the London Borough of Hackney. The prospect of a bid for a UK Olympics based in East London raises a number of issues for Hackney. Largely these centre on community benefits and disbenefits and the impact on our local economy.

11. While we hope such a venture could benefit the UK as a whole and leave a lasting legacy of regeneration for East London, we believe that these benefits can only be realised locally if the Government's decision to host the 2012 Olympics is swiftly followed by a schedule of regeneration, transport and infrastructure schemes drawn up with stakeholders. These schemes need to include the delivery of an underground Crossrail 2. Additionally if the bid is to be made then there should be no room for important initiatives being abandoned or further delayed should the bid not be successful. This should reduce the potential for planning blight to hit the east of London whilst the bid is being considered.

12. We are aware that other areas, from Barcelona to Sydney, that have successfully bid to host the Olympics, have benefited from significant new infrastructure not just in the field of sports but also in terms of transport, housing, and new public services. Urban design standards have also tended to be higher in larger co-ordinated developments than in more piecemeal development and there have also been economic benefits, especially in relation to inward investment.

13. The East of London as part of the Thames Gateway area has been identified by Government as a region of the country that can help sustain the national economy and through the development of brownfield sites, provide more housing and jobs and contribute to an urban renaissance. The development of sites such as the Stratford rail lands are already beginning to work towards this agenda and proper preparation for the Olympics can go a great

way further in assisting to deliver this. By creating the infrastructure necessary for the Olympics we can at the same time create the infrastructure needed to grow east London.

14. We are however also concerned that proposals could potentially have a negative impact and create planning blight for Hackney if not addressed with imagination and early infrastructure wins.

15. The issues for Hackney centre primarily on transport and economy as well as those of sport and leisure. The major direct impact for us is for the area called Hackney Wick where there are considerations to place sporting events and athletes housing and I will explain the key issues here.

16. As I am sure you are all aware, the London Borough of Hackney like our neighbours Newham and Tower Hamlets is one of the poorest areas in the UK and has many deep rooted problems.

17. However there are some issues for Hackney that set us apart from our neighbours. Given that we are an inner London Borough next to the City, our unemployment rate, the highest in London, is staggeringly high at nine per cent (UK level is 3.2 per cent) and our only large employers are public sector agencies. Our economy is mainly made up of micro businesses that currently have few opportunities to expand to become small to medium enterprises within the borough. Given our proximity to central London it is perhaps surprising that Hackney does not have any direct links to the London Underground. We believe that these two issues are linked and that both can be assisted by thorough physical preparation for Olympic bidding.

18. We see transport infrastructure as crucial both to a successful bid and to negate detrimental impacts for Hackney. While we are not the only inner London borough to not have a tube station, we are the only one on the north bank of the Thames and we are surrounded by boroughs with tube stations. This makes us appear to have poor public transport links and has a detrimental effect on the borough and its regeneration potential. In terms of attracting and growing local business, transport links is one of the key factors that deter business from moving into the borough.

19. The East London Line extension is set to put us on the tube map with connections to South London and Finsbury Park. This will however only affect a small section of the borough and we believe that an underground Crossrail, linking the centre of the borough to both central London and Stratford is necessary to include in Olympic preparations to both benefit local people and improve access to the sports facilities.

20. Therefore while it is true that with International Rail connections to Stratford there are good connections for international visitors, if London as a whole is to benefit economically from hosting the Olympics it is essential that good public transport links are established from Hackney Wick through Hackney Central to the West End. It is this, above all else, which would lead to a lasting regenerative legacy for Hackney.

21. Research carried out locally has shown us that there are a number of people who will not travel far to access work, so our strategy besides training people for jobs elsewhere is to retain and where possible expand the number of jobs available locally. Hackney Wick is our major if not only significant area zoned for industrial activity where we have a realistic opportunity to grow the number of jobs available locally.
Consequently it is important for us to:

- Have good transport links to new potential jobs, including those in construction;
- Have early sight of the job types so we can train local people for them;
- Retain business and industrial uses on the Hackney Wick site (even if temporarily used for other purposes).

22. Hackney and the east end in general is an area of great cultural diversity and can use this diversity to make athletes and visitors from around the globe feel welcome.

23. The local provision of facilities to an international standard, would encourage greater participation in the various sports and create many sports related jobs. It can also be marketed to promote health living and be a valuable resource to encourage young people away from crime and into sport. However some new facilities may need to be developed on greenfield or public sites and could encounter local opposition if issues around community benefits, accessibility, affordability, compensation and who pays for upkeep after the event are not factored in from the beginning.

14 January 2003

Annex

LONDON BOROUGH OF HACKNEY FACTS AND FIGURES

- The London Borough of Hackney has an area of 1,898 hectares and a population of 202,819 (Census 2001) of which almost a quarter is under 16 years of age. The percentage of the population aged under 44 years is 74 per cent compared to just over 60 per cent for England and Wales. The population has been projected to increase by 11 per cent over the 10 years from 2001.

- The population of Hackney is constantly changing. In a recent MORI survey (October 2001) 19 per cent had lived in Hackney for less than five years.

- According to the Government Index of Deprivation 2000, Hackney's average ward ranks make it the second most deprived area in the country. All 23 old wards (out of 8,414 in the whole country) are in the worst 10 per cent nationally and nine wards are in the worst 3 per cent. Hackney's teenage pregnancy rate is the fourth highest in the country.

- Almost 40 per cent of Households have an income below £15,000 (source: CACI, Paycheck 2001). Net equity per head of population halved from almost £3,000 in 1995 to just £1,400 in 1999. During the same period the average across inner London increased from £2,260 to £2,950.

- Historically, Hackney has attracted a diverse range of immigrants, refugees and asylum seekers from all over the world, which continues to this date. A recent survey found people from 22 countries in one hostel alone. According to recent ONS mid-year estimates, almost 40 per cent of the population are from ethnic minority groups, of which the largest group is Black (25 per cent). Stamford Hill is home to the largest Jewish community in Europe, while the Vietnamese and Turkish speaking communities are also strongly established in the borough. All ethnic minority groups in the borough have a younger age structure than the white population, 50 per cent of children under 4 years of age come from ethnic communities other than white. A recent survey amongst 12 year olds in Hackney schools indicated that nearly 80 per cent of these pupils were from nationalities other than English, Scottish or Welsh. Another survey in Hackney schools showed that the total number of languages spoken other than English is 88: these include Turkish, Bengali, Punjabi, Gujarati, Urdu, Somali, Chinese, Vietnamese and French.

- Council Housing is no longer the dominant tenure (33 per cent compared with nearly 60 per cent in 1981). This change is as a result of regeneration programmes which have seen housing transferred to Housing Associations and refurbished—or demolished and rebuilt. Hackney has demolished 15 tower blocks since 1986.

APPENDIX 9

Memorandum submitted by the Lee Valley Regional Park Authority

WINNING THE 2012 OLYMPICS

In Support of Bidding to Host the 2012 Olympics in London

1. As a body intimately involved in sport, the Lee Valley Regional Park Authority is fully supportive of a bid to host the 2012 Olympics in East London. Apart from the prestige that staging the world's premier sporting event would bring to our capital city and the boost the nation would receive from seeing its athletes winning medals on home soil, the true benefit of the Games would be the legacy they would leave behind.

2. This legacy would not be just for the benefit of sport, although sport would be a prime and most deserving long-term beneficiary from the facilities. Staging the Games would have a much broader regenerative effect on the severely deprived area of East London, delivering much needed long-term social and economic benefits and environmental improvements. The very act of bidding itself will promote participation in sport across the nation with subsequent cultural and health benefits and as the Arup report states, the "catalytic impact on the regeneration of the Lower Lee Valley" from a decision to bid will be significant.

The Authority's Potential Role and Contribution

3. The Lee Valley Regional Park Authority is already a significant provider of sporting opportunities to London and the South East through a range of facilities in the 10,000-acre Regional Park. Its strategic goal is to play an even more significant role in both sports provision and sports development through the 21st Century by:

- Providing, facilitating and promoting high quality, regionally significant sports facilities

- Facilitating and enabling regionally significant development programmes through partnerships that help to deliver pathways for winners and champions

- Effectively contributing to the regional delivery of sport by engaging in debate and contributing to the strategic decision making process

- Supporting and encouraging quality initiatives to improve the delivery of sport by actively pursuing continuous development

- Contributing to Sport England's objectives of 'More People, More Places and More Medals'

4. The Authority sees itself as having a key role to play in:

- The development of an Olympic bid and is already engaged with the 'Stakeholder Group' which commissioned the Arup Report and the Steering Group led by London International Sport. Through its environmental remit, the Authority is also well placed to play a leading role in 'managing' the environmental considerations relating to the staging of the Games and has expressed its willingness to do so to the Steering Group.

- The delivery of the required facilities and the Games. The Authority led the National Athletics Centre project, from which it gained extremely valuable experience, and is responsible for the development on behalf of UK Athletics, the English Institute of Sport and Sport England of the London Region High Performance Centre for Athletics at Picketts Lock. In addition, the Authority also owns sites in the Lower Lee Valley Olympic Zone of strategic importance to bidding for and hosting the Games, most notably the Lee Valley Sports Centre and Lee Valley Cycle Circuit sites at Eastway, Stratford, totalling 91 acres.

- The future of the legacy sports facilities post-Olympics, consistent with its Sports Development Policy.

9 January 2003

APPENDIX10

Memorandum submitted by Mr David Sparkes, Chief Executive of British Swimming

WINNING THE 2012 OLYMPICS

1. A decision for the Government to support an Olympic bid for London in 2012 is one that should be given very careful consideration. For Sport however it is essentially an easy decision there is everything to gain and nothing to lose. The opportunity to play sport at the very highest level, the Olympic Games, at home in front of a partisan crowd must be every athletes dream. The staging of the Games in London whilst challenging is well within the capability of British Sport and our people. This would be a wonderful opportunity to showcase the nation to the world as we have never done before.

2. Manchester 2002 and the Commonwealth Games showed what we can do. The European Football Championships was a great success, but the Olympic Games is another world, it is simply the greatest and most magnificent sporting occasion on this planet. We have staged the event twice before but the time could never be better to stage it once again. The investment the Government has made in sport has and will continue to make a difference. For the first time ever we are beginning to invest in schools sport to inspire our youngsters with sport, and we are supporting our élite athletes as we have never done before and the results are coming. We can and should do more but having begun to support sport in 1997 with Lottery and now Exchequer funding we should showcase the results of that investment in 2012 in London at the Olympics.

3. However sport is not the only reason to tackle the staging of the Olympics. What about the people of London. In London there are many fine and wonderful sporting facilities—Wimbledon, The Oval, Lords, Twickenham etc, but what do we have for everyday people, the answer is a crumbling infrastructure of dilapidated and uninviting facilities perhaps starkly demonstrated by the national disgrace of Crystal Palace. What an opportunity to have a strategic plan to build a legacy of sporting facilities for the people of London, located close to public transport and available at affordable prices. London is also a multi-cultural society and some parts of that society perhaps do not value sport as highly as others, what an opportunity to inspire them as to the value of sport.

4. The Olympics would without doubt be a catalyst for change and regeneration in London, it would as Manchester did, inspire the nation to again celebrate being British and everything that is good about sport and young people. There are moments in history when we have to be bold and make lifetime decisions that will change society forever; this is one of those moments. The accountants and economists will argue about the value and cost and in reality we will only know when the Games are over who is right. The people however want Government to govern and lead not recklessly but lead. We are at a moment in history, all parties see the value of sport, the time is right to seize the moment and make that bold decision to change forever British sport through bidding for and winning the Olympic Games in 2012.

20 January 2003

APPENDIX 11

Memorandum submitted by UK Athletics

INTRODUCTION

1. UK Athletics welcomes the opportunity to submit evidence to the CMS Committee ahead of their inquiry into the merits and prospects of a bid to host the 2012 Olympic Games in London.

2. For many people, the Olympic Games are synonymous with athletics; the home victory for Cathy Freeman in front of 110,000 supporters in Sydney being the enduring image of the 2000 Games for example. An Olympic medal is certainly the most prized reward in athletics, and the prospect of British athletes competing for the Olympic title on home soil for the first time in over 60 years is tantalising.

BENEFITS OF A LONDON BID AND GAMES

2003–2005:

3. The bid phase should see British sport as a whole benefit from the acceleration of measures to modernise the relationships between Government, its agencies (the sports councils) and the governing bodies of sport. The experiences of the abortive London 2005 World Championships and the early stages of Commonwealth Games preparation show the perils of unclear relationships and changes to key personnel. The scrutiny to which an Olympic bid will be subjected will quickly uncover such weaknesses and fatally undermine London's prospects.

4. To maximise fully the 'home' advantage of staging the Games in London, it will be necessary to increase investment in our élite athletes—particularly targeting the emerging élite aged 16 to 18 who will be our best medal hopes (mid to late twenties in 2012). To ensure that athletes peak in 2012, it would be necessary to start this additional investment immediately. It would be dangerous to wait until 2005; whatever the outcome of the bid, some benefit will be felt wherever the Games are held.

5. Finally, as a show of seriousness, it is assumed that the bid phase will also see some capital developments begin. Clearly the choice of facilities to be developed will depend on land availability and potential for meaningful use should the bid fail, but, if carefully chosen, then London's sports facilities should see lasting improvements even from the bid phase.

2005–2011:

6. Should the bid be successful, the years leading up to the Games offer Britain an unparalleled opportunity to develop our sporting culture and infrastructure. With a clear focus, and modernised sporting structures, a coordinated programme can be put in place from schools upwards to harness the interest and enthusiasm that a London Olympic Games will generate.

7. At school level, as well as inspiring sporting interest, the Olympics offer a cultural opportunity for international linkages and exchanges with the competing countries alongside the opportunity to learn from the values of the Olympic movement. But it is the sporting benefits that are clearly of most interest to UK Athletics: the staging of an Olympic Games in the UK makes a statement about the seriousness with which Government treats sport. This seriousness needs to be mirrored in its investment in school sport, without which the opportunities offered by a London Olympics will not be fully realised.

8. As previously mentioned, additional investment in the élite athlete programme will be necessary to maximise the medal haul in 2012. These programmes will inevitably be tuned to deliver results in London, but during the years leading up to 2012 we should see improved results at World, European and Commonwealth levels.

9. There will clearly be major capital developments taking place throughout the lead-in period, not just the competition venues but also the vital facilities across the UK for training and pre-Games holding camps for other competing nations. The benefits to London sports facilities are obvious, but the benefits from improving the existing network of élite sporting facilities to use as holding camps are also important.

2012:

10. It hardly needs stating that a well-run Olympic Games—as at Manchester 2002— would be a tremendous experience for athletes, spectators, volunteers and officials.

11. In athletics terms, the home advantage would be a tremendous inspiration to the GB team—hopefully pushing the athletes to produce medal-winning performances. The statistical benefits of competing at home are frequently cited in terms of overall Olympic medal hauls—in athletics this effect is even more marked, perhaps as a product of the atmosphere in the stadium driving on the home team. This effect was evident in Manchester, and with the right preparation, should be repeated in London.

Post 2012:

12. Without long-term benefits, it is unlikely that Government would be persuaded that the Olympic Games represented a good value for money investment. Others will make the regeneration and tourism case, but as a sports governing body, we would anticipate that with careful planning, London 2012 could leave a very healthy legacy for British sport.

13. In performance terms, there would need to be continued investment in the élite squads, but if the experience of other Olympic host countries is anything to go by, there should be a sustained improvement in performances in major events—perhaps not quite reaching the peaks of the home performance, but certainly well exceeding those achieved before staging the Games.

14. The facilities legacy is an obvious long-term benefit. London has long been identified as lagging behind the rest of the country in terms of sporting facilities at both community and performance level. The Olympics offers the 'once in a lifetime' opportunity to rectify this. To do so, the design briefs need to be carefully considered to balance short and long-term needs—as the Manchester Aquatics Centre did.

15. An often-overlooked benefit of staging mega events such as the Olympics is the improvement to the sporting human resources of the UK that would develop—both in the paid sports administration sector and in the voluntary sector from the vast numbers of volunteers that would be trained to deliver a successful Games.

16. Perhaps most important long-term benefit, though impossible to quantify, would be the generation of young Londoners who will be inspired by the staging of the Games in the capital to take an active part in sport, whether as a competitor, coach, official or volunteer.

THREATS TO A LONDON BID AND GAMES

17. Previous CMS Select Committee inquiries and reports have looked at Wembley, London 2005 and Manchester and reached similar conclusions: that Government involvement in such projects needs to be clear, consistent and unswerving—with Cabinet representation to ensure co-ordination between Government departments. It goes without saying that all this is true of an Olympic bid, with the added threat that the scale of the Olympics dwarfs those projects previously considered by the Committee.

18. Political commitment to a bid for London 2012 has to be cross party, at both national and London level, and absolute. The damage done in international circles by withdrawing from staging the 2005 IAAF World Championships in Athletics was partly rebuilt by the spectacular success of the Manchester Commonwealth Games. However, the IOC (and other bidding cities) will be looking for weaknesses in political support, and Government backing must be utterly unequivocal.

19. Public support for the Games will be determined by the success with which they are staged. There is likely to be public (and press) cynicism right up until the Opening Ceremony—this was the case even in Australia. A strongly led Organising Committee with full Government backing can ensure that the staging is slick, but the vital added ingredient is British success. This galvanises support from the public, whether inside the venues or watching on TV, as Manchester proved. It is essential therefore to enhance the support given to élite athlete support over the next ten years to ensure British medalists —to not do so threatens the public support for the whole event.

20. A long-term threat that should be considered is that of the Olympic facilities being left in the ownership of London boroughs. The threat of total 'white elephants' in usage terms can be overcome with the right balance being struck between Games and after-use in the initial design, but many of the facilities are still likely to operate at an annual deficit. These are facilities that would have London-wide benefits; to burden a local borough with the cost of upkeep would be illogical and could threaten their long-term use. The establishment of an Olympic trust to own, or at least revenue fund, the facilities would seem sensible.

CONCLUSION

21. UK Athletics fully supports the BOA's proposal to bid for the 2012 Olympic Games in London and also their stance not to proceed with the bid unless it receives unequivocal Government support. The benefits to British sport at all levels would be widespread and long lasting. It is hoped that the CMS Committee reach a similar conclusion and put their weight behind the potential bid at this crucial time.

7 January 2003

APPENDIX 12

Memorandum submitted by the Lawn Tennis Association

1. I am writing in regard to the Select Committee's forthcoming inquiry into the merits and prospects of a bid to host the 2012 Olympic Games in London.

2. As Chief Executive of the Lawn Tennis Association (LTA), I would like to express my association's overall support for London bidding to host the 2012 Olympics. I believe that staging the Olympics in London would be a huge boost to the game of tennis in this country and would be invaluable in encouraging and inspiring more players to take up the sport.

3. In terms of practical considerations, the existing courts and facilities at the All England Lawn Tennis Club, Wimbledon could be used in the event of London staging the games, which critically, would require little or no extra capital investment. The added advantages of using the facilities at Wimbledon are that there would be no issue surrounding their future use and that excellent transport links are in place and have been proven during The Championships.

4. If you or the Committee require any further information as part of your deliberations please do not hesitate to contact me.

8 January 2003

APPENDIX 13

Memorandum submitted by Sport England

INTRODUCTION

1. Sport England is the country's leading sports development agency, accountable to Parliament through the Department for Culture, Media and Sport (DCMS). Our mission is to foster a healthier, more successful nation through increased investment in sport and active recreation. We are the largest distributor of Lottery and Exchequer funding for sport in England, having invested some £1.6 billion since 1994.

QUALIFIED SUPPORT FOR A LONDON OLYMPICS

2. Sport England is broadly supportive of a London Olympics on the basis of certain assumptions. It is essential that any bid for 2012:

- Does not divert investment away from grass roots sport
- Has a robust, achievable business plan
- Delivers a substantial and sustainable sporting, social inclusion and regeneration legacy
- Is not reliant on Sport England Lottery funding
- Contributes to the overall Government objective of increasing participation in sport
- Recognises the role and success of volunteers
- Has broad public, political and business support from the start.

3. If these objectives can be met then Sport England believes a London Olympics in 2012 could be a major boost for sport and sports development in London, which is short of world-class facilities, and for the whole nation.

PARTICIPATION IN SPORT AND PHYSICAL RECREATION COMES FIRST

4. The recently published DCMS/Strategy Unit report *Game Plan: a strategy for delivering Government's sport and physical activity objectives*, states that by 2020, 70 per cent of the population should be "reasonably active". This is a laudable aim which, given appropriate support from Government, has the potential to make a significant positive impact on the nation's health, particularly in reducing the incidence of obesity and coronary heart disease.

5. However, a London Olympics on its own, in isolation, will not achieve the Government's vision for sport, nor its wider physical activity and public health objectives. What will is significant new investment in sport at every level: in school sport, in club and coach development, in grassroots facilities in both urban and rural areas; in sport volunteering programmes; and in local government support for sport. It is these types of investment—coupled with a sea change in attitude towards sport and physical activity in central and local government and across the medical profession—that will ultimately help to deliver the Government's vision of a physically active nation.

IMPORTANCE OF LEGACY PLANNING

6. A London Olympics could prove to be an important catalyst for sport in England. But for this to happen, the legacy of a London Olympics—the facilities, the volunteers, the broader infrastructure, and the passion and interest created—must be carefully woven into a much broader strategy for sport encompassing the whole of England.

The legacy of a London Olympics must outlast the two weeks of the actual Games and be felt for many years both before and after 2012.

LEGACY OF THE MANCHESTER COMMONWEALTH GAMES

7. The 2002 Commonwealth Games held in Manchester—to which Sport England provided £165 million—demonstrated the positive impact mega sports events can have on engendering domestic interest in sport, and on boosting sports participation and volunteering in sport.

8. The consultancy firm Cambridge Policy Consultants, employed by Manchester City Council to produce a cost-benefit analysis of the 2002 Commonwealth Games, has concluded that 250,000 additional visits will occur each year to both new and existing sports facilities in the northwest as a result of the Games .

9. 10,500 Volunteers—from all walks of life—gave their time and effort during the Games. Of these:

— 500 have so far signed up to Sport England with a view to volunteering in sport (we are working in conjunction with sports County Partnerships and do-it.org to match volunteers with sports clubs/opportunities

— 280 have signed up with the Experience Corps

— Manchester City Council have written to all Games volunteers to encourage long term volunteering (of the 1350 returns to date, 761 have expressed an interest in sport related opportunities).

10. Residents in the North West of England have benefited from the physical legacy of the Commonwealth Games. For example:

• The National Squash Centre in Manchester is hosting squash development courses for up to 7,000 local children. The Centre is also being used as a 'pay & play' facility for local residents

• As part of the Lottery Funding Agreement, Sport England has negotiated a tenancy agreement with Manchester City FC (MCFC) and Manchester City Council resulting in MCFC becoming the anchor tenant of the City of Manchester stadium. As the anchor tenant, MCFC is responsible for all maintenance, repair, and renewal of the facility as well as all operational risk. MCFC will also pay a rent to Manchester City Council, based upon a percentage of ticket sales at the stadium above 32,500 providing MCFC is competing in the Premier League, which will be re-invested into sports facilities and programmes in Manchester and the North West. In addition, the stadium will be made available for community use for 100 days each year - this will include use of the pitch for local youth football competitions.

• In its first 12 months of operation (September 2000-September 2001) a total of 675,331 visits were made to the Manchester Aquatics Centre - of these more than 350,000 were casual swimmers

• The Commonwealth Games indoor athletics track and warm-up track are now being used by local Manchester athletics club Sale Harriers

• All the gymnastic equipment used during the Games at the G-MEX Centre has been awarded to a new gymnastics high performance centre, which will be used by a local gymnastics club—Gorton—once the centre is constructed.

11. Manchester 2002 delivered a significant sporting legacy for the people of the North West. A London Olympics, given the size and magnitude of the event, can make a significant contribution to the people of the South East and beyond. But it is imperative that relevant legacy planning for a London Olympics is started at the earliest possible stage.

THE LOTTERY AND AN OLYMPIC BID

12. There has been some debate about using the Lottery to help fund a London Olympics. It is important, however, to stress that Lottery income for sport has fallen significantly over the past 5 years - both as a result of falling ticket sales and the creation of the New Opportunities Fund (NOF) in 1998, which receives one third of all good cause money.

13. In 1997–98 Sport England's Lottery income was £268 million which we invested right across sport eg, to national governing bodies, to grass roots and community sport; to élite athletes and facilities. However, 2002–03 will see our Lottery income fall dramatically from the 1997–98 peak to £170 million per annum. This significant decline is extremely worrying. Consequently, unless Sport England's Lottery income increases radically, we will be hard-pushed to play any meaningful role in the funding of a London Olympics.

CONCLUSION

14. Sport England support a London Olympics on the understanding that the prime objective for staging the Games is to stimulate increased investment and involvement in grass roots sport in London and across the country. We are encouraged that the Secretary of State shares this position.

15. Current funding for sport is under extreme pressure. A bid must not be at the cost of investment in grass roots sport in England. It should complement a much broader sport and physical activity strategy aimed at delivering the Government's objective of getting 70 per cent of the nation 'reasonably active' by 2020.

14 January 2003

Supplementary Memorandum submitted by Sport England

1. We were grateful for the opportunity to present evidence to the Committee yesterday in respect of your inquiry into the Olympic Bid for London.

2. I thought it would be useful to clarify a number of points that arose yesterday in relation to the National Stadium and its potential role within an Olympic context. I trust that you will find this helpful in your deliberations.

3. The purpose of the Sport England Lottery Fund grant for the National Stadium project at Wembley was to develop a stadium for three sports—primarily for football and rugby league, and with the capability of hosting athletics should the stadium be required by the organising committees of either the World Athletic Championships or the Olympic Games. The project was not developed primarily for the 2012 Olympic bid.

4. In 1999, when the key decisions regarding the development of the Wembley project were being taken, the BOA were not in a position to formally commit to Wembley, in part as it had not determined whether to bid for the 2012 Games.

5. Sport England wanted to ensure that the National Stadium would have the capability to be the centre-point of any future Olympic bid for years to come. That is why we wrote into our Lottery Funding Agreement conditions that state that the National Stadium must be made available at a cost-basis for the Olympic Games.

6. Whilst the BOA could not formally commit to Wembley at this time, both they and the Government were focusing their thoughts and activities on Wembley as the centrepiece for any future bid, as the following extracts from previous reports of your Committee demonstrate:

> In consultation with the English Sports Council, it has been agreed that the redeveloped Wembley Stadium will have the ability to cater for top level athletics competition whilst retaining sufficient capacity to satisfy the demands for Olympic Opening and Closing Ceremonies.

> *BOA written evidence, 4 March 1999*

> It must be more than a football stadium. It is called 'the national stadium'. It is an absolute requirement that it is a stadium that will stage athletics events, Rugby League events and indeed it will be very much the Olympic stadium if and when a successful bid is mounted. It will be for London. This is something that the British Olympic Association is saying, not me, so apologies to all Members who do not come from London. That is their statement, not mine. Wembley is absolutely crucial to that. We are only progressing on the basis that Wembley will be used to stage athletics world championships, or at least one athletic world championship and, we hope, an Olympic Games.

> *Oral evidence, Minister for Sport, Tony Banks MP, 22 April 1999*

> The BOA has always seen Wembley as being the focal point for a future London Olympic bid. The feasibility study which the BOA has been preparing for over 18 months, involving the running of four working groups, was centred around Wembley's ability to act as the main stadium.

> *BOA written evidence, 18 January 2002*

7. At yesterday's hearing, the Committee was interested in how important it was that the village be located adjacent to the Olympic stadium. This was in relation to a view that Wembley might not be suitable, as a village could not be located alongside the stadium.

8. At the time of our consultation on the future of Wembley, no issues were raised by the BOA in relation to the juxtaposition of Wembley and the Olympic village. Indeed, the BOA had at that time identified options for Olympic venues including the village, based upon a West London option with Wembley as the focus.

9. The BOA submitted the following evidence to the Committee:

The location of the Village is crucial to the success of a future bid. Taking into account the need to house up to 15,000 athletes and officials for the duration of the Games, as well as the requisite ancillary facilities, a minimum site size of 50 hectares is required to be located within reasonable proximity of all major sporting venues.

BOA written evidence, 4 March 1999

10. The 2002 Arup report has focused on an East London option. We believe that the BOA, working with the Mayor and the GLA, have placed the bid in the context of emerging regeneration priorities for London (the GLA was not in existence when the original Wembley decisions were made), and that this is the primary reason for the proposals for the location of the stadium in East London rather than its juxtaposition with the Olympic village.

11. In summary, therefore, Sport England has created the opportunity for Wembley to be utilised within an Olympic bid - either as the main stadium, for football or for other purposes. There were options for the village based upon a West London bid option under consideration in 1999. The BOA has chosen not to pursue those options. Ultimately, decisions regarding the bid are for the organising committee to make, based upon a wide range of factors related to planning, transportation and other issues.

12. I hope this is useful, and would be happy to provide further information if required.

16 January 2003

APPENDIX 14

Memorandum submitted by UK Sport

SUMMARY

13. Early in 2002, a group including the British Olympic Association, the Greater London Authority, the London Development Agency, the Government and UK Sport commissioned an independent cost-benefit analysis report into London staging the 2012 Olympic and Paralympic Games. The report by Arup clearly demonstrates that a coherent solution for the Games can be delivered in London, optimising existing facilities and providing new build in easily accessed locations. It also concludes that bidding for and staging the Olympics and Paralympics in London would result in an overall cashflow position of between plus £82 million and minus £145 million.

14. As the government agency responsible for co-ordinating the bidding and staging of major events in the UK, we firmly believe that securing the Games would be one of the most significant factors in helping UK Sport achieve its overall goal of making the UK one of the world's top five sporting nations by 2012.

15. The Games would also bring enormous economic and social benefits to the East End of London and the country as a whole. The football competition is required to be staged in a minimum of four different cities, whilst the sailing would take place on the south coast. Additionally, 199 countries would be sending teams to the Games, many of whom would require a training base somewhere in the UK.

16. At its November 2002 meeting the Council of UK Sport debated the possibility of a London bid for the Olympic Games of 2012. It considered the report undertaken by Arup and a winnability assessment. In light of current UK Sports Council policy objectives and the assessment undertaken, Council express its full support for a London bid for the 2012 Olympic Games with the following caveats:

(a)   Any bid must have political priority and cross party support.

(b)   There must be committed political will to drive the necessary leadership, coordination and cooperation of the many delivery and impacted organisations.

BACKGROUND

17. The Arup Report was considered by the Major Events Steering Group of UK Sport at its June meeting in order to help inform the preparation of a winnability assessment which had been requested by DCMS. This assessment was submitted in September and forms part of the overall consideration being prepared by DCMS.

18. In order to assess the feasibility of a London Games the consultants prepared a specimen bid solution which formed the basis of their analysis. This assumes an east London focus with the majority of sporting venues located in the Lee Valley corridor and two options for the Olympic village—Stratford or Bromley-by-Bow. The study has clearly demonstrated that a coherent solution can be achieved that optimises existing facilities and provides new build in easily accessed locations centred on the Stratford transport interchange. It further establishes that the necessary ancillary accommodation is deliverable and that the transport system can cope with the high demand if managed to an unprecedented degree. It also concludes that Crossrail would enhance capacity and accessibility but acknowledges that immediate decisions would need to made on this major infrastructure project for it to be in place for 2012.

19. Importantly for UK Sport, the report includes the necessary investment (£167 million) in high performance sport needed over the eight year run-in period to 2012 to deliver a GB team of the highest standard with optimum medal potential.

20. The report also stresses the absolute necessity for full government support and a willingness to put in place the necessary legislation and executive bodies to deliver a world class event.

UK SPORT POSITION

21. The stated goal of UK Sport is for the UK to be one of the world's top five sporting nations by 2012. Further, it is a major events policy objective of UK Sport to see the UK stage the Olympic Games at some time in the near to medium future as a demonstration of our commitment to, and capacity to deliver, world class events. Improved sporting performance

22. UK Sport believes that the securing of the Games in 2012 would be one of the single most significant factors in helping UK Sport achieve these goals and would transform the high performance system. The impact of staging the Olympics and Paralympics on élite performance in the UK would be tremendous. Evidence from previous Olympic Games demonstrates that a host nation's performance and position in the medal table is nearly always improved:

Country	Host city & year	Gold medals at Games 4 years previous	Gold medals won when hosting the Games
Korea	Seoul, 1988	6	12
Spain	Barcelona, 1992	1	13
Australia	Sydney, 2000	9	16

23. The reason for the improved performance is down to a number of factors, some quantifiable and some not. Investment in élite sport in the UK has lagged far behind our international competitors for a number of years and would undoubtedly increase if we were to stage the Games. Hosting the world's largest sports event would focus the minds of Government and sports agencies throughout the UK into preparing a Great Britain and Northern Ireland team of optimum medal potential to compete at the Games.

24. Anecdotal evidence also suggests that competing in front of a home crowd boosts athletes' performance. Competing in a familiar climate, at facilities where you have trained and competed before, added to the desire of wanting to do well in front of partisan home spectators, can substantially affect an athlete's performance. This was ably demonstrated by Paula Radcliffe at the highly successful Manchester Commonwealth Games.

25. London is considered by the BOA to be the only option for a winnable bid from the UK and UK Sport agrees with this position. A bid for 2012 could well be the last opportunity to assemble the necessary package of land and produce a coherent Games truly based in the capital. At present it seems unlikely that such an opportunity will arise again for a generation of more.

26. The Games will provide new sporting infrastructure for élite competitors. The Olympics and Paralympics would require up to 100 training venues, which would provide real sporting legacy, for use by both grass roots and élite sport. Refurbished school gyms, leisure centres and community facilities in London would directly benefit from this. By using existing exhibition hall space for temporary competition venues, costly permanent indoor facilities will be avoided ensuring only sustainable facilities are built with long term community use in mind. Early discussions have been held with potential users of the stadium again to ensure no unnecessary 'white elephants' are built.

BENEFITS THROUGHOUT THE UK

27. An area of interest for British cities is the concept of holding camps for overseas teams. An example of this is the Team GB camp which was set up on the Gold Coast of Australia in 2000. This contributed over £1 million to the local economy over 12 months. Given that there are 199 international National Olympic Committees, there is considerable scope for cities across the UK to attract this lucrative business.

28. At present the football tournament is required to be staged in a minimum of four different cities presenting an opportunity to take the Games to other parts of the UK and helping to create the feeling of a nationwide celebration of sport. Sailing will also take place outside of London integrating another region of Britain into the Olympic network. The location of both of these sports outside of the host city is catered for under present International Olympic Committee regulations.

COMMUNITY BENEFITS

29. A large impact could be expected through increased social cohesion and the promotion of diversity through an Olympic and Paralympic cultural programme. London is one of the most culturally diverse cities in the world and the Games could be used to celebrate local communities and ensure that the socially excluded have every opportunity to engage with the event. An aim should be that after the Olympics and Paralympics, a legacy in terms of improved community leadership, enhanced cultural networks and a close engagement with the education sector will remain.

30. Both the Sydney Olympics and the 2002 Manchester Commonwealth Games showed the benefits of having a dedicated and enthusiastic pool of volunteers. The experience of Sydney has shown that this culture of volunteerism has been continued, with people becoming auxiliary police officers, community workers, teaching assistants or carers for the elderly. Manchester's programme of recruiting and training disadvantaged groups and long-term unemployed through pre-volunteer training enabled the necessary skill development and employment potential of many to be realised.

REGENERATION

31. The proposal is based around a specimen Olympic Games proposal with Village and venues located in the heart of East London. This is currently an area experiencing high levels of deprivation (for example the Borough of Newham has an unemployment rate three times above the Greater London average). Much of the targeted area also has objective two regeneration status, although the potential positive impact of European Union funding has not been included in this report. A point to note is that Greece has just been awarded 1.4 billion euros from the EU for Olympic and Paralympic-related transport projects.

32. The Games would provide a critical focus to the regeneration in the East of London providing directly for the regeneration of approx. 100 hectares of land and the construction of 160,000 square metres of employment floor space. The development of the Olympic Village would provide close to 4,000 new housing units - all built upon brown-field land. Large-scale reclamation of contaminated, derelict and under-utilised land will have a significant impact on regeneration opportunities in the wider locality.

TRANSPORT CONSIDERATIONS

33. The report concludes that: "Projected flows can be accommodated without delays and without unacceptable disruption to normal travel in London". An effective transport management scheme can deliver the necessary capacity for athletes, officials and spectators. Sydney implemented a well-publicised scheme to get people to take public transport to competition venues. In effect, no public car parking was provided and spectators made the journey via rail, bus or ferry. The long-term impact has been that the Games are now credited with changing many preconceptions about travel by public transport.

ECONOMIC COSTS AND BENEFITS

34. The assessment of costs of the Games in the Arup Report used a public sector investment methodology recommended by the Treasury. This involved establishing base case costs and benefits, together with a provision for risk, all in 2002 prices and discounting the cash flows (15 years) to give a present value in 2002. Subsequent work by the Government has included an understanding of the maximum downside risk for each key stakeholder if the best laid plans go awry, thereby significantly increasing the provision for risk in the totals. We agree with the consultants that whilst this is an important exercise to undertake, we do not think that the provision of these eventualities should be included as base cost in the evaluation. The effect of so doing would be to assess the benefits and costs of a badly managed and/or a very unlucky London Olympics.

WINNABILITY

35. A key factor is the winnability of any bid. The Olympics are one of the most sought after events in the world with the stiffest of international competition. All bids will have strengths and weaknesses and we have undertaken a detailed assessment of the relative positions of the known bidding cities. It is UK Sport's assessment that with the necessary sensitive and charismatic leadership, full and ongoing political support and a real commitment to deliver a quality Games, a London bid has a serious chance of success. No bid can be considered a certainty and as a nation UK Sport believes we should be bold enough to go for what is one of the ultimate prizes in international sport. Our polling shows that the British public wish to see more of this level of event staged in the UK and in hosting a Games an entire generation of the British public would be given the unique opportunity to be involved with an event of truly global importance.

8 January 2003

APPENDIX 15

Memorandum submitted by the English Tourism Council

1. The English Tourism Council (ETC) welcomes the inquiry by the Culture, Media and Sport Select Committee into the merits and prospects of a bid to host the 2012 Olympic Games in London. ETC submits the following as a submission to the inquiry.

2. The English Tourism Council was created in 1999 to replace the English Tourist Board (ETB) established by Parliament under the Development of Tourism Act 1969. ETC and the British Tourist Authority are in the process of merging into a single lead body for tourism in Britain. The new agency will operate from 1 April 2003 and be responsible for the marketing of Britain overseas and tourism in England. Sports tourism is a buoyant and growing market sector within the tourism industry—which itself is a major success for UK Plc contributing £74 billion to the economy, supporting over two million jobs and underpinning many more. This economic importance will continue to grow.

THE MERITS OF A BID TO HOLD THE 2012 OLYMPIC GAMES IN LONDON

3. The 2012 Olympic Games in London represents a major 'once in a generation' opportunity for UK tourism. It will strengthen London's claim to be one of the world's top five cities and promote huge opportunities for tourism to Britain, both during the Games and for many years' afterwards. It will create jobs, generate wealth and be a major catalyst for regeneration, both for the benefit of residents and London's visitors.

4. Sports tourism provides huge direct and indirect economic benefits. The 2002 Commonwealth Games created a substantial boost for tourism to Manchester and the region, and enhanced the image of both the North West and Britain as a whole. Staging the Commonwealth Games generated 300,000 additional visitors, 6,100 Full-time equivalent jobs, with immense direct and indirect knock-on effects for the local economy. Holding a Six Nations international match at Murrayfield in Edinburgh creates an injection of around £20 million for Scotland.

5. Holding the Olympics in London in 2012 has the potential for far greater impact.

6. The long-term effects of holding the Olympic Games in both Barcelona and Sydney are proven examples of the positive benefits for a city of holding the world's premier sporting event. Barcelona was rejuvenated by the Games and transformed into a world-class visitor destination with overnight stays rising by 70 per cent from 4.1 million in 1991 to 7 million in 1997.

7. Immediate public investment and strong leadership from Government is critical for a successful bid, with Ministers committed to this opportunity with the determination and confidence that breeds success. Of particular importance is the need to ensure improvements to the city's infrastructure. Substantial upgrading to transport systems, together with investment in the support facilities, such as London's accommodation stock, will be essential to maximise the positive impact of hosting this event.

8. The impact on London would be unprecedented and the returns would leave a lasting legacy for the future.

9. I look forward to seeing the result of the inquiry.

10 January 2003

APPENDIX 16

Memorandum submitted by the British Tourist Authority

1. We are grateful for the opportunity to submit a short memorandum in relation to this Inquiry. In the interests of brevity, this submission is written on the assumption that the Committee does not require any introduction to the British Tourist Authority's (BTA) role or on the value of tourism to the economy.

2. There can be little doubt that the staging of a successful Olympics in London would be beneficial in the longer term for inbound tourism to Britain as it would provide an unparalleled opportunity to showcase London—and Britain—to the world and provide BTA with a valuable legacy to exploit in promoting the whole of Britain overseas. This legacy would be twofold: the positive image of London and Britain portrayed and the infrastructure that would remain in place following the event.

3. If the Olympics were not successful - or perceived overseas as not having been so - the effect could be a negative one resulting in a downturn in overseas visitors in the years immediately following the event. It would be essential to learn lessons from Sydney where, as well as ensuring that the transport, sporting and accommodation infrastructure was in place, the level of welcome and service extended to athletes and visitors was exemplary, due in no small part to the fact that the venues were so well managed, and the media was well catered for.

4. Despite the undoubted long-term benefits of a successful Games, overseas visits to the host country may suffer during the year in which the Games are staged. The majority of people attending the event tend to be residents: overseas visitors who do not wish to go to the Games are often deterred from visiting the host country because they perceive that it will be overcrowded, and that prices will be at premium level. (Forecasts prepared by KPMG for the Manchester Olympic bid suggested that only five per cent (i.e. around 300,00) of tickets would be bought by overseas visitors.)

5. Domestically, staging the Games in London may well result in displacement with people choosing to spend time at events rather than to visit other regions of England and Scotland and Wales. On the other hand, some visitors would be deterred from visiting London and choose to visit other parts of the country instead.

6. On balance, the legacy of a successful event would more than counter-balance any downside in tourism terms during the year of the Games - if indeed this proved the case.

14 January 2003

APPENDIX 17

Memorandum submitted by Mr Mark Dolley

1. Your questions regarding London's bid for the 2012 Olympic Games are a clear reflection of careful and commendable consideration on the Committee's part. I shall do what I can to answer them, based not least on recent experience of bidding for the 2012 Olympic Games, with the Bay Area Sports Organizing Committee. Of eight US cities, San Francisco made the final pair. Our bid lost to New York City in the race to represent the USA, receiving some 40 per cent of the vote, after emotionally-charged presentations to the US Olympic Committee on 2 November 2002.

Summary:

- The scars of recent British fiascos have healed and are fading. History and recent successes offset them;
- London has the basis for a stronger bid than New York City, Paris and other likely 2012 contenders;
- London's estimates for the cost of bidding are reasonable;
- Bidding and losing can still improve sport in London;
- Facing strict IOC rules, 2012 bids must demonstrate transparency, great technical competence and immense creativity;
- The IOC has mandated a more cost-efficient approach to operating costs than that adopted by Arup;
- Operating excesses from hosting the Olympic Games can pay for fresh sporting and transport infrastructure;
- Sporting and financial benefits would accrue to the entire UK but would disproportionately favour London.

2. The Picketts Lock, Wembley and Euro 2006 issues have already been offset by Commonwealth Games perceived internationally as a great success. In 2005, when the IOC makes its decision, those mistakes will have faded further from memory and can be further offset by the continued and even expanded staging of international events in the UK. Concerns about Britain's ability to influence international sports bodies merely echo those voiced by other nations. For example, the USA's ability to influence international sporting opinion was called into question in 2002, when Americans were surprised to lose the 2007 Pan American Games to Rio de Janeiro.

3. Historically, London has been the city capable of hosting the Games even when no other city was ready. It has bid against international competition before, for the (cancelled) 1944 Games, and won by a country mile. And whereas ten years ago British athletes had their unemployment benefit cancelled for competing in the Olympic Games, now they are properly funded. Such initiatives have not gone without international respect and admiration.

4. *Managed properly and supported wholeheartedly, London has the basis of a better technical bid than its likely competitors.* The area chosen for London's bid, the Lower Lee Valley, lends itself to an attractively compact design for the Games. There would be only minimal distances between key sites. Such is the basis of a technically superb bid. Together with its press and broadcasting centres, London's Olympic Stadium, swimming pools, gymnastics facilities and sites for more than a dozen other sports would all lie within two miles of the Olympic Village. New York City 2012, for example, places only its track cycling, badminton, archery and beach volleyball venues within two miles of its proposed Village. Indeed, in the face of the same opposition that derailed Mayor Giuliani's earlier plans for a Manhattan stadium, NYC 2012 has already named Flushing Meadows Park as a backup location for its Olympic Stadium: more than six miles from its Village and further still from its media facility.

5. Paris was previously mentioned by the Select Committee as likely to submit a strong 2012 bid. In the absence of an independent report, as suggested by the Committee, UK Sport's report on 2012 bidders also appears to favour Paris. But Paris will not be able to put forward a compact venue plan, on account of new development around the Stade de France. On 10 December 2002, Paris 2008 head Claude Bebear said: "A Paris bid for 2012 is possible but it will more difficult than in 2008, mainly because the land for the planned Olympic village is no longer available." Paris's 'less difficult' 2008 bid received 15 of 112 first-round votes. Istanbul received 17.

6. *London's estimate of some £15 million (2002 prices) for bidding operations is reasonable and is comparable to US bid city projections.* Apart from necessary land acquisition, additions to that total should include only elements certain to further improve the quality of sporting life in a clear fashion. Examples might be the sponsorship of sporting events in London, or upgrades to existing venues (such as the creation of an international-standard swimming facility at Crystal Palace) as a requirement of hosting sports events. The opportunity to attract private support to assist with such projects—under an Olympic banner—is a good reason to bid.

7. Even bidding and losing is likely to leave London richer in terms of sporting heritage. San Francisco for example, has added to its annual sporting calendar in ways not possible without the support generated by its 2012 bid. The San Francisco Grand Prix, a world class bicycle race now two years old and enjoyed by 400,000 spectators, is a prime example.

8. The 2012 bidding process will follow the same rules as the 2010 bidding process. They preclude visits from IOC members, the soliciting of IOC members in any way and ban all international campaigning. These rules are stricter than those in force for 2008. Under the latest rules, for example, Beijing would not have been able to implement the international PR campaign that helped it overcome international criticism of human rights abuses. Differences in IOC contact by the lead 2012 contenders will be marginal, as bid teams assemble in the same lobbies of the same hotels at international sporting events, hoping to catch the attention of passing IOC members.

9. The quality of final presentations will be crucial. *Tied to an immaculate technical bid, the ability of the London 2012 team to harness the commercial creativity that has put the UK at the forefront of world advertising will be crucial. Transparency will also be vital. Secrets and surprises will have no place in a successful 2012 bid and the Select Committee is to be commended for its previous recommendations in this regard.*

10. In order to be successful at the IOC level, London will have to put forward an operational budget more modest than that outlined in the Arup report. In 2000 money, Sydney's operating costs were £793 million. In 2002 money, Arup predicts operating costs that are more than double that. On the contrary, the IOC's recommendations are clear. The final report of the IOC Co-ordination Commission for the Sydney 2000 Games stated: "Measures will have to be taken to control the future growth of the Games. The Games certainly must not be allowed to grow any larger, otherwise they will present a major risk."

11. In all fairness, both San Francisco and New York City prepared operating budgets similar to those prepared by Arup. It was only in November of 2002 that the IOC clearly indicated the new way forward: "An effort must be made to stop the current benchmark inflation by clearly establishing what must be delivered for the purpose of the Games. A thorough study of the evolution of service levels will help define a reasonable standard to be provided in the bidding stage . The effort to stop this benchmark and service inflation must begin at the bidding phase. Bid cities should be better educated in order to avoid over-bidding and making unnecessary promises. The need to address sustainability aspects in the bidding stage should be stressed," stated the interim report of the Olympic Games Study Commission.

12. Following the adoption of this new, more cost-conscious approach, the IOC has already told Beijing's Organising Committee to cut back some proposed venues and completely eliminate another. *The IOC's new approach will allow London to satisfy the needs of the IOC at considerably less expense than Arup's predictions, which were based on extensive comparisons with other bids and major sporting events.*

13. While operating costs for future Games will be kept in check, revenues are likely to continue to rise at pace. 2012 operating revenues are likely to exceed operating costs by hundreds of millions of pounds. By assuming responsibility for infrastructure projects, a London Organizing Committee of the Olympic Games could use Olympic revenue to pay for significant capital improvements to the Lower Lee Valley. Meanwhile, the benefits from increased tourism will account for hundreds of millions more, paying for further infrastructure improvements and leaving a legacy of jobs to complement new sports facilities, increased national pride and greater sports participation.

14. *The Olympic Games can pay for fresh sporting and transport infrastructure in London.* But infrastructure attributed to a London Games could cost billions more. Argue that Crossrail is an Olympic project and the Games will clearly never be a profitable enterprise. Regardless of new transport projects with an Olympic label, in 2012 two Underground lines, the Docklands Light Railway, multiple overground rail links, the Channel Tunnel Rail Link and an airport will serve the Lower Lee Valley. Currently, the site of New York City's proposed Olympic Stadium is not even on that city's Subway map.

15. A London Olympics would deliver fresh revenue throughout the UK. The football tournament, for example, would spread the financial and also the intangible wealth. Training camps for visiting teams will be another important source of revenue, pride and involvement for those outside the capital. *London, however, must remain the sole focus of the Games. The IOC will not consider bids involving multiple host cities.*

27 December 2002

APPENDIX 18

Memorandum submitted by the North and East London Sports Network

BID TO HOST THE OLYMPIC GAMES IN LONDON IN 2012

1. The North and East London Sports Network is a sub-regional organisation representing members drawn from seven local authorities, three universities and other key stakeholders involved in sports initiatives which make a positive contribution to the sub-region. Initiatives include health improvement through increased physical activity, tackling social exclusion, regeneration and other key Government priorities.

2. The Network is strongly backing the bid to host the 2012 Olympic Games in North and East London sub-region for the following reasons.

TOURISM

3. Major sports facilities and events can play a key role in attracting new audiences, as seen in Barcelona and Sydney. Recently London's share of the world's tourism has declined. The Games would be the catalyst for using sport to play a more significant role in tourism and would reinforce London's position as a World Class City, with tangible benefits to the whole of the UK. (Barcelona shared the Games with 17 other cities).

INCREASED INTERNATIONAL PROFILE

4. A successful Games would reflect our ability to stage a world class event and be a world class force in sport. It would follow on from one of the key objectives of the Manchester Games: "to make the UK the centre of International Sport, able to host international events."

ELITE PERFORMANCE

5. An array of élite athletes from Sir Steve Redgrave, Paula Radcliffe, Jonathan Edwards and Dwain Chambers has given their support to a London Olympics. The results at Manchester's Commonwealth Games demonstrate the impact of competing in your home nation. Furthermore we need to support the immense human endeavour displayed by individual athletes in the past—often at huge personal cost, despite help from the public through the lottery. This is the time for politicians to make a real contribution to sport.

FEEL GOOD FACTOR

6. The Games would have an electrifying effect on the City. The whole country would have its spirits lifted, providing "the spark to regenerate an area which has been neglected for decades." (*Sir Steve Redgrave*)

URBAN RENEWAL

7. Games could be a catalyst to one of Britain's biggest and most significant schemes of urban renewal. Both Barcelona and Manchester used the Games to lever in significant investment and drive its wider and much longer-term local regeneration strategy. Manchester attracted additional investment including £52 million from New Deal for Communities, 325 million from SRB, £3 million from SureStart, plus European Union Objective 2 funds.

8. The Games could be used to accelerate the enormous task of redevelopment and restructuring in the Thames Gateway and specifically in the Lower Lee Valley. We will need to harness the Olympic 'effect' and investment it will bring to create wider investor interest in the 'Olympic Zone'. Sydney grew in five years from a derelict munitions dump to a gleaming new suburb in the heart of the City.

9. The Games will redress the balance of the city, providing qualitative growth. An East London focus will challenge the distribution of historic patterns of major grant to support museums, galleries and venues in West and Central London. It can be used to rebrand and reposition the place of East London within the City, emphasis its sporting and cultural infrastructure, within a Cultural Quarter and Tourism Action Zone.

10. Barcelona's approach was to "Make the Games for the City… to do in five or six years what had not been done in 50 years."

ECONOMIC IMPACT

11. In 2,000 spending on sport was £15.2 billion (Sports Market Forecast, SHU), representing three per cent of total consumer spending. (This was 70 per cent higher than 1990)

12. Studies into the economic impact of major sports events measuring the additional expenditure of visiting spectators, competitors officials and the media within the city staging the event reveal that the they can generate a significant economic impact on the local economy if properly planned and implemented:

- London Marathon brought £33 million to London alone and £66 million to the whole country.
- Euro '96 Match in Sheffield brought £6 million or 150 full time equivalent jobs.
- Masters Swimming Competition in Sheffield brought £3.59 million to the city.

13. The economic impact of the Games to North and East London, the region and the nation would be substantial. Although we must ensure that contracts for the majority of goods and services required by the Games go to local companies.

HOUSING

14. The Olympic Village could provide four thousand new houses which could be used as post games accommodation for low-paid key workers. Manchester's regeneration plan saw an increase of 12,500 new homes and improvements to 7,000 more.

EMPLOYMENT AND EDUCATION

15. Staging the Games would involve 63,000 operational personnel of whom 47,000 will be volunteers, including stewards, marshals and drivers as well as highly skilled IT staff and those with appropriate skills needed to procure, co-ordinate and manage the Games. Huge resources of skills and expertise will be attracted to the sub-region.

16. The impact of the Games, plus the new infrastructure would also encourage relocation of businesses.

17. Currently Sports Action Zone status is being sought in parts of East London that will be involved in the bid. However, the Games could be used as a catalyst to develop a 'Sports Economic Zone' in the sub-region. The sub-region could establish a sport and leisure employment and service sector, (currently the focus of a research project funded by the LDA) concentrating on research and development, technology, product design and innovation as well as manufacturing. It could also specialise in sports development, sports facilities and services, other aspects of the sports industry, research, consultancy and academic research into sports medicine and sports science as well as attracting major events.

18. N&ELSN is already working with the Learning and Skills Council using sport and leisure to develop education and employment opportunities, particularly aimed at traditionally socially excluded groups.

19. The success of Manchester's Pre-Volunteer Programme which engaged thousands of local people and gave them training and experience, not just for the Games but also to improve their chances of long term employment in the leisure industry could be replicated in London. The Olympics should be seen as the pinnacle of sport as a dynamic, emerging sector and driver of long term job creation.

TRANSPORT

20. The Olympics should also be seen as a driver to improve the transport infrastructure. It would focus the minds of key decision-makers and funders running our transport system. Again it will help to address the imbalance in current poor transport in East London.

21. The smooth running of the Games would be greatly enhanced by Crossrail and/or River Crossings—but astute management of transport will enable the Games to run without it.

SPORTS LEGACY

22. The Olympics will leave a substantial legacy of facilities, which should be integrated into the City's infrastructure for all those who live, work and visit London.

23. This legacy of new facilities will engage young people and support the efforts of young athletes forced to train in sub-standard facilities. It is necessary that the link between grassroots participation and the need for top class facilities is recognised and not used to play one off against the other.

24. Local authorities should benefit as widely as possible from the need for training facilities both before and during the Games.

TACKLING SOCIAL EXCLUSION

25. The Games would help to address the concerns identified in the London Plan, the need to reverse increasing polarisation within communities in London and create a fair, just and ultimately sustainable community. The Games could provide a common focus for all those living within the community and deliver a legacy of training facilities for a generation of those who live, work and visit London.

26. London has a strong and historic tradition of sport, with the greatest number of world class athletes based within the region. Despite the growth of private facilities, especially health and fitness clubs, public facilities are generally poor. Londoners face massive increases in housing which needs to be balanced by adequate leisure facilities, to avoid a significant decrease in the quality of life of most Londoners. This is particularly relevant in East London which has the greatest deficit of leisure facilities, lowest participation rates and greatest health problems.

27. London's has one of the biggest populations of deprived children in the developed world, with very restricted leisure choices. New facilities need to be focused in areas of existing deficiencies (identified as areas of opportunity in the London Plan) which fall within the Lower Lee Valley area.

28. The Olympics should be seen as a vehicle of social change. Despite the DDA of 1995, there are currently few accessible leisure facilities or programmes for people with disabilities in London. London should build on the benchmark of access and inclusivity set by Manchester, aiming for a fully inclusive Games, with a real and lasting legacy for all. The Games have received support from Paralympic Association.

29. Barcelona used the Games to unite people with cultural and language difference, without losing its identity. The Games needs to make a difference, but also identify the similarities and unity within local communities. Local communities and sports organisations must be involved from the start to enable them to buy in to the overall package of improvements to enhance the image of the sub-region and create greater social complicity and consensus.

HEALTH BENEFITS

30. There has been a huge explosion of major health problems influenced by our increasingly inactive lifestyles, particularly obesity, CHD, Cancer and diabetes—especially in young people. The World Health Authority identifies inactivity as one of the top ten leading causes of death and disability. Statistics from the British Heart Foundation reveal that a 10 per cent increase in PA could reduce premature deaths by over 6,000. Savings in excess of £2 billion a year. Health inequalities are particularly problematic in East London, with some of the lowest participation rates and poor access to leisure facilities. The Olympics could not only leave a legacy of facilities, but also begin to change the attitudes and behaviours of the community towards exercise.

FINANCIAL IMPLICATIONS

31. Economic assessments have been thoroughly carried out. The Arup Report estimated that economic benefits could bring a surplus of several hundred million. Although the overall net costs of the physical infrastructure and costs of staging the Games exceed the revenue by £494 million, conservative estimates of the wider quantifiable benefits (mainly from tourism) could result in a surplus. Furthermore, unquantifiable benefits include national prestige, legacy of facilities, sports development programmes and participation, promotion of the cultural diversity of London and improvements to social cohesion and leverage of inward investment opportunities.

32. The major financial implications are too big for a city or local authority to carry on their own. The London Plan suggests a pooling of resources to support sub-regional projects which may help with the necessary training and support facilities for the Games. However, despite a great deal of funding coming from the private sector, the Government and other public sector funders need to be totally behind the Games and to be full and active partners.

INCREASED PROFILE OF SPORT

33. The recent support of the media is a crucial factor. However it needs to be partnered by greater political support. The Games would raise the importance of sport within Whitehall. A successful bid will need the wholehearted support of the Prime Minister and Chancellor and will require a concentration of political focus and priority in favour of an East London Olympics in 2012.

34. The Games will also need a charismatic, strong leader and organising committee with appropriate resources, powers and authority.

IN CONCLUSION

35. N&ELSN support the proposal to bid for an East London Olympics in 2012 as a catalyst for change and regeneration, levering resources and providing a legacy that will increase sports participation and health benefits for London (especially NE London). This premier international event should be seen as a driver for regeneration and sustainable growth in this key area of London, linked to low cost housing, employment, sports infrastructure and transport improvements (including airports). It would celebrate the diversity of East London, tackle the increasing polarisation of communities highlighted in the Plan and unite people through sport.

9 January 2003

APPENDIX 19

Memorandum submitted by the London Business Board

INTRODUCTION

1. The London Business Board (LBB) is an overarching body, comprising the London Chamber of Commerce and Industry, the London CBI and London First. As such, it speaks on behalf of its members and thereby represents business in London.

2. This submission from the LBB to the House of Commons Select Committee on Culture, Media and Sport is in response to the Committee's announcement that a short inquiry will be carried out into the merits and prospects of a bid to host the 2012 Olympic Games in London. The arguments it puts forward deal with the impact that we anticipate such a bid will have on business and what business can do to support such a bid. It is not intended to be a universal assessment of the arguments surrounding this debate.

3. The LBB believes that a world city of the stature of London could win the bid. This would obviously be dependent on the bid being well constructed. That means two things: that Government (national, London and local) wholeheartedly supports the bid. And that business is involved right from the very start, from the initial stages of the preparations through to the submission itself. Achieving this means being focused on realising all the benefits of the Games, both at the time around the event itself, and also thinking ahead about the legacy it will leave. We believe that the quality of the business acumen and skills of the person who is chosen to lead the bill will be crucial to this success.

4. It is absurd to think that a city of the nature and stature of London could not win. We are already considered a global centre in other fields and, when it comes to major world cities, we are on a par with the best. As a nation and a city we have the skills and expertise to make this happen.

5. The business community very much hopes that those conditions will be satisfied as it keen to play its part in supporting a bid, in the full knowledge that this will require financial support without the certainty that the bid will be successful. It is also keen to be involved substantively in the development process from the beginning, and on through the bidding and implementation stages, in order to ensure the best chance of success. Preparation for a bid should also look at the lessons—both successes and failures—of other host cities as part of our preparation. Most importantly bidding should focus on delivering a legacy for London and the UK.

6. The LBB believes that we have within the London business community the skills and resources to make this happen.

THE MERITS AND PROSPECTS

Favourability in the International Olympic Committee

- It is widely acknowledged that the International Olympic Committee (IOC) is considering a bid from Europe for the 2012 Games. Jacques Rogge, President of the IOC, has publicly encouraged a bid from London and has said that he is impressed with the opportunities to deliver regeneration in East London. . So a bid from London should be well received. The only other serious, likely European bid is Paris; we believe that London is capable of beating Paris.

- The LBB is also of the view that London does have the size and status to be selected and that the timing is right, so a bid is realistic.

- If the British Olympic Committee (BOC) does not submit a bid from London (the only city in the UK from which the IOC have said they will accept a bid) then the chances of being realistically considered again are not expected to come around until 2024 at the earliest. This is because the IOC operates a rotation basis and it will not consider Europe in the subsequent rounds. This would mean that the UK has not hosted an Olympic Games for virtually three quarters of a century. A gap of this length undermines London's status as a city of stature and our attempts to both promote and support our sportsmen and women in a sporting environment.

- It is vital that we take this opportunity to demonstrate that we are a great city and a nation that can host major world-class events and deliver infrastructure projects whilst also promoting and supporting our sportsmen and women in a sporting environment.

Benefits for the area East London and the Thames Gateway

— Regeneration and housing

There are potentially huge benefits for regeneration of the area considered in the specimen proposal—already acknowledged as one of the most deprived areas of Europe, suffering particularly from high levels of unemployment and poor health. The games would:

- provide a focus for the continuing regeneration of the east London and the Thames Gateway area

- reinforcing existing and planned investment (both public and private) in the area including the Channel Tunnel Rail Link, ExCel, the Jubilee Line extension, DLR, the Dome and Greenwich Peninsula

- create real incentives and a deadline to deliver improvements to transport and other infrastructure including sports and healthcare facilities which are vital to successful regeneration

- improve infrastructure, including the provision of at least 4,000 new and much needed homes in East London

- stimulate a comprehensive upgrade of the East London environment and provide a catalyst for site assembly

- stimulate a comprehensive upgrade of the environment and the development of contaminated and under-used land

— Employment and skills

7. Staging a Games will generate additional opportunities for employment and inward investment before, during and after the games. It is estimated that it would create around 9000 new, full-time jobs, of which 3000 are thought to be in the East London economy. In addition, there will be a large number of volunteers that will acquire new skills that will be attractive to employers in growth sectors, including hospitality and customer services.

— Inward investment

8. Bidding for and hosting the games will raise the profile of the area and the tremendous opportunities it offers, nationally and internationally. This is a key element of the inward investment strategy for the area. This change of image, together with improved technological and transport links and access to better skills, would be an incentive for business to relocate to the area.

— Existing capacity

9. Current indications are that existing accommodation capacity in London and airport capacity are sufficient to tolerate the extra influx of visitors that hosting a Games would bring. The amount of available accommodation is thought to compare very favourably with other cities.

10. The Thames Gateway area has been identified as an opportunity for tourism and has already seen an increase in moderately priced accommodation.

Wider Benefits

11. This is a British bid to host the games and the benefits will be nation wide. The Games gives the Britain an opportunity to showcase itself to the world.

— Political cohesion

12. Staging the Games would require improvements to infrastructure projects, wider transport provision and other similar works. Major projects in, around and supporting the capital have frequently and publicly been bedevilled in the past, due to political wrangling. The LBB, while acknowledging the very real difficulties such projects have experienced, is strongly of the view that the prospect of hosting a Games would help diffuse this and help bring about an even more successful outcome to infrastructure projects already in the pipeline. As we said in our letter to the Financial Times, "…this is an opportunity to confront our sceptics and prove that we can do it". All the main opposition parties are believed to be in favour.

— Wider infrastructure benefits

13. Much of London's and the UK's infrastructure is long overdue for improvement and requires real investment. Hosting the Games presents a realistic opportunity for Britain to give a boost to its capital city in this way, with the chance to concentrate minds and release extra funds. Many of the projects would benefit those from outside London using the capital city, providing real, lasting and concrete benefits that would last long after the Games is over. It is worth noting that the cost/benefit analysis conducted by Arup quite reasonably did not include in its quantified benefits the potential of European funding for which it is thought the UK could then apply (the area proposed is currently eligible for Objective 2 funding). This has been the case with Athens who has funding for transport on this basis. The LBB would welcome the additional availability of such funding for infrastructure improvements that are long overdue anyway.

— Other UK cities

14. It is not only London that would benefit. Other parts of the UK would benefit from the staging of events such as the sailing competitions and the use of multiple football stadia. UK cities will act as training camps and bases for overseas teams. The camps will provide an incentive to improve the facilities (both sporting and for accommodation) already on offer as well as leading the way for improvements in provision elsewhere. The Great Britain camp for the 2000 Olympics was located in the Gold Coast and it contributed over £1 million to the local economy over a 12 month period.

— Tourism and inward investment

15. With Britain centre stage, we have an opportunity to develop co-ordinated National campaigns for tourism and inward investment. An independent study has shown that there was over £2 billion in inbound tourism spending in Australia attributable to the staging of the Games in Sydney in 2000. An Olympic Games gives us a unique chance to showcase what Britain has to offer to a global audience.

16. Inward and outward UK investment, expertise and the raised profile of staging the Games would have a beneficial impact on UK exports. Staging the Sydney Games enabled Australian companies to win 10 per cent of capital projects in Beijing, bringing in £1.1 billion.

— Industry

17. Staging the Games would also bring a significant boost and other benefits to a wide range of industry sectors. Sectors that are likely to benefit include construction, property, hospitality, leisure and retail, ITC, healthcare, higher and further education, media and the creative industries. The Premier of New South Wales reported that the Sydney Games created bookings for £233 million worth of international business conferences.

— Social inclusion

18. The Olympics, followed by the Paralympics, would provide a good environment to celebrate and promote diversity in the UK whether it is age, sex, race or religion.

— Society

19. Hosting the Games would encourage participation in sport and that in turn would benefit society, as, anecdotally, participation in sport appears to bring about a reduction in youth crime and acts as a stimulus for education. There are also obvious health benefits.

— 'Feel good' and 'can do' factor

20. There is an unquantifiable 'feel good' factor that is associated with the staging major events, such as an Olympics. We have already had a taste of this from the Manchester Games and the Queen's Golden Jubilee. The benefits of a 'feel good' factor are most directly shown in the higher tally of medals that host countries often win. As it has been suggested that the money the Government will need to spend on submitting a bid could be better spent on supporting athletes to further enhance their chances of success, the LBB argues that failure to support a bid on this ground would be misguided.

21. These factors are also manifest in how London performs as a player on the international stage. London is already a world-leader in fields such as finance; hosting an Olympic Games would entrench and develop this perception of our capital city. This in turn would encourage subsequent opportunities and roles for London, creating a longer lasting benefit.

— Sports and community legacy

22. The provision of facilities for both élite and grass roots sports would leave an obviously defined legacy to the world of sport. Up to 100 training venues will be required in the form of refurbished school and community facilities.

SECURITY

23. Security has always been a major concern for organisers of the Olympic Games, and there is also a history of terrorist incidents. In the wake of September 11, concern in this area can only have increased still further. Given the political stance of the UK, our 'special relationship' with the United States, and recent arrests in connection with a possible toxin attack, the attraction of a Games in London to militant terrorists cannot be ignored. The IOC may take the view that a bid from London would represent a particularly high-risk location. However, London also has a particularly high level of experience and success in dealing with counter-terrorist activity, not least as a result of IRA activity on the mainland. While Paris may seem a lower risk European bid, it is worth noting in this context that other bids from outside Europe, including New York.

PUBLIC SUPPORT

24. The Evening Standard has commissioned YouGov to conduct a survey which found that overwhelmingly Londoners have given their backing to a bid with 69 per cent in favour of the financial risk of bidding. Support falls off slightly for the older age groups. When respondents are reminded about the Dome and Wembley fiascos support falls just below the half way mark, to 45 per cent. There is also support across the board from celebrities and former gold medal winners, including Sir Steve Redgrave and the Princess Royal. The ICM poll in the Daily Telegraph, commissioned by the Government, found a similar but slightly higher percentage of Londoners are in support of a bid. These figures represent high levels of support.

CONCLUSION

25. The London Business Board has three main strands to its argument in favour of submitting a bid for London to host the 2012 Olympic Games. These are:

(i) London is a city that is on the global stage. It would be absurd for us to say that we are unable to compete with other such cities and put on such an event. We have the resources and skill within the business community to construct a successful bid.

(ii) Business must be involved in the preparation for a bid from the very beginning. Without the skills and resources—including the financial support that is required in addition to Government money—any resultant bid will be the poorer for it. And therefore less likely to succeed.

(iii) It is vital that the Government supports a bid. This must be wholehearted and genuine support, not lip service. This support must also come from other tiers of Government, both London and local government.

26. Unified and wholehearted support for a London bid is key to achieving success and winning this prize for London. We would urge the Government to seize this opportunity with both hands and go for Gold.

10 January 2003

APPENDIX 20

Memorandum submitted by European Sponsorship Consultants Association

1. I write on behalf of the UK members of the European Sponsorship Consultants Association (ESCA) which is an independent, authoritative body comprising professional sponsorship consultants with the aim of promoting the effective and professional application of sponsorship practices throughout Europe.

2. As a body we represent over £300 million of sponsorship money. We talk to clients on a daily basis about marketing opportunities in this country through which they can promote their companies and brands. Their marketing activities actively assist the commercial and economic climate of the country.

3. This has been proved recently with the Commonwealth Games, through which £30 million of sponsorship money was raised—money which might otherwise have been lost to the economy.

4. There is no doubt that a successful bid by London to host the Olympic Games in 2012 would benefit the sponsorship industry. However, this is not the sole reason for this letter.

5. The Manchester Commonwealth Games achieved a number of valuable benefits for the country as a whole. First, there was the successful regeneration of East Manchester. Without the Games it is likely that this area would have lingered in deprivation for some time to come. The staging of major sports events not only provides improved sporting facilities for the event and for longer term use by sports bodies and the local community, but also leads to other capital development in terms of housing and business investment.

6. Second, there was a creation of a significant number of jobs in the area, both during the Games and continuing after them as one of the legacies. The economic impact of major sporting events has been proven on many occasions, both in terms of visitor expenditure, but also in respect of long-term employment and other income generation.

7. Third, as anyone in the local communities will testify, the Games brought a general uplifting spirit to the area, the benefits of which are uncalculable. The level of success of élite athletes is raised considerably through national motivation and home crowd support, as well as use of the improved facilities. Additionally, public support by spectators and the television audience is enormous, as was shown during Euro '96 and the Commonwealth Games. The interest in sport at this level is enormous, and affects most people throughout the country.

8. A successful London bid could bring similar benefits to East London, an area much in need of regeneration and possibly without any hope of seeing any tangible changes within the next two or three decades without a boost of this sort. Together with the general prosperity that bringing the Olympics to the country's capital, it seems impossible to believe that the Government won't give the go ahead to making a bid.

9. There seems a reluctance on the Government's part to believe that sport plays a part in the nation's well-being. There are plans afoot to bring tangible evidence to bear to prove this point. Certainly, in terms of the impact on Manchester, all the evidence suggests that the Commonwealth Games were the catalyst for major investment and regeneration for the city, and for the north west.

10. If the Government decides to back a bid for 2012, ESCA urges this decision to be supported at the highest level, with cross-party backing, and that there is input at Cabinet level to support this bid, as well as the staging of the Games if the bid is successful. Central funding will be needed to support the bid and the Games, and ESCA trusts that this will be found through additional expenditure, since the existing Lottery and exchequer funding for sport is already severely stretched. We believe that, despite the costs of backing a bid by London for the Olympics, the value in terms of promotion of the UK and the city of London overseas, the value of the newly required facilities, and the economic impact of such as major event on the whole of the country, not just London, will fully justify the financial resources that are required.

11. ESCA urges the Government to support a bid to bring the Olympics to London and follow the example set by Sydney. Australia's Government saw an opportunity to bring the country and its people a life-changing experience, an uplifting experience which would benefit Australia in a myriad of ways

12. This letter, on behalf of the UK members of ESCA, urges the UK Government to say 'Yes' to giving London, the UK and its people the same opportunity, but only if the full resources and support of the nation are put behind this initiative.

8 January 2003

APPENDIX 21

Memorandum submitted by Helen Day Consulting

1. I have already written to the Committee on behalf of the association of which I am Vice Chairman, the European Sponsorship Consultants Association (ESCA), particularly emphasising the economic effects in terms of sponsorship and support for sport, should the Olympics be staged in London. However, I wanted to add a few further points from my own perspective.

2. As background, I am an independent freelance consultant, specialising in advising on the staging of major sports events. Having been solely responsible for staging the 1995 World Skating Championships in Birmingham (one of the very few events in recent memory to have actually made a profit of over £0.5 million), I gave evidence before the Committee as part of its consideration on the Staging of International Sports Events in 1998.

3. Recently, I have provided expert advice on event management to a number of major sporting events. Employed either by Sport England or UK Sport on behalf of the Lottery, I have provided pre-event advice to World or European events in judo, modern pentathlon, netball, and the Millennium Youth Games, as well as assessing the bid documents and business plans for athletics, boxing and basketball. Additionally, I have undertaken detailed post-event Monitoring and Evaluation reports for Disability Athletics, World Football for Players with Learning Difficulties, World Senior Boxing, the World University and Commonwealth Rowing Championships and am currently working on the World Indoor Athletics to be held in Birmingham this March.

4. Most relevantly, last summer I was contracted by KPMG as their sports expert to provide input regarding all the sporting aspects of the Commonwealth Games in Manchester, working on behalf of the DCMS, Manchester City Council and Sport England to assess the Lessons Learned from the Games. My report was supplied to KPMG for incorporation into their document, which I understand the Committee has recently considered. Hence, from my above experience, and the fact that I am a member of London Sport, I wish to comment on the potential bid for the 2012 Olympics, based on the commercial aspects of organising such as major sporting event.

- The staging of major sports events is virtually always a catalyst for public interest and enthusiasm in sport, as well as for economic impact and regeneration. The goodwill created, and the business generated as a result of a major sporting event is unquestionable. Additionally, the incentive to élite participants, and to the grass-roots participants is incalculable in the long run, in terms of results, and of health and social aspects.

- Britain has a long history of staging highly successful sporting events, in terms of administration, media coverage and organisational ability, such as Euro '96. While the international sporting reputation of the UK is not high at the moment, particularly due to the cancellation of the World Athletics Championships and the long delay in the planning of Wembley.

- It is a very costly exercise to put on a major international one-off event, since the scale of the organisation is vastly bigger and the costs in terms of financial commitment and cashflow, facilities needed and the higher quality of delivery that is required, than any other national event that a sport will have run before. Prior to the essential support of the Lottery, many national sports federations could not even consider staging major sports events, and even so, they will virtually always run at a loss. Additionally, the extra time and effort put in to organising the event can take a major toll on the resources of sport, at a time when it should be gaining extra benefit from having the event on home soil.

- At the Commonwealth Games, from my investigations, it is clear that the early planning was done without sufficient research into the budgets needed and the potential cost. Most of the plans put together by Manchester were based on a break-even budget put together by people with no previous experience on staging sports events, whereas in reality, it proved to be a much more costly exercise.

- While the Commonwealth Games were an undoubted success in terms of impact, new facilities, regeneration of a deprived area, economic income, sporting success and local community benefit, the longer term sporting benefits are much harder to measure. In organisational terms, not enough money within the budget was put aside to support the sporting administration within the Games, with too few people of limited experience, so that in future, there is not the legacy from Manchester that there ought to have been to put that knowledge to good use in future for sports event organisation in the UK.

- The initial report into staging the Olympics was written before the experience of the Commonwealth Games, and there is now a great deal more background information available upon which to base a realistic budget and to develop plans. It is suggested that more time is spent immediately to go into greater depth in looking at the strengths and weaknesses of staging the Olympics, using wider expertise and more relevant information—so that the problems that arose in Manchester of under-funding and changes in organisational direction and the scale of the event, are not repeated in the case of an Olympics.

- I cannot comment on whether London is the only suitable venue in the UK to attract an Olympic Games to the UK, but while there are some advantages of staging in the capital city, there are distinct problems in terms of the massive size of the city in terms of transport and communication. Manchester proved a wonderful sized city, in that it could cope with the influx of people but it was accessible and had a great atmosphere throughout the city.

- If the UK wishes to bid of an Olympic Games, it is only viable if this has the whole-hearted support of the Government, both vocally and in financial terms. The experience of Australia over three successive campaigns, where the first bid came from a city, followed by one supported by the state, and finally the successful bid which was undertaken by the national government for Sydney. Unless the Government (and all parties) agree to give full backing for the bid, it will not be successful—and even if it was, then the event could never be staged without the 100 per cent backing of the Government. Not least, since London does not have a metropolitan authority, but is made up of many local councils, it requires the national government to pull all the stakeholders together into a cohesive group, in order to be able to deliver a highly successful and co-ordinated Games.

- While the proposal to bid for an Olympic Games is being put forward by the British Olympic Association, there are many other bodies that have an interest in this, notably UK Sport as the recognised co-ordinating agency for major sports events, and Sport England, from the facilities and Commonwealth Games experience. It is imperative that these, and the sports federations, work closely together on any bid, and that they utilise the existing expertise within the public and private sector, to give the UK the best advantage to secure the Games.

- If there is not across-the-board support of a bid to stage the Olympic Games in the UK, and if the Government do not give unequivocal support at this stage, then it is my view that the relevant agencies cannot risk staging the Games themselves, and should not enter the bidding.

- However, the benefits to the UK from staging an Olympic Games are so enormous, to the sporting world, to the community of London, to the economy, and to the wider national public interest in major sport, that it is definitely worth bidding to stage the Games in the UK.

- In conclusion, it is proposed that the Culture, Media and Sport Committee use its best efforts to persuade the government to give full, unequivocal support and financial backing to a bid from the UK to stage the Olympic Games in London in 2012.

8 January 2003

APPENDIX 22

Memorandum submitted by the East London Line

1. The East London Line Group is delighted to submit evidence to the Culture, Media and Sport Committee in connection with its inquiry into Winning the 2012 Olympics.

2. The Group is a consortium of local authorities, regeneration agencies, public-private partnerships and other interested parties, seeking the earliest possible construction of northern and southern extensions to the East London Line.

3. The extensions would deliver numerous transport benefits across North, East and South London which have been set out in considerable detail elsewhere. It is clear that the extended line would provide substantially improved access to many of the potential Olympic centres and vital transport connections between the major sites, relieving congestion on other major routes and river crossings:

- The proposed swimming pool at London Fields, the cycling, archery and softball site at Hackney Marshes and the modern pentathlon site at Crystal Palace would be situated within close proximity of the new line, as extended under the initial phase of construction. Should a further phase of construction lead to an extension to Wimbledon, this would facilitate access to the proposed tennis site there.

- The interchange between the Jubilee Line and the East London Line at Canada Water means that access to the proposed Olympic sites in Docklands from North and South London would be facilitated by the East London Line extensions

- Access to the proposed stadium at Stratford could also be provided by the East London Line extensions, if the disused eastern curve at Dalston was brought back into use, to allow services to run onto the North London Line towards Stratford.

4. The cost of the East London Line extensions scheme is currently estimated at £800 million, which means that it could be completed at a fraction of the price of other major rail infrastructure schemes which would bring benefit to London and enhance the viability of an Olympic bid.

5. The extensions scheme makes considerable use of existing or former tracks which means that it could be completed within a relatively short timeframe. In TfL's annual report, published last month, it was noted that the opening of the line could be achieved by 2008. This means that, unlike other major London infrastructure projects, the new East London Line could be fully operational well in advance of the potential London Olympics in 2012.

6. The East London Line extensions will boost £10 billion of regeneration and economic development around London, of which a large part will be concentrated in inner East and North East London, close to the major potential Olympic site. This means, if the East London Line extensions are given the go-ahead, not only will key transport infrastructure be in place by 2012, but also jobs, investment and economic infrastructure. We have attached a brochure outlining the regeneration benefits which would accrue as a result of the extensions.

7. The extensions scheme has almost universal support from London and national stakeholders. The project was cited as a top priority in the *Government's Ten Year Transport Strategy*, published in July 2000, and was also listed as a key project several times in the *Mayor's Transport Strategy*, published in July 2001 and his London Plan, published in July 2002. The project has also gained endorsement from MPs, GLA members, all major players in the rail industry, and local stakeholders who are members of the East London Line Group.

8. Despite this, the project has stalled in recent months. The business case, which contains proposed service patterns and a funding plan, was submitted by the Strategic Rail Authority to ministers in late summer, but has still not been signed off. Until this happens, funding cannot be allocated to the scheme, and contractors cannot be appointed to construct the extensions.

9. The construction of the East London Line extensions would increase the viability of a successful Olympic Games and indeed greater certainty about the future of the extensions project would increase the viability of a bid for the Olympics. Conversely, the Group believes that if the government is unable to complete what is essentially a small and simple infrastructure project, it is surely unable to support a successful Olympic Games.

10. The Group hopes that all of the above points are borne in mind by the Committee, and that pressure is applied on the government to sign off the business case as soon as possible and facilitate the earliest possible construction of the line.

11. The Group would be happy to supply supplementary evidence, if the Committee felt that this would be helpful.

10 January 2003

APPENDIX 23

Letter from Mr Michael Cunnah, Wembley National Stadium Limited

1. I am writing in reference to the Culture, Media and Sport Committee inquiry into the merits and prospects of a bid to host the 2012 Olympic Games in London.

2. The new Wembley National Stadium is currently under construction and on target to open in 2006, as a 90,000-seat stadium. When it is completed, we believe it will be the best stadium in the world, offering fans, participants, officials and broadcasters unparalleled facilities.

3. I understand that the British Olympic Association is proposing the construction of a venue in East London for the Olympics, but I would like to reiterate that Wembley would be available for whatever uses were deemed appropriate—whether as a secondary venue or as the centrepiece stadium as per our obligations under the terms of our funding agreement with Sport England.

4. Though designed primarily for football, Wembley can be configured for athletics by means of a temporary platform solution, which has also been adopted by New York City, for its Olympic Bid. The IOC defer to the IAAF with regard to all technical matters relating to a stadium's suitability for athletics and the IAAF re-endorsed the Wembley design as recently as March 2002. It has also been approved by UK Athletics and Sport England following a detailed technical review in the first half of 2002.

5. We have correspondence from the IOC (dated 9 July 1998) confirming that there are no specific rules regarding the minimum capacity of an Olympic Stadium and that 65,000 would be an appropriate amount. Wembley's capacity for athletics events is 68,400—a figure that could be increased to more than 70,000 by the addition of temporary seating.

6. If a bid for the Olympics is mounted, it would be extremely beneficial for London's case that the city will boast a truly world-class venue already under construction and near completion by the time of an IOC inspection visit.

7. If you would like copies of any relevant correspondence, or would like to ask me any further questions, please do not hesitate to ask. I would also like to take this opportunity to extend an invitation to the Committee to visit the site at any time for a guided tour of the site, which is currently in the demolition phase. More information is also available from www.WembleyStadium.com

10 January 2003

APPENDIX 24

Memorandum submitted by Southern Lea Valley Federation

1. The press have been reporting the Government's need to make a decision about supporting an Olympic Bid in the next few weeks. Our federation represents many groups that have been active in the southern part of the Lea Valley for decades. We are concerned that proper consideration is given to what we regard as 'a tranquil green lung' close to central London and not an area of 'derelict land needing restoration'.

2. There is a lack of information about sites in the Arup Report, which we take as indicating that green open spaces are available as required. We will vigorously oppose any development on our precious open spaces.

3. East London is densely populated and the green open space is important for the liveability, health and well-being of people living in East London, and hence for its regeneration. The risk is that for 17 days of sport, some temporary jobs, facilities that may get some occasional use post Olympics—and possibly some good publicity—the open space and hence the quality of life is being put at risk.

4. Another issue is planning blight. Hackney Wick SRB has a Master Plan whose aim is to encourage jobs into Hackney Wick. The impact of an Olympic bid would be to put a stop to any planning for inward investment until decisions are reached, unsettle those companies already in the area and risk current economic activity. Those who will benefit most from this are the fly tippers and the companies that hope to clear up the mess ahead of the concreting over of the area for car parks, Olympic village etc.

5. There are many areas that we would like to see improved and schemes have been talked about for years. If money is available to bring the Olympic Games to London why is it not available to enable these schemes to be completed? We are concerned at the damage the Games could do to our "playground" and tranquil open spaces for very short-term gain.

6. In particular, having fought the M11 Link road for 30 years, we would not want to see a road constructed from Stratford up the Lea Valley. We want public transport improved and we would welcome Crossrail, the Hackney to Chelsea line and the restoration of the Low Hall curve to enable trains to travel from Chingford to Stratford.

7. We urge you NOT to support the Olympic bid but to invest in a long-term rejuvenation of this area protecting the open spaces that make it an attractive place to live.

8 January 2003

APPENDIX 25

Memorandum submitted by New Lammas Lands Defence Committee

OLYMPIC GAMES PROPOSALS IN THE LEA VALLEY

1. We are appalled by the current possibility that the Government might support a bid to host the 2012 Olympic Games in the Hackney Marshes area of the Lee Valley, East London's precious 'green lung'.

2. Most of the Valley is a Regional Park containing large amounts of green open space (much of it common land), as well as several nature reserves, bird sanctuaries and SSSIs. It is a pleasant and tranquil place much used for formal and informal recreation, once described as a 'playground for Londoners'.

3. We are very concerned that much of this welcome green haven in our overcrowded city could be destroyed and concreted over, simply for the sake of less than three weeks of Olympic sport and athletics activities. No amount of temporary jobs could compensate for the complete destruction of this much-loved area and the detrimental effects on the quality of life of East Londoners.

4. We enclose a copy of a letter that we have written to the Minister for Sport requesting that if a bid is to be made for Britain to host the Olympics then more suitable (possibly brownfield or derelict) sites should be sought elsewhere.

5. Rather than wasting public money making the proposed bid, surely tourism to the existing attractions of the Lee Valley could be more certainly enhanced if the Government were to spend more on improving Hackney's public transport links (there is still no tube service!) or cleaning up and regenerating the Hackney Wick area and its under-utilised waterways?

Annex

Letter, dated 10 January 2003, from the Chairman of the NLLDC
to Rt Hon Richard Caborn MP

OLYMPIC GAMES PROPOSALS IN THE LEA VALLEY

1. We write to express our deep concern at the current reports in the media about the possibility that the Government might support a bid to host the 2012 Olympic Games in the UK, and that a possible venue for this would be in the Lee Valley area of East London.

2. The New Lammas Lands Defence Committee (NLLDC) is a large pressure group which was set up in the autumn of 1993. Our purpose is to protect the former Lammas Lands of Leyton, Hackney and Walthamstow from inappropriate development and encroachment, and to maintain the right of all members of the public to full and free access in perpetuity to all of the former Lammas Lands. Most of the lands with which we are concerned fall within the Lee Valley Regional Park and some of this area—including Hackney Marshes—is registered as Common Land.

3. The Lee Valley is East London's precious 'green lung'. Much is past and present Common Land, and the Regional Park contains several Nature Reserves and SSSIs. The Lee Valley is a pleasant and tranquil place, once accurately described by the late Dame Joan Littlewood as 'a playground for Londoners'. We are very concerned that this welcome green haven in our overcrowded city could be destroyed simply for the sake of three weeks of organised sport and athletics activities. We therefore write to request that your Department should please drop any thoughts you may have of ruining our Valley for this, or any other, purpose and instead consider more suitable (possibly brownfield or derelict) sites elsewhere.

4. On 23 March 2000 two gentlemen called Steve Lawrence and James Burland attended a meeting of the Stratford and Temple Mills Partnership Board in Stratford, and presented a scheme to build an Olympic Stadium and Village on the Bully Point Nature Reserve, part of Hackney Marshes and the Westdown (Temple Mills) area of Leyton. The then Chair of the New Lammas Lands Defence Committee, Ms. Katy Andrews, was at that time a member of the STMP Board as the representative of Voluntary Action Waltham Forest. She reported the scheme to our group, and at that time we simply thought it was rather bonkers (very close to April Fools' Day) and frankly a bit of a joke.

5. After that, everything went very quiet, until we recently heard in October 2002 that the UK Government was considering whether to put in a bid for the UK to host the Olympic Games. Arup had by then prepared their consultants ' feasibility report, and Londoners were informed that if it was decided by the Government that London would be allowed to bid, then it would almost certainly be a bid based in East London. Even more frighteningly, we understand that Mayor Ken Livingstone supports the scheme.

6. Please would you see sense and drop this idea. Not only would the bid as presented to the STMP involve building Olympic stadia and an Olympic Village on Hackney Marshes and the Bully Point Nature Reserve on Stratford Marshes (which would be destroyed), but it would ruin our valley—probably forever. No amount of temporary jobs could compensate for the complete destruction of this much-loved area and the detrimental effects its loss would cause in terms of the quality of life of East Londoners.

7. Rather than supporting this unwanted bid, could the money that would otherwise be used not be put to some better use, such as improving Hackney's public transport links (there is still no tube service!) or cleaning up and regenerating the Hackney Wick area and its waterways?

8. We urge you and your Department to look elsewhere for a venue and leave our valley alone. We are utterly opposed to any Olympic bid involving Hackney Marshes and the surrounding area and will oppose it as vigorously as possible. We feel certain that should this proposal to build an Olympic Village in our area be taken any further then the Government will have another Twyford Down on its hands.

13 January 2003

APPENDIX 26

Letter from Mr Robert Craig

If London is not a suitable venue for the Olympic Games, how about Bristol? It has ready access north and south along the M5, and east and west along the M4. It has a vibrant cultural scene. There is accommodation in the adjacent towns such as Bath and Weston-super-Mare besides Bristol itself, and across the bridge in Wales.

23 December 2003

APPENDIX 27

Letter from the Hackney Environment Forum to the Prime Minister

LONDON BID FOR 2012 OLYMPICS

1. I am writing to you as Chair of Hackney Environment Forum, an umbrella group for a variety of environmental groups in Hackney, London. Our activities include a series of Environmental Question Times which brings together local politicians and local people to discuss environmental issues of local concern.

2. We are writing to bring to your attention the perspective of local groups towards a possible London Olympics Bid for 2012. We consider that the benefits of the regeneration value of the Olympics are grossly overestimated because they fail to recognise the environmental value of East London's open space and the work of Regeneration Agencies. Precise information about the bidding process has been provided, but even at this comparatively late stage, there is very little information available about where in East London key events are expected to take place and the site of the Olympic village. There is little discussion of public transport implications for in Hackney's Lee Valley: it would seem that access to events in the Lee Valley is likely to be by car.

3. A London Olympics (if the bid were successful) would bring visitors into East London for the 17 days of the events. It would produce several venues which bodies such as Lee Valley Park might then be able to use for sports provision. However, we are unconvinced by arguments that a London Olympics would provide a valuable regeneration legacy. Any benefits an Olympics Bid/ London Olympics might bring have to be compared with the costs and losses incurred by local people and local communities, as outlined here.

4. The Olympics could rob East London of large areas of open space. We are concerned that rumours we have heard about the site of events (eg archery on Hackney Marshes) and Olympic Village (eg Waterden Road and the open spaces of Arena Field and Wick Woodland) suggest that the open spaces, Common Land and Metropolitan Open Land in Lee Valley and Hackney Marshes are at risk of being covered in buildings. Open space is particularly at risk because it is quicker and cheaper to build on green spaces than brownfield sites: there are no worries about sites being contaminated or the time and expense to clean them up. It is also quicker and cheaper to build on sites which are already in public ownership because less time and money are taken up in bringing together and purchasing parcels of land.

5. Hackney and other East London boroughs are already densely populated. As argued in Planning Guidance (PPG 17), our open spaces are important for our day to day quality of life. Against the benefits of 17 days of entertainment and the legacy of some sports sites have to be set the deterioration in the quality of life of local people of concreting over open space in Hackney and Lee Valley.

THREAT TO NATURE CONSERVATION VALUE OF LEE VALLEY

6. GLA recently designated Lee Valley as a site of Metropolitan Importance for Nature Conservation- the highest possible nature conservation designation. Heron and kingfisher— two flagship species of London's and Lee Valley's Biodiversity Action Plans live in Hackney's Lee Valley. Wick Woodland was planted over six years ago as the result of a considerable amount of inward investment and a partnership between local people, Groundwork Hackney and London Borough of Hackney, and is cared for by the local community. It is home to wide variety of birds, insects, butterflies and animals, plants and semi-mature trees (such as native black poplars especially grown by London Wildlife Trust). Wick Woodland is part of the River Lea floodplain—it flooded last in 2000.

PLANNING BLIGHT AND DETERRING REGENERATION

7. Regeneration is already underway in East London. Hackney Wick Regeneration Board has been supporting regeneration in Hackney Wick and Waterden Road for five years. As a community partner on that Board, I am aware of the work of job creation and environmental improvement in which the Board and its Regeneration Agency have been engaged. This work will come to a halt if a decision is made to back a London Olympics bid. The area will become a no-go area until a decision is reached in June 2005: firms will not want to move in and those firms operating in the area and providing local jobs will not want to invest further while their futures are uncertain. The area will be blighted even more by fly tipping and illegal occupation. As Hackney Wick SRB programme has demonstrated, there are quicker, cheaper and more certain ways of helping regeneration in Hackney and Lee Valley than an Olympics bid.

LACK OF INVOLVEMENT WITH LOCAL COMMUNITY

8. Noticeably absent from debates about London Olympics/Olympics bid is the negative impacts for Hackney and Lee Valley, and questioning of the regeneration argument. There has been no attempt to inform or consult with local communities, reinforcing our sense that there would be few long term benefits for the people of East London.

9. We feel strongly that the Government could support regeneration in East London in cheaper and more effective ways than through their support for bid for 2012 London Olympics.

8 January 2003

APPENDIX 28

**Letter to the Chairman of the Committee from Mr Michael D J Liebreich MA, MBA
British Olympic Ski Team, Albertville 1992**

1. The upcoming debate on a potential London 2012 Olympic bid in Parliament is an excellent opportunity to bring into the open worrying information about the inadequacy of the preparations for a potential bid.

2. The backers of the bid, and in this I am including the Rt Hon Richard Caborn and Tessa Jowell, as well as the BOA and London Mayor Ken Livingstone, are relying on a cost/benefit study by Ove Arup which states that the Games can be staged for £1.8 billion and would result in a profit, as well as increased investment in British sport.

3. As I pointed out in my letter to the Evening Standard of 17 October 2002, Ove Arup won awards for their construction engineering work on the Sydney Olympics and stand to gain from early involvement in any successful bids. In any case have no competence as economic forecasters and their report misses large cost items, such as the cost of security outside Olympic venues, the cost of bringing forward and rushing infrastructure spending, and collateral costs inevitably borne by local and central government departments such as immigration, customs and social services. In short it is rubbish.

4. There are reports of internal Government figures of £5.2 - £5.4 billion. These sound more sensible. If they are correct, this raises the question of why the Department of Culture Media and Sport spent taxpayers' money on a cost-benefit report from Ove Arup, rather than from a competent and independent source.

5. The technique used by bid backers of restricting their budgets to a fraction of total costs while claiming the benefit of speculative revenue is not new. I attach information on the Sydney and Athens bids. According to the Auditor-General of New South Wales, Sydney 2000 ended up costing over twice the pre-bid figures. The total costs of Athens will be at least four times the bid committee's initial budget; the "Olympic Legacy" of airports, railways and roads is being paid for by £13.1 billion of (largely) EU taxpayer money, and not by either the £1.2 billion Organising Committee's budget or by the £2.75 billion the Greek Government was forced to throw into the pot subsequent to winning the right to host the Games.

6. As a former British Olympian, I go as misty-eyed as anyone over the prospect of top-level sports. But in a post-Olympic-scandal, post-Enron/WorldCom world, the Olympics must be squeaky clean. The attempts by the backers of London 2012 to confuse public and politicians over the costs of the Game give me very serious cause for concern. I trust you will represent these concerns during your Committee proceedings and in the debate on the 2012 bid.

25 December 2002

Annex

LONDON 2012: THE TRUE COST OF THE OLYMPICS?

INTRODUCTION

1. In the debate about a potential London Olympic bid it is essential that there is openness about the true costs and benefits of hosting the Games.

2. We are repeatedly told by the bid backers that the cost of the Games will be less than £2 billion, that they will make a profit, that they will cost the tax-payer less than £500 million and that they will leave as their legacy an enormously improved sporting and transport infrastructure. These claims are based on a report commissioned this summer by Sport Minister Richard Caborn and Mayor of London, Ken Livingstone, and on the experience from recent Games.

3. We should be very sceptical.

4. The cost/benefit report in question was undertaken by construction engineers Ove Arup and property consultants Insignia Richard Ellis. Ove Arup, you will note, are not economic forecasters. They are, of course, winners of several awards for Sydney 2000 Olympic venues. As for Sydney and Athens, closer inspection of their economics, including not just the costs met by the Organising committees but also those borne by the public purse, shows a very different picture. According to the Auditor-General of New South Wales, Sydney 2000 ended up costing over twice the pre-bid figures. In Athens, the extent of Government and EU spending on infrastructure is so huge it's hard to establish an exact figure, but total costs will be at least four times as high as the bid committee's initial budget. The "Olympic Legacy" of Athens is in fact being largely borne by EU taxpayers.

5. Before it backs any bid, the government needs to do the following:

- Release the full Ove Arup report (not just a summary) and the British Olympic Association's bid dossier as other bidding cities have done, so that they can be properly scrutinised.

- Undertake and publish a credible, independent assessment of the cull costs of the Games, including the impact on public budgets in areas such as policing, customs, immigration, social services and local government which are missing from the Arup report.

- Publish an assessment of the infrastructure projects (including, presumably, Crossrail) that will be essential for London to hold the Games successfully, indicating whether or not the associated investment is incremental to existing spending plans, and the extent to which these projects will need to be accelerated.

- Explain how it is going to finance the resulting extra public expenditure. Will it be borrowed? Will it be levied as tax, and if so from Londoners or from National Taxpayers. Even taking only the direct operating costs of the Sydney Games, the public subsidy provided by New South Wales would have been equivalent to an average £187 one-off charge on Londoners' council tax (see below).

- Undertake market research among Londoners, once the above information is in the public domain, to ascertain support.

- Require the British Olympic Association to publish and adhere to a set of principles on ethical behaviour, community involvement, transparency and good governance.

6. If, after a proper public debate, the public (and in particular Londoners) want to proceed with a bid, then and only then is it proper to do so. Otherwise stand by for another unpopular and expensive White Elephant, by the same team that brought us the Millennium Dome!

SYDNEY 2000: CONDEMNATION BY THE AUDITOR GENERAL OF NEW SOUTH WALES

7. When researching the costs and benefits of the Sydney Olympics it is common to come across figures talking about many billions of Australian dollars of 'business outcomes' and infrastructure spending.[2] All of these figures, however, are measures of spending, not the value created by that spending, and they completely ignore the cost of economic distortions caused by raising taxes. For them a pound taxed and spent on the Olympics is always a full pound of benefit—clearly an absurd position.

8. The best analysis of the costs and benefits of the Games was undertaken by the Auditor-General of New South Wales in 1998, and updated in 2002. This is what he found:

(a)   When Sydney bid for the 2000 Games, the bid committee estimated a total cost of $AUS 3.0 billion (£1.0 billion), of which just $AUS 363.5 million (£125 million) would be borne by the public. By 1998, however, when the Auditor-General of New South Wales first reviewed the costs and benefits of the Games, it had become clear that this figure was a huge understatement. He estimated that the true cost of the Games was more like $AUS 5.9 billion (£2.1 billion), of which the public would be paying $AUS 2.3 billion (£800 million).[3] These figures excluded major infrastructure projects that had been accelerated by the needs of the Games.

(b)   The reason for the huge discrepancy was that the bid budget was based on "only those direct costs which have an additional cash effect on the budgets of relevant agencies." In other words, the budget had excluded many capital costs for facilities and infrastructure, as well as, for instance, most of the costs of providing security, which naturally fell on the public purse. The original budget had also excluded costs which might crystallise after the Games, for instance in the form of redundancy payments, as well as the costs of disruption to public services. The original Sydney bid budget did, however, include in its calculations all potential revenues, including $AUS 600 million of putative increases in tax income to the Government.

(c)   In the words of the Auditor-General: Limiting the costs to direct costs but allowing revenues to reflect indirect revenues mingles incompatible concepts." This sort of financial shenanigans is why it is important that the plans and budget for a potential London bid are made public in advance of any decision by the Government whether or not to bid.

(d)   The Auditor-General also made a point of condemning the excessive secrecy which surrounded the Sydney bid budget and the subsequent operations of the Games Organising Committee. "One of the issues which has provided a backdrop to this audit is the unnecessary secrecy which has been associated with the preparations for the Sydney 2000 Games."

(e)   In 2002 the Auditor-General of New South Wales updated his audit, confirming that the Sydney Games had ended up costing $AUS 6.6 billion (£2.3 billion), and had cost the public purse somewhere between $AUS 1.7 and 2.4 billion (between £580 million and £830 million), depending on your estimate of incremental tax revenues.[4]

9. A shortfall as modest as Sydney's for a London Olympic Games would add a one-off charge of £187 to each London household's council tax.

10. The cost of a London Olympics would, however, be far higher than those of Sydney. Firstly because of the enormously under-invested state of London's sporting facilities and transport infrastructure, and secondly because of the massively increased cost of security since September 11th. Perhaps Athens would be a better guide to what a London Games might cost?

ATHENS 2004: COSTS SPIRAL, SUBSIDISED BY EU BILLIONS

11. The absolute minimum cost of Athens 2004 is going to be £6.5 billion, all but £1.1 billion of which will be public money. Published estimates have been as high £9.4 billion.[5] In order to arrive at an accurate figure, the following elements must be taken into account:

•   Budget of the Athens Organising Committee (£1.2 billion). The bid committee initially estimated ATHOC would spend $1.57 billion (£1.0 billion) and generate a profit of $36 million (£23 million).[6]

---

[2] Business and Economic Benefits of the Sydney 2000 Olympic Games, Price Waterhouse, April 2002
[3] The Sydney 2000 Olympic and Paralympic Games Performance Audit Report by the Auditor-General of New South Wales, 1998, available at http://www.oca.nsw.gov.au/resource/fin_cont_report.pdf
[4] Cost of the Olympic and Paralympic Games Auditor-General's report to Parliament 2002, available at http://www.audit.nsw.gov.au/agrep02v2/costofolympicgames.pdf
[5] Athens 2004 is 'Back on Track', Tom Knight, Telegraph, 4 May 2001 http://www.telegraph.co.uk/sport/main.jhtml?xml=/sport/2001/05/04/soolym05.xml
[6] Report of Bid Committee into expected benefits Athens 2004, 22 July 1997. Summary available at the Greek Embassy to Washington DC website http://www.greekembassy.org/press/newsflash/1997/July/nflash0722d.html

Since then the Organising Committee budget has increased to Eur 1.96 billion (£1.23 billion), of which just Eur 235 (£149 million) will be public money.[7]

- The Greek Government's own Olympic budget (£2.75 billion). Prime Minister Costas Simitis has set aside a further 1.493 trillion drachmas (£2.75 billion) of Governmental spending to cover Olympic venues and activities, including a rowing and sailing centre and the athletes' village.[8]

- Infrastructure financing cost (£2.4 billion). The success of Athens 2004 depends entirely on accelerated completion of infrastructure projects costing a total of Eur 20.9 billion[9] (£13.1 billion) as follows:

	Eur
Athens International Airport	2.5 billion
Athens Ring Road	2.5 billion
Athens Metro Extension	2.0 billion
Pathe Motorway	2.0 billion
Egnatia Motorway	2.3 billion
Upgrading of Telecommunications	5.0 billion
Athens-Halkida suburban railway line upgrade	1.5 billion
Rio Antiro Bridge	750 million
Water and sewerage programmes	375 million
Health and welfare programmes	375 million
Energy and gas projects	920 million

Bringing forward expenditure costs money. Assuming these projects have been accelerated by an average of three years, that is a hidden financing cost for Athens 2004 of £2.4 billion (£13.1 billion x 6 per cent financing cost per year assumed by Ove Arup x 3 years).

In addition, of course, the fact that these projects have to be rushed through at once is contributing to enormous inflation in the Greek construction industry, the unquantified costs of which hit the rest of the Greek economy. Athens 2004 will use all this infrastructure at no charge.

Of course all potential 2012 host cities have a similar list of required infrastructure investments. For example the figure for San Francisco's failed 2012 bid was $31.8 billion. The real question, for London 2012, of course, is what is the list of similar projects required and who is going to pay for them: London, British or EU taxpayers?

The real scandal of Athens 2004 is that the projects generally referred to as the 'legacy' of the Olympics are in fact being paid for not out of the ATHOC budget, nor even out of the Greek Government Olympic budget, but out of the European Union's regional development funds, but no one from the EU is auditing them.

The majority of the Eur 20.9 billion costs are being met by the Community Support Frameworks II and III for Greece (Eur 18.5 billion and 26.6 billion respectively), with much of the remaining funding taking the form of subsidised loans from the European Investment Bank.

Amazingly, despite the huge sums being doled out, the EU does not maintain a list of projects supported by CSF III. Money is distributed to qualifying projects by selected local "partnerships". They only inform the EU of the individual projects when the whole programme is closed (ie all the money is gone). CSF III is not expected to close until 2009. Until then, the Greek Government can effectively direct the EU money-hose wherever it wants. The EU does not even have a list of projects, let alone any financial information it could audit, for nearly a decade.

---

[7] Athens 2004 official website http://www.athens.olympic.org
[8] *Olympics budget to stay at 1.5 trillion drachmas, government decides*, ANA, Athens, 16 January 2002
http://www.greekembassy.org/press/newsflash/2002/January/nflash0116e.html
[9] Infralympics Athens Conference Material, November 2000 http://www.hirc.gr/events/infra/Org_New_Infra_Brochure.pdf

CSF II was grossly misapplied by the previous Greek Government. The EU is currently (behind a veil of secrecy) trying to recover Eur 2.9 billion that was spent on non-qualifying projects.[10]

And who is the EU Commissioner in charge of ensuring that Greece can "absorb" (EU terminology) these multi-billion dollar sums without waste or fraud? None other than Michel Barnier, President of the Albertville 1992 Olympic Organising Committee!

- *The Cultural Olympiad (£74 million initial cost).* This is an ambitious monumental roving showcase of Olympic and Greek culture.[11] Resources to the tune of 40 billion drachmas (£74 million) have already been allocated through the [Greek] state budget ... to this amount one should also add the additional resources that will be allocated during the 2001-2004 period through the current budget, the Ministry of Culture lottery tickets, funds for Ancient Olympia and the Olympic Youth Festival and Olympic Education, not to mention the funds allocated for specific Ministry of Culture activities with regard to the 2004 Olympic Games. These funds are earmarked solely for activities and not for any infrastructures, which will be covered by the resources derived from the 3rd Community Support Framework."[12]

- *Indirect costs (unquantified).* In addition to the costs listed above, Greek police, customs, military, social services, health, environment and other public services are having to deflect very substantial resources away from other priorities because of Athens 2004. These public costs have not been quantified. There are also costs to disruption of business up to and during the Games, again unquantified.

LONDON 2012: KEY QUESTIONS

12. So where does all this leave London? Before the Government supports a London 2012 bid, the public needs answers to the following questions:

13. *What would be the real costs of the Games?* How can we believe the Arup figure for operating costs of £779 million when the cost of security alone for Athens is going to be more than £400 million? What has been left out of the Arup total cost figure of £1.8 billion in addition to most security, customs, immigration, social services and local council costs? How can it be so far below the total costs of either Sydney or Athens?

14. *What revenue assumptions are made in the bid budget?* Are the Arup figures predicated on higher TV licence revenues than Athens or Beijing? Who bears the risk if the current slump in advertising market continues? You can ask the Football League what that feels like.

15. *What new transport infrastructure will be required?* If a London Olympic bid is successful, there will be a list of infrastructure projects to which the Government is committed, including presumably Crossrail. These projects will be given priority over other national projects. The public has a right to what they are and what it will cost to prioritise them.

16. *How would a London Games impact London Underground PFI?* A successful London Olympics would require considerable upgrading of the London Underground. Is this included in the existing PFI contracts? If not, how will its costs be covered? Will the Mayor concede his power to run the tube to an Olympic transport authority during the Games?

17. *How will new infrastructure and facilities help London?* Will the athletes' village help solve London's affordable housing crisis? Will new infrastructure be in the right place to solve London's well-known transport problems?

18. *What liabilities will Londons taxpayers underwrite?* According to the Olympic Charter, host cities have to underwrite the total cost of the Olympics. Based on potential costs of £5 billion and three million households, that is equivalent to every London household writing a £1,670 insurance contract. Could this liability not be shifted to the capital markets?

19. *How will the public expenditure be funded?* Even a public funding requirement as small as Sydney's would be equivalent to a £187 one-off surcharge on Council Tax for Londoners. How will the full public costs be funded—will it hit only Londoners or the whole country? Note that even the optimistic economic scenarios rely on huge public spending, later recouped through tourism—which relies on higher taxes followed by a treasury windfall some years later.

20. *Who will run the bid, and any eventual Games?* In Sydney, the chairman of the Games Committee was a Cabinet Minister. Is that appropriate? How will other members of the Committee be selected? How will the views of the public be incorporated into plans?

---

[10] Kathiemerini, 8 June 2002, *EU pressing Athens for huge refund*
http://www.ekathimerini.com/4dcgi/_warticles_politics_100005_08/06/2002_17381
[11] Cultural Olympiad 2001–2004 website http://www.cultural-olympiad.gr
[12] Helenic Ministry of Culture website http://www.culture.gr

21. *Where does new Wembley National Stadium figure in all this?* The project's delay and much of its cost related to providing an athletics track. But is Wembley, or is it not, an Olympic site? If it is, then shouldn't its £161 million public subsidy be added to the Olympic budget?

22. *Would a London Games require new public order legislation?* Under the Olympic Charter the Mayor and Government have to guarantee that large swathes of London will remain advertising—and protest-free during the Games. Will this require new legislation? Will recent anti-terrorism legislation be used to uphold this commitment?

23. *How will the public be assured that a London bid is clean?* In the wake of Enron/WorldCom (not to mention the recent Olympic bribery scandals) it is absolutely essential that a London bid and any resulting Games are clean, transparent, ethical and open. The IOC is still an un-elected body completely lacking in modern governance. What safeguards will the government put in place to ensure a London bid committee is different? How will the Government ensure transparency and high ethical standards? How will the public scrutinise the award of London Olympic contracts? Who will audit Olympic expenditure by Bid and Games Committees, Government, Local Authorities and the GLA?

24 December 2002

APPENDIX 29

Letter to the Chairman of the Committee from Mr Robert Wolton

1. I was very concerned to read the report in *The Times* of December 24 of your apparent comments that it would be madness to bid for the 2012 Olympic Games to be staged in London and that the cost and problems with transport links should rule it out.

2. You may of course be right, however, this could not be said of the rejection of Picketts Lock for the World Athletics Championship in 2006 where the site was offered free of charge and where there are motorway links to London and to Stansted airport.

3. Quite frankly with the thinking behind the rejection of Picketts Lock it must be doubtful if any suitable site can be found in England for locating any world class stadia.

4. And yet we have Wembley, where the present transport problems are horrendous and the cost is more than twice the cost of providing similar facilities in Birmingham where there is an international airport and motorway links to the rest of Britain. So sentiment rules at Wembley whatever and however the cost is derived.

5. Certainly costs are difficult to estimate. Everything should be priced at present day value which is normal practice including benefits and disbenefits.

6. Stratford would benefit greatly from an infusion of new infrastructure in the form of a fully developed international rail link with the continent of Europe and the rest of Britain plus roads, housing and other facilities which, whilst temporarily used by the competing athletes and officials, would become part of the future complete development of the area.

7. The cost of all or most of this provision should be charged to redevelopment not to the provision of the Olympic bid only.

8. Estimation of the cost and its apportionment will be greatly influenced by the strength of purpose and vision of those responsible for compiling any bid for the 2012 Olympic Games.

9. In other words, where there is a will, there is a way. Where this is no will, there is no way. Lord Seb Coe has expressed a strong interest in the preparation of a London bid, so I would encourage you to get him, or someone like him, for example David Hemery, on board as one of the evaluators to provide some will and vision to balance the machinations of the technical experts and politicians.

10. I would have thought that it would be much more to the credit of the chairman of the Commons Culture Committee if he were to press hard for a successful bid, even if it were to fail, rather than to scupper it.

29 December 2003

APPENDIX 30

Letter to the Chairman of the Committee from Mr John H Smith

1. I read with interest and full agreement your views that Britain should not make a bid for the Olympics in 2012. It is fundamentally, indeed morally wrong, that significant sums of money should be devoted to a healthy, young sports group of people while other essential services for the poor and elderly are still wholly inadequate. Many of the major agreements for and against are well-rehearsed but I would like to make a few observations.

FINANCIAL BENEFITS

2. Much is made of the benefits which will arise at the time of the Games and thereafter from increased tourism etc. but what about the 6-7 years in the lead-up to the Games? I have attended the last two Summer Games; my son is a member of the British swimming squad, and from my discussions with local people at Atlanta and Sydney, they suffered years of disruption, aggravation and frustration and could not wait for the Games to be over. London currently operates at full capacity with respect to the transport system etc; the inevitable disruption during the period 2005-12 must lead to a loss of economic activity in London, which could be a permanent downside. In Sydney, we rented a property 30 minutes from the main Olympic complex, a significant number of people in the area had rented their properties - this got them away from the Games and they made some money!

LONG-TERM SPORTS LEGACY

3. It is true that countries like South Korea in 1988, Spain in 1992 and Australia in 2000 exceeded their previous Olympic medal winning performances. However, South Korea and Spain have not maintained their new level and are now back at the level they were before they hosted the Games. It would be interesting to monitor Australia's performance at Athens. There appears to be no evidence of sustained sporting improvement for countries hosting the Games.

ETHICS

4. One of the reasons advanced for host countries doing so well is that the pressures to succeed are so great, given the level of investment, that countries step over the acceptable and normal rules of fair play. In South Korea, there were home team decisions for boxers. In Barcelona, the Spanish middle-distance runners did exceptionally well amidst suspicion of EPO doping. Already one or two Greek swimmers have been banned for drug abuse; the top Greek athletes rarely compete outside Greece, never in the Athletics World Cup meets, thus avoiding the drug testers.

DATE OF EVENT

5. No city in recent time has the number of major sporting events which London stages. Presumably the Olympics in London will be staged during the soccer closed season. In 2012 there will be a European soccer championship which will end around mid-June (and dominate TV coverage). The next football season will start in early August with the Community Shield match at the Lazarus stadium (old Wembley). In that 6-7 week period London will stage Wimbledon, Henley, at least one cricket test match and some one-day cricket matches. Where is the three week window for the Olympics? Some of these events, as well as the Open Golf Championship are listed events and will be covered by the BBC who presumably will be the host broadcaster for the Olympics. Can London cope with overlapping these events? Can the BBC cope?

SELF-PRESERVATION

6. Obviously, the BOA and the Olympic sports are going to give full support to the bid but this comes from a strong sense of self-protection amongst the leading officials in their organisations. Lottery funding is decreasing and if a sport like swimming fails to deliver at Athens, funding will be drastically reduced and the organisation will have to be pruned. However, a successful Olympic bid will guarantee levels of funding, almost irrespective of performance, and the organisation will be preserved up to 2012. In my experience, sporting officials are interested much more in their personal position than the athletes they purport to represent.

7. I look forward to the debate on the Olympic bid and trust you will be successful in your opposition to the bid.

2 January 2003